ICEBOUND IN ANTARCTICA

Other books by David Lewis

The Ship Would Not Travel Due West
Dreamers of the Day
Daughters of the Wind
Children of Three Oceans
We the Navigators
Ice Bird
From Maui to Cook
Voyaging Stars
Voyage to the Ice
The Maori
The Aborigines

ICEBOUND IN ANTARCTICA

David Lewis with Mimi George

To Bob Gerhard

with best wishes for great boating

[signature] David Lewis   *[signature] Mimi George*

W·W·NORTON & COMPANY
NEW YORK   LONDON

Juneau April 1988

ISBN 0-393-02487-3

W. W. Norton & Company, Inc., 500 Fifth Avenue,
New York, N.Y. 10110
W. W. Norton & Company Ltd., 37 Great Russell
Street, London WC1B 3NU

1 2 3 4 5 6 7 8 9 0

Dedication

To Major H. W. Tilman, mountaineer, explorer and cruising yachtsman extraordinary, who was lost at sea in 1977–8, *en route* to Antarctica to climb yet one more peak at the age of eighty, this book is dedicated with humility.

Contents

List of Illustrations

Maps

Acknowledgements
The photographs are by Mimi George, Gill Cracknell, David Lewis and
Jannik Schou, with the exception of 1, which is by Karen Keys.
The publishers wish to express their thanks to Graham Johnston for Map
2 and Tony Mould for Map 1.

Acknowledgements

Literary

The quotation from T. E. Lawrence's *Seven Pillars of Wisdom* is by permission of the Seven Pillars Trust and Jonathan Cape Ltd.

The quotation from Ezra Pound's *The Seafarer* from his *Collected Shorter Poems* is by permission of Faber and Faber Ltd.

The inscription by Mawson in the copy of *Home of the Blizzard* that he presented to Edgeworth David in May 1915 is reproduced by permission of Miss Mary Edgeworth David, the explorer's daughter.

The article on Rates and Mechanisms of Iceberg Ablation by Harry and Karen Keys is reproduced as an appendix by permission of the authors and the International Glaciological Society, publishers of the *Journal of Glaciology*.

The article on Weddell Seal Vocalization is reproduced as an appendix by permission of co-authors Dr Jeanette Thomas, Dr Rhys Puddicombe and the journal *Hydrobiologia*.

The quotation from *Clancy of the Overflow* by Banjo Patterson (*The Collected Verse of A. B. Patterson* © Retusa Pty Ltd) is by permission of Angus & Robertson Publishers.

The quotations from the diaries of Dr Eric Marshall and Frank Wild are reproduced from *Shackleton* by Christopher Ralling with the permission of BBC Enterprises Ltd.

The quotation from R. K. Nelson, *Hunters of the Northern Ice*, is by permission of The University of Chicago Press.

The letter to *The Times* (24 March 1986) is reproduced by permission of the Royal Geographical Society.

General acknowledgements

The following individuals and organizations all contributed in various ways towards the 1981–2 and 1982–4 expeditions and, indeed, they alone made the expeditions possible. Their contributions are gratefully acknowledged, whether they were in time, money, equipment, food, or other supplies. So many were involved that it is simply not possible to thank every individual who contributed in some measure; to do so adequately would require a book in itself. Nor can we be certain, due to several changes in ORF secretaries, that every commercial donor and important helper has been included. To any whose name has been inadvertently omitted we tender our most sincere apologies.

Organizations and Individuals

The Board and members of the *Oceanic Research Foundation* and the willing helpers gathered around them, of course, *were* the expeditions, quite as much as those of us in the field. The Board during the period of the expeditions consisted of:

Lord Shackleton KG PC OBE (Patron)
Don Richards
Robin Miller (Ms)
Margaret Huenerbein
Philip Rowe (Accountant)
Ron Barragry
Dick Smith (Chairman during the first expedition)
David Lewis (President until 1985)

Active helpers included Dick Smith, Dr Carl Edmonds, Dr David Taylor, Geoffrey Campbell, Tony Nelson, Barry Lewis, a whole group of radio hams and innumerable others.

The Antarctic Division in Kingston, Tasmania, loaned us equipment that would not readily have been available elsewhere, arranged communications facilities and scientific cooperation. We are particularly indebted to Clary McCue, the Director during most of this period, to Jim Bleasil, his successor, to the Equipment Officer Rod Leddingham, to Harry Burton, Senior Scientist, and to Lt-Colonel John Godwin of the Australian Army Psychology Unit.

Professor Bill Budd and Dr Ian Allison of Melbourne University and Dr Neil Stretton of the Bureau of Meteorology gave us ice information. The following ship's masters did the same and helped us in other ways: Captain J. Jensen formerly of *Nella Dan*, Captain Gisli Gunnarson of *Nanook S*, Captain Gordon Williams of *Lady Franklin*, Captain Arne Sorenson of *Nella Dan*, Captain Joe Smith of the US Coastguard icebreaker *Polar Star*, and the Master of the Soviet ice-strengthened ship *Kapitan Markov*.

Outside Australia grateful mention must be made of the late Professors Victor Turner and Edwin E. Erickson of the University of Virginia; Jim Caffin, editor of the *New Zealand Antarctic Journal*; Dr James Lester of Washington, DC; Dr Jeanette Thomas of the Hubbs Sea World Research Institute, San Diego; and Dr Y. Korotkevich, Deputy Director of the Arctic Antarctic Scientific Research Institute, Leningrad.

The French bases Dumont d'Urville and Ile Amsterdam accorded us the most generous hospitality, as did the Australian base at Davis. We wish to tender particular thanks to the Davis base leaders Peter Briggs and Phil Elliott and to their splendid 2/ic's, and to radio operators, electronic technicians, mechanics, engineers, cooks and others among whom we found adventure-minded soulmates. Perhaps the thoughtful and understanding David Payne, who thought up monthly gifts, can stand as representative of his colleagues.

Sponsors and donors

Aim
Air Express International
Alexander Roberts Co. – sheet winches
Alliance Foods
Amalgamated Wireless of Australia
Ampol Ltd – fuel of all types
Ansett Airlines
The Armoury
Arnott's Biscuits Pty Ltd
Arnott's Milling Pty Ltd
Australian Bacon Ltd
Australian Dried Fruit Sales Pty Ltd
Avon Products Pty Ltd

Barry and Sargent
Beaufort Air-Sea Equipment – gift of liferaft and boat
Belersdorf Ltd (Australia)
Blackmore Laboratories
Blackwood and Sons
Brandts
British Paints
Bullivants
Buttland Industrial Ltd, New Zealand
Buttrose

Cadbury-Schweppes Pty Ltd
Cadilac Plastics
Carnation Co. Pty Ltd

Cascade Cordials
Champion Spars
Channel 7 TV – our major sponsor
Clothing and Camping Ltd
Colgate-Palmolive
Colourful Canvas
Cottee's General Foods
CSIRO
CSR Inner Circle Rum

Dairy Farmers Cooperative
Dalgetty
Damart Thermolactyl – superb underwear, etc.
Del Cerro
Dick Smith Electronics Pty Ltd
Dr Basil Donovan
Dulux Australia Ltd

The Egg Marketing Board
Arthur Ellis Fairydown, New Zealand – parkas and sleeping bags
Emtronics Division of Emona Pty Ltd

Fermentation Industries of Australia
Fesq
Findlay Communications Pty Ltd – radios

G.E.C. Australia Ltd – electrical equipment for whole ship
Geography Dept, University of Woolongong
Golden Circle
Peter Green, Chandlers
Greenwich Marine – gift of Furuno radar
W. Gregg and Co. of New Zealand
W. A. Grubb Pty Ltd
Gunnersons

Hannas Health and Bulk Foods
Harmony Marine
Harris Coffee and Tea
Hawkins Heat Wave – gift of heaters
Heinz
Higgins and Neild
Howe and Bainbridge

ICI

John West Foods
Julian's Lodge of Falls Creek

Mr M. Keys
King Gee Clothing Ltd
Kingtread
Klisser Bakery, New Zealand
Kraft Foods Ltd

Lars Larsen – Eskimo sledge
Leeds-Northrop
Eli Lilly and Co.
Line 7, New Zealand
Liquid Air, Australia
Living Simply of New Zealand

McLeod Flour Mills
Macpac
Marine Navaid Systems
Marlin International – storm clothing
Marner Fasteners
Marson
Mayfair Ham and Bacon Co
Metalworkers
Metco No. 2
Metzler Wave Overseas
Microcomputer House
Mogulair, New Zealand
Mountain Equipment
Mudgee Honey Co

Nabisco
Namco
National Geographic Magazine
National Panasonic
Nestles
James North
North Sails

Outboard Marine – gift of four outboards

Panair
Pasta House Pty of Balmain
Patra Sales
Peters Ice Cream
Phillips Industries
Pier One
Plumrose
Polaroid

Polygram Records

QANTAS

Rank Xerox, Australia
Barry Rawson
Red Mill Rum
Rennet Co. Coop Farm, Butlands New Zealand
Rice Marketing Board
Richards McCallum Pty Ltd
Roche Products
Russells Bulk Buy Health Foods
Ryvita Co., Australia

Sanitarium Health Foods
Sanyo
Leon Sawyer
Mr Schou sen.
Selbeys
Sidchrome
Smith Markwell
Smith and Nephew
South Seas Philatelic
SPC Ltd
Squibb and Sons
Sun Herald

TAA
Tamar Knitting Mills – warm clothing
Tip Top
Tooths
Trio Kenwood Australia
Tupperware – gift of excellent containers

Unilever
Union Carbide
Univas Trading Co

Vegetable Oils Pty Ltd
John Vose

Watties, New Zealand
White Wings
Wilderness Experience, Los Angeles – parkas
Wilderness Products, New Zealand
Wormold International
W. E. Woods Industrials
Woolworths

Prologue

Winter Ordeal, 1983
by Mimi George

Sea ice is unpredictable. Even in the depths of winter vast areas may, without warning, be driven out by blizzards or by distant Southern Ocean storms. Only the previous year three British explorers were caught in just such a breakout and lost their lives.

It was late July, a month past midwinter, when Gillian, with her fieldwork partner Jannik, David and I set out from *Dick Smith Explorer* [the expedition's ship] on our seventh field trip, but the first seriously to push southward over the frozen ocean beyond the shelter of the Rauer Islands, where our ship had been locked in these four months past. Our objective was to reach the emperor penguin rookery at Amanda Bay while the chicks were yet perched, swaddled in down, on their parents' great vascular feet. This particular emperor rookery had never previously been visited before full summer season. The Alcan sledge behind the little 430 cc Yamaha snowmobile was piled high with food, fuel and gear. I drove with Gill riding pillion and Jannik and David standing on the sledge runners grasping the load for support. The little machine laboured heavily in the recurrent drifts, obliging the passengers frequently to jump off and put their shoulders to the sledge. We camped that night at Cape Drakon, the last mainland rocky promontory in the Rauer area, our jumping-off point for the open sea ice beyond.

The next solid land *en route* would be the northern Brattstrand Bluffs, a straight-line distance of twenty-one miles to the southwest. We would be entirely on our own since our field radio had broken down some time ago. What would the going be like, we wondered? In May and June we had pushed on foot nearly to the Ranvik Glacier tongue that jutted out from the continental ice plateau fifteen miles away athwart our course. Did the berg field off Ranvik mask a jumble of rough ice that could stop our vehicle? No matter how favourable the going we would have to camp on the sea ice, a procedure emphatically frowned upon by experts. Hope-fully, we could make it to the Ranvik berg field before camping, for here grounded bergs and the offshore Svenner Islands might be counted upon to anchor in the fast ice. There was good reason to distrust the stability of the intervening sea ice. On 3 April and again on 21 April it had broken out in blizzards along much the same irregular line. We had found the new ice still unsafe on 15 May but, as tested by pick axe ('high tech', David called it), a more reasonable seven inches thick by 4 June. Our current doubt was as to the effect of a ninety-knot blizzard which, four days earlier, had disintegrated right up to the ice cliffs a five-mile stretch of sea ice north of the Rauers. Had this storm affected our southward route as well?

At Cape Drakon we had earlier laid down a well-stocked supply depot and Gill, Jannik, Jamie and Norm had built an igloo, which we found to our chagrin had sagged on one side, leaving room for only two occupants. Gill and Jannik begged to sleep there and, after jumping on the roof to test its strength, David consented. He and I pitched the polar pyramid tent.

It is hard to convey what it was really like to camp and sledge over the sea ice in the polar night. The experience is certainly seared into my memory for ever. Although the sun was newly resurrected after five weeks below the horizon, it only arched red and low above the frozen ocean to the northward for two hours each day and brought little warmth. The weather was much colder than before. The thermometer had gone down to $-38°C$ a few weeks since. The few daylight hours had to be reserved for travelling, which demanded that we break camp in the dark. We would stumble about in an agony of frozen fingers, tripping over guy-lines and struggling with recalcitrant ice-gripped tent-pegs.

Then, after a day's man-hauling or snowmobile riding, we must erect the tent in the dark again. Frozen breath and condensed steam from cooking coated the insides of our tents so thickly with rime by morning that four gallon-sized buckets full of ice crystals had to be scooped off the walls. Flashlight batteries were inoperative in the cold and a smoky wick lamp was the only illumination we had. Our double sleeping bag and inner bags became wet with condensation, which quickly froze. They had to be aired, draped over tent or sledge whenever opportunity offered. Modesty went by the board. Each morning I would help David balance precariously on a tupperware 'pee' bucket on a wobbly nest of sleeping bags and he would do a like service for me.

Our departure from Cape Drakon on 28 July was delayed until afternoon by the need to sort out the depot and reorganize our loads, all taking longer because we were inexperienced as yet, so that a lengthy re-packing of the sledge was necessary. Extra drums of kerosene for the primuses and outboard fuel tanks filled with petrol for the snowmobile were loaded, some to be cached further south, together with plastic sacks of rice, muesli (granola in American), long-life sliced bread, sugar, canned and dehydrated foods. Among key items of equipment were two sturdy 40 lb Beche tents, ice-axes, shovels, wooden planks for bridging tide-cracks, and two American fibreglass man-haul sledges for use if the snow-mobile was irrevocably damaged.

Primus kerosene pressure stoves were vital life supports that had to be perfectly maintained, for this whole southern continent, larger than the USA and Mexico combined, is devoid of liquid fresh water for three-quarters of the year – and melt pools and streamlets are few and far between even in summer. Before breaking camp we filled plastic bottles with hot water and slipped them into the inner layers of our clothing for drinking *en route*, knowing full well that within three hours they would be frozen solid.

That morning the thermometer stood at − 30°C and the wind off the Polar Plateau cut like a knife. It struck through my two pairs of Damart long johns and sleeved singlets, through a heavy wool shirt, two pullovers, down pants, a full set of windproofs and a quilted Dacron jacket and trousers. My head was muffled up in a balaclava helmet, inner and windproof hoods and goggles. I was wearing Damart gloves inside thick woollen mitts inside polar overmitts and insulated 'Mickey Mouse' boots with three pairs of socks on my feet. Still I was cold.

David was anxious about possible breakouts from the recent ninety-knot blizzard. While the rest of us sorted and packed, he clambered up the headland above our camp to a vantage point from which to peer into the frost haze to the southward. He stood on the tops of bluffs for an hour or more exposed to the chill wind. Visibility was poor with low overcast cutting down shadows and masking contours, so he came down again. Then the sky cleared somewhat and David hastily re-ascended for another hour's scanning. The information gleaned with such effort was minimal. The route appeared to be intact, though how far seaward the firm ice extended was uncertain.

By the time we finally set off, an hour after noon by the sun, David was thoroughly chilled. 'It's all right for you,' he shivered. 'You have spent a winter in Chicago, so this is nothing to you. We Kiwis are semitropical.' I urged postponing travel, but that meant unpacking the sledge and starting over again next morning. 'No, we mustn't delay any longer,' David decided, adding impatiently, 'Of course I'll be all right.'

Once again I drove with Gill behind me and Jannik and David standing on the bouncing sledge runners. This was easy enough for Jannik, who is tall. Not so for David. 'I'm only little and I've got little short legs,' he complained ruefully. The load now towered over him so he could only cling tightly to the netting, awkwardly off balance, and try to anticipate upcoming bumps.

The going was reasonable for the first two hours: some patches of newer ice to check, some tide-cracks to cross with a rush, some jolting over icy cobbles and weaving in and out to avoid wind-scalloped snowdrifts of upended ice blocks. The modest speed of our passage was enough to intensify the pitiless wind. Our tiny caravan, dwarfed by the vast plain of the frozen sea, crawled over the most unstable stretch, outside of which we could now discern a lead of open water to seaward; and we seemed an interminable time passing the landward ice cliffs. It was a scene of savage splendour. The ice cliffs, purpling in the thickening twilight, were dwarfed by the awesome majesty of the continental ice sheet behind, which rose tier on tier until it merged into an infinity of space and sky. No living thing stirred save only ourselves.

Now, as the light was beginning to fade, the ice surface changed drastically. It became so jumbled that we had to zig-zag constantly, achieving even our meagre forward progress only at great risk of damaging the vehicle. I switched on the headlight and kept direction by the ghostly silhouettes of the bergs that were frozen into the sea ice some way ahead.

About now I began to be worried about David. Several times, and now ever more frequently, he had loosened his grip on the sledge load and stumbled free of the runners. I urged him to walk on at intervals to try to warm up. He did so but he still shivered uncontrollably and what could be seen of his face was chalky white. I dared not bear him behind me on the pillion because, if he fell off, the Alcan sledge, which with its overload weighed a ton at least, would inevitably crush him.

'Keep your eye on him every minute,' I urged Gill. Several times she signalled me to stop to give David a chance to regain his footing on the runners when protruding ice chunks swept his feet from under him.

'I'm all right,' David insisted with obvious untruth. 'We should hurry on to those bergs ahead. This place is dangerous.' That was rational enough. I knew the barometer had fallen 6 mb since last night and a storm could well be making up. A blizzard could very easily break out the ice where we were now standing and send us all into oblivion. Patently, this was no place to linger. For safety's sake we must attempt to reach the lee of one of the large grounded bergs ahead. Even if it did not offer the same security as the Ranvik berg field it should at least stabilize the fast ice in its shelter. But what about David? Could he last out? He was obviously severely chilled and hypothermia (the drop in core body temperature which, if not arrested, is ultimately fatal) must be developing. Might this bring on a stroke too, I fretted? In either case we should camp as soon as possible.

I had Gill take David's arm and walk him ahead while I stood up on the snowmobile's seat to look for the best route to the shelter of the nearest berg. Our progress was no faster than a walking pace.

The final mile or so seemed never-ending. The ice became much worse. We lunged and crashed through a maze of upturned broken and refrozen slabs. I fought to keep the little vehicle moving along alleyways of less formidable blocks and speeded up when I could, so that when the snowmobile jarred to a halt at an obstacle, the momentum of the jack-knifing sledge would jerk it forward over the obstruction. The underside of the engine cowling dented badly but the vital track assembly and the tough little motor survived the appalling punishment unharmed. Time and again we would be stopped by an impassable barrier and I would run ahead to find another way. Gill would walk David in the interludes.

Nearly in the lee now. A smoother stretch. Then Gill pounded on my back and yelled that David's knees were sagging. We skidded to a halt. David was mumbling and staggering about, unable to stand without support. His skin was icy cold to the touch. There was no doubt about the hypothermia now.

'We need to get him into a tent and a sleeping bag as fast as we can,' I told the others.

'Gill, stand next to him on the runner and hold on to him.' I jammed David's arms tightly into the netting over the load. 'Jannik, push to start us off and then put your weight on the pillion to give some traction to the track.'

At last we drew up in the rather dubious shelter of a round tabular berg ringed with caves scoured out by last summer's restless waves before the freeze-up arrested their motion. Gill and Jannik had our tent up in a trice. I hurriedly spread out the sleeping bags and bundled the semiconscious David into them, pausing only to pull off his boots. I threw off my outer clothes and snuggled down against him and took him in my arms in a feverish attempt to arrest the decline in his body temperature. The others passed in the sledging box and I quickly got the primus going to melt snow for a hot drink and to warm the tent. Whatever could we do if we lost David's leadership, I wondered? Would I be able to hold the expedition together? Some time later, when I again tried to force hot, sweet coffee between his chilled lips, David opened his eyes halfway. 'Rum,' he murmured feebly, and I knew that the worst was past.

During the night a strong katabatic wind got up and roared down from the polar plateau out over the frozen sea. The tent walls flogged and vibrated but stood firm. So did the sea ice.

David's memory for these events is completely obliterated for six hours, and he retains only wavering shadows of another twelve, an indication of the severity of the chill he experienced. Without everyone's prompt action, he wrote later, he would probably not have survived.

This scary incident, recalled in Mimi's journal, underlined for me (David Lewis) how fragile were our life-support systems in the stark Antarctic wilderness – much as they would be in outer space or the underwater world. The experience rammed home the lesson that our very survival, not to mention the success of our programme, depended on unremitting vigilance and meticulous care in everything we did. Nothing but excellence would do.

Introduction

Antarctica: The Frozen Frontier

A word about the main protagonist in this story, Antarctica itself, is timely here. The great southern land is about the size of the continental United States plus most of Western Europe. Roughly 95 per cent is covered by an ice sheet averaging one mile in thickness, often two miles in West Antarctica. On the 5 per cent of exposed rock no permanent rivers run, no flowers bloom. Only the most primitive plants – lichens and mosses, sparse grasses towards the tip of the Antarctic Peninsula (the northward extension of the continent below South America that extends to within 600 miles of Cape Horn) – cling to a precarious foothold.

Seven countries: Britain, Australia, New Zealand, Argentina, Chile, France and Norway, but not the USA or the Soviet Union, make claims to territory. Argentina and Chile have even invoked the Papal Bull of 1498 that divided the world between Spain and Portugal in support of their rival claims. Since both countries could claim with equal justification to be Spain's heirs, nothing was resolved. In December 1959 an Antarctic treaty was signed that largely put an end to territorial bickering. The claims would be held in abeyance, it was agreed, for the thirty-year duration of the treaty (it is open for revision in 1991). Thus without acrimony the United States set up bases in New Zealand's Ross Sea Dependency and on the Antarctic Peninsula, where Britain, Chile and Argentina have overlapping claims, while the Soviet Union moved in force into the enormous Australian sector.

Antarctica has thereafter been administered by an exclusive club – the sixteen Antarctic Treaty Consultative Parties plus a further eighteen acceding nations (the number increases almost daily). A multinational civil service establishment called the Scientific Committee on Antarctic Research (SCAR), which is heavily influenced by the National Science Foundation in Washington, virtually runs the continent. The accent is on scientific research, but in the words of Roland Huntford, iconoclastic author of *Scott and Amundsen* and *Shackleton*, 'the official establishment has become ossified. The projects are repetitive, dominated by the earth sciences and redolent of academe of the late 50s.' The treaty powers are also responsible for regulating the exploitation of living 'resources' like krill, fish and seals, and ongoing thorny negotiations are in progress to set up an oil and minerals regime.

It must be stated in all fairness that the treaty has in the main been highly successful. The conservation record has been generally excellent. Neither is there any cold war among the icebergs. Soviet and Western scientists work on each other's bases. At the height of the Falkland Islands war British and Argentine representatives sat down peaceably together to discuss minerals. What then is missing from the continent? There are no citizens.

Heavy investment in the krill and fishing industries by Japan, West Germany, the Soviet Union and others has even now depleted fish stocks in the Atlantic sector of the Southern Ocean and threatens the basic food of penguins, seals and seabirds, a scenario for disaster equivalent to the near-extermination of the great whales. Projected oil drilling on the deep berg-strewn continental shelves and mining on the limited ice-free areas ashore are alike fraught with environmental peril. Formidable pressures can be exerted on the international Antarctic bureaucracy by immensely powerful multinational commercial concerns, especially in the absence of accountability to a resident population. Admittedly, oil and mineral extraction is not yet a paying proposition. But governments and firms are already jockeying for position, and with the recent entry of new countries into the arena (Japan, China, India, Poland, Uruguay and Brazil, among others, have established bases) infighting is more than likely to increase.

The fact that Antarctica is unique among continents in having no permanent inhabitants to speak on its behalf leaves the field open to manipulation by the establishment and commercial interests. Base personnel, who usually rotate annually and are either government employees or dependent on the government monopoly of transport and shelter, are hardly independent citizens. SCAR does its best to discourage 'interlopers' and many private innovative ventures have been squeezed out.[1] But not all by any means, and there are signs that the tide is turning, as we shall see.

Remote as it is, the ice-age frontier is of vital concern to every one of us. It has been aptly termed the world's weather factory, because of the global effects of its turbulent overlying air masses and the movement to

[1] Argentina and Chile are alone in welcoming independent expeditions and rendering them every assistance. Indeed their record goes back to the Argentine rescue of the Nordenskold expedition at the beginning of the century and Chilean help to Shackleton in bringing back his men from Elephant Island.

the Equator and beyond of its chilled bottom water. Meteorological changes in Antarctica can influence the type and amount of precipitation, the length of crops' growing seasons, and sea level perhaps most of all. Ninety per cent of the earth's fresh water is locked up in the mile-thick ice cap. Should polar melt rates be materially increased by human agency – the carbon dioxide 'greenhouse effect' from ever increasing combustion warming up the atmosphere, smog deposition reducing the albedo (reflecting power) of the ice, or 'atomic winter' cutting off the sun's light, all come to mind – the level of the oceans would rise to flood major cities and lowland farmlands. Even a partial melting would be catastrophic. The recent discovery that the ozone layer that shields us from cosmic radiation is periodically breached over Antarctica has stimulated a massive research effort to find the cause. Being canvassed as likely culprits are carbon dioxide released by the combustion of fossil fuels and fluorocarbons from aerosols.

Antarctica is too important to the world, it seems to us, to be left to the tender mercy of governments and autonomous multinational corporations alone. This last great wilderness, sealed off by two thousand miles of storm-torn and ice-strewn ocean, is largely closed to the very people who could best appreciate it and be vigilant in its defence – mountaineers, naturalists, bird watchers, sea mammal watchdogs, skiers, scuba divers, venturesome tourists, environmentalists and the like. Only yachtsmen, at some peril, can utilize their own means of access.

Wilderness areas are needed for our mental health and spiritual renewal, and so impelling is the frontier-directed imperative that, despite daunting financial and logistic problems, a citizen sector of Antarctic exploration, research, and adventure has become re-established for the first time since the early heroic age of exploration. In face of all the odds it is growing steadily.

Of course no one in their right minds would consider small-scale ventures to be in any way in competition with the elaborate and high-technology official undertakings with their enormous resources. They are supplementary, that is all.

One of the independent organizations we have alluded to, and one which features in this story, is the Australia-based Oceanic Research Foundation (ORF), which I helped to found in 1977 after my solitary voyage to Antarctica in 1972–4 had impelled me to learn more of this strange land. I subsequently led ORF expeditions south in 1977–8, 1981–2 and 1982–4.

This book is an admittedly personal account supplemented by other people's often conflicting opinions, very briefly of the 1977–8 *Solo* and 1981–2 Mawson Anniversary Expeditions (the latter of which really deserves a whole book to itself), and at length of their 1982–4 Frozen Sea successor. It may well be controversial, as was my November 1984 *National Geographic Magazine* Frozen Sea article, in which I wrote the truth. An overwhelming proportion of the letters Mimi and I received, about thirty to three, supported my honesty. Jim Caffin, the respected editor of *Antarctic*, the journal of the New Zealand Antarctic Society, commented on the article 'in which you were old-fashioned enough to forget the humbug and say what really happened during the winter. Nowadays nobody in this part of the world seems to be completely honest about anything.'

But some were affronted, especially Norm Linton Smith, who was our engineer–radio operator, who felt a 'public defamation' of Jamie Miller and himself. It is with great satisfaction, therefore, that I have read Norm's views in *Aurora* magazine. I will quote him extensively, especially over debatable incidents, for it is only right that he should have his say. No individual participant in any undertaking can be completely objective, try as he may, and the only way to arrive at the truth is by allowing all points of view to be aired.

Our expeditions revived and updated simpler technologies of an earlier day in low-cost flexible operations. We used an auxiliary sailing vessel for transport, thereby saving fuel and making space available for people and gear. The 65-foot three-masted schooner *Dick Smith Explorer*, which carried the 1981–2 Mawson Expedition, was afterwards wintered in a frozen-over Antarctic bay in 1982–4 as a scientific base that would not harm the environment – the Frozen Sea Expedition. We also adopted simple techniques for traversing the ice once the sea had frozen – man-haul sledges, skis, tents, and time-tested kerosene pressure stoves. The updating of classic methods included *Explorer*'s modern diesel engine, radar, satellite navigation, synthetic fibre clothing, outboards, inflatable boats, wind and solar generators and that spunky little vehicle, the snowmobile. We came into closer contact with the fierce environment than is customary nowadays, when centrally heated enclaves have become the rule, and this intimate interaction with the polar world called for the utmost responsibility. The stakes for carelessness were high, the stresses were sometimes severe, and high standards of performance were demanded of everyone. None of us passed the test of excellence unscathed – the author, since he carried the overall responsibility for every act of commission and omission, perhaps least of all.

The Oceanic Research Foundation, which organized these and several other undertakings, is a shoestring non-profit society that is funded entirely by the public without government financing. Preparations for both undertakings took months and even years and involved hundreds of people. To detail every aspect and episode or to mention, if only by name, all the people who deserve to be mentioned would merely produce an unreadable catalogue. The *dramatis personae* are, therefore, mainly the actual expedition teams.

Our research in these expeditions fell into two, sometimes overlapping, categories: original projects and others programmed by scientists from such bodies as the Australian National Antarctic Research Expeditions (ANARE) and institutes and universities in Australia and the USA.

Since encounters with polar ice in its various forms is the theme of this book, something about different kinds of ice may not come amiss. *Icebergs* are floating or grounded ice islands calved off from the mile-thick ice cap that covers most of Antarctica and flows century by century down to the sea as glaciers or enormous ice shelves (the Ross Ice Shelf alone is the size of France). Icebergs float anything between five-sixths and two-thirds submerged, depending on their density, and some are more than a hundred miles long.

Pack ice is sea water that has frozen. Usually about three to five feet of ice are added each winter, so that the multiyear pack averages about nine feet in thickness. It guards the southern continent in a belt hundreds of miles across, forever cracking apart or else squeezing so close that it buckles into pressure ridges or rafts like a monstrous pack of shuffled cards, producing sheets up to a hundred feet thick. A practical point for the explorer is that, although pack is frozen salt water, the salt leaches out in the course of a year or so, leaving old pack ice drinkable.

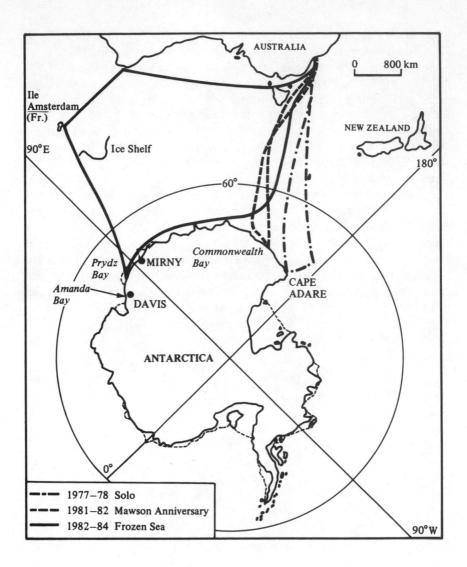

AUSTRALIA

0   800 km

Ile
Amsterdam
(Fr.)

NEW ZEALAND

90°E   Ice Shelf

180°

60°

Commonwealth
Bay

Prydz
Bay   MIRNY

Amanda
Bay   DAVIS

CAPE
ADARE

ANTARCTICA

0°

—·—·— 1977–78 Solo
— — — 1981–82 Mawson Anniversary
———— 1982–84 Frozen Sea

90°W

I

Baptism of Fire: The ORF's First Two Expeditions, 1977–82

The Solo *Expedition, December 1977–March 1978*

The Oceanic Research Foundation's first true 'baptism of fire' was an expedition to the Antarctic Balleny Islands, Cape Adare and Macquarie Island during 1977–8. The crew were Lars Larsen, deputy leader, engineer and radio operator (Greenland sledge dog patrol and Antarctic veteran); Dr Peter Donaldson, biologist; Dr Pieter Arriens (Antarctic veteran), geologist; Jack Pittar, electronics; Fritz Schaumberg, Himalayan mountaineer; Dorothy Smith, mountaineer; Ted Rayment, yachtsman and TV director-cameraman; and myself as skipper.

The 55-foot, 25-year-old steel ex-racing yacht *Solo* had only six bunks for the eight people aboard and her cockpit was open. She was low in the water and very wet, so comfort was minimal.

We sailed from Sydney on 15 December 1977. Three weeks later the hull was holed by pack ice and was repaired with Neoprene and cement, a frightening incident 1,300 miles from the nearest repair facility. We managed to reach the remote Balleny Islands through the pack, and were the first ship ever to anchor at any of them – at Sturge Island, largest of the group, where we spent twenty hours in an anchorage now officially known as 'Solo Harbour'. We were only the second party to set foot on this island and the first to arrive by sea. Bottom samples were dredged up and oriented rock samples collected, as well as soil samples from a penguin rookery on a neighbouring island.

Cape Adare on the Antarctic mainland was subsequently visited and two long-neglected historic huts filmed – Borchgrevink's, where the first men wintered in Antarctica in 1899–1900, and the hut of Scott's 1911 Northern Party.

Iceberg measurements were made at sea and the yacht called at sub-Antarctic Macquarie Island on the way back to Sydney, which we reached on 4 March 1978.

The Australian Broadcasting Corporation made 'Voyage to the Ice', a TV special that was first shown throughout Australia in September 1978. I wrote a book of the same name about the expedition, which was published by the ABC in association with William Collins of Sydney in 1979 (it is available from the ORF, PO Box 247, Windsor 2756, Australia).

The scientific results of the expedition are recorded in appendices to that book, except for Dr Arriens' meteorological observations, which were sent to the Meteorological Bureau, Melbourne:

Appendix 1. Observations by Dr Donaldson on marine samples, bird log, whale log, and his own hazardous studies of sea temperatures and salinity around three free-drifting icebergs.

Appendix 2. Dr Elizabeth Kerry studied soil samples collected under sterile conditions in the vicinity of a penguin rookery and found namatode worms, bacteria, yeasts and thirteen species of fungi.

Appendix 3. Dr Pat Quilty examined and reported on foraminiferida and diatomaceae in the dredged-up samples.

Appendix 4. Dr B. Embleton reported on the magnetic properties of the rock samples collected by Dr Arriens.

All in all, these were encouraging results from such a modest, low-cost venture.

The Mawson Anniversary Expedition, December 1981–March 1982

The place was Cape Denison, Commonwealth Bay, in George V Land, far south of Tasmania, involving a 2,000-mile[1] voyage each way in *Explorer*. The main aim was to compare the current state of affairs with that found by the great Australian explorer Sir Douglas Mawson seventy years earlier, particularly the abundance of wildlife, and the position of the margin of the continental ice sheet. New photographs placed alongside the legendary photographer Hurley's old pictures would show whether the ice was advancing or retreating, a key factor in Antarctica's and the world's future climate.

Dr Harry Keys, assisted by his wife Karen, was to study iceberg melt rates, essential data if bergs are ever to be used as a source of fresh water. The Adélie penguin population of the cape and nearby Mackellar Islets had never been counted. A penguin census was one of the jobs of biologists Jeni Bassett and Paul Ensor. Their counts would contribute to the international programme, Biomass, which seeks to increase our knowledge of the food web of the Southern Ocean, by assessing the mass of living things dependent ultimately on the lowly but ubiquitous plankton.

I was President of the Oceanic Research Foundation during this period,

[1] The term 'miles' in this book means nautical miles, approximately one-tenth longer than a land mile.

but much of the time was fully occupied in the field. We on the ship
parties were merely the 'tip of an iceberg', whose main bulk was the ORF.
No radio appeal for extra gear or funds from *Explorer* was ever dis-
regarded. Our expeditions were thus made up of an advance guard in the
field and a main body, the main body being the members of the Oceanic
Research Foundation.

Plans for the Mawson Anniversary Expedition were well in train by
early 1981 and were locked into an immutable timetable, the need to use
the summer weather slot, for the only time the pack ice melts enough to
allow a ship to approach the Antarctic coastline is in December, January
and February. We must therefore set out by mid-December. There was
just one snag. We had no ship to sail in.

The specifications for an ideal vessel had been drawn up by a volunteer
team of naval architects in the anticipation that the cost of construction
would be within our means. But when we put the plans out to tender,
construction estimates were staggering: she would cost three-quarters of a
million dollars at least, far and away beyond our each. So we had no ship
in prospect and the scheduled departure date was less than a year away.

It is unfortunately true that privately funded projects have one grave
disadvantage. You must mount a media campaign to obtain funds; if you
fail to publicize, nobody knows anything about you. But by announcing
your plans beforehand you are under the distasteful necessity of stating in
advance all the 'clever' things you are going to do. A certain momentum
builds up if you are lucky. Should you once falter, however, this momentum is lost and you are done.

So it came about that members of the Oceanic Research Foundation
and as many friends as we could rake together were scouring waterfronts
from Perth to Darwin and round to Sydney in a desperate effort to find a
strong, roomy auxiliary sailing vessel fit for the polar seas, and at a price
we could afford.

Ironically, when we found the right ship it was where we least expected,
at our own back door as it were, in Lavender Bay in the shadow of Sydney
Harbour Bridge.

'That fishing boat over there was built to sail and has a deep ballasted
keel,' a friend remarked casually. I had already noted the slim lines of the
motor fishing vessel but had not suspected she was so deep in the water
and able to carry sail, a necessity for our purposes if we were to cross the
2,000-mile-wide Southern Ocean with capacity to spare for anything other
than fuel.

She proved to be just what we wanted. *Tunny*, as she was then, was a
65-foot long-liner superbly constructed in quarter-inch steel by a magnificent craftsman of the old school. She was very narrow, her beam a
shade under thirteen feet, and her six-foot unladen draught was not enough
for good windward performance in the open ocean but would be a boon

for entering shallow uncharted bays. Her cross-section was steeply V-ed, so that ice pressure would squeeze her upwards rather than pinch and crush her hull. The engine was a fifteen-year-old 120 hp Mercedes diesel and the fuel capacity an ample 2,000 gallons. The ship was an enlarged version of the famous American designer Francis Herreschoff's *Marco Polo*. *Tunny* would need many modifications and additions, but the essentials were there.

Money was the problem. By dint of selling tee shirts and postcards, running film shows and barbecues, screening a TV appeal, and so on, the Oceanic Research Foundation had amassed funds over the years. One large school had raised more than $1,000; a golf club secretary in an inland town had organized community activities bringing in no less than $1,800. Donations had come in from people who had overflown Antarctica, from aged pensioners, from business houses and men and women in every walk of life. But in all it came to $40,000 or so. This was not nearly enough. I was brooding one day over these matters, sitting at the surgery desk of a doctor I was relieving. The phone rang.

'Dick Smith here. Have you been able to raise enough to buy your boat?'

'No.'

'Well, is this *Tunny* I hear about what you want?'

'Certainly.'

'All right, then. I will loan the ORF up to $100,000 and charge you the going rate of interest. Can you buy her for that?'

I was speechless. This was precisely the lift we needed. I knew Dick well. He was a 35-year-old electronics genius and self-made millionaire, an adventurer besides, and a sponsor of adventures. A daring rock climber and pilot, he was currently preparing for the solo helicopter flight round the world that has deservedly made him famous. He is a monumental egoist too and not always easy to work with. But no matter. We would have our ship after all.[2]

Good fortune never comes singly. Ted Thomas, the manager of Channel 7 TV in Sydney, agreed to purchase all the media rights to our two proposed expeditions (Mawson Anniversary and Frozen Sea) for the generous sum of $100,000 each. The Channel would film both expeditions. The magazine rights were subsequently sold by them to *National Geographic Magazine*. Apart from these major sponsors, a philatelic organization printed special covers for us which ultimately netted a goodly sum. A great many firms donated their products – a marine radar, most of our food, all our fuel, an inflatable boat, outboard motors. The seemingly endless list is given in the acknowledgements (p. xii); how very well these gifts served us will become apparent as the story unfolds.

Tunny, subsequently renamed *Dick Smith Explorer*, had naturally to

---

[2] We borrowed $65,000 and were able to repay $19,000 before we sailed.

pass survey and go through acceptance trials before we bought her. Mimi (of whom more later), who had come to stay with me in Woy Woy, sixty miles north of Sydney, where I was recouping my scanty finances by relieving another doctor, was on board for the final trial. The owner, a brawny fisherman with arms thicker than my thighs, claimed to revel in storms, an attitude considered by Mimi and me to smack of masochism if not downright weakness of mind. Casting off from the mooring buoy, he negligently pulled up the rusty gear lever one-handed (it took two of us to even budge it a fraction) and spun the wheel to head down the sunny harbour to the open Pacific. When, some hours later, we returned, Mimi stared round, perplexed.

'I can't see the mooring buoy anywhere. Where is it?' she asked.

We came upon it five hundred yards away, bobbing around, drifting free. In the absence of appreciable wind and tide, much less the drag of a moored vessel, it was hard to see how the heavy chain could have parted. Not unless the massive steel links had rusted right away, an eventuality only conceivable if the mooring had been neglected for years. We would soon know. A tackle was rigged and the truant buoy with an attached length of weed-grown mooring chain was brought aboard. A six-inch link had indeed rusted right through. The owner regarded it pensively.

'Well, there was only *one* weak link!' he remarked defensively.

So *Dick Smith Explorer* was purchased early in 1981. The list of modifications demanded by the Antarctic was daunting. The well deck had to be raised to bring the deck flush (the same height all over) to increase buoyancy amidships and to give added space below, both at a premium, for *Explorer* is as long and narrow as a canoe.

From front to back there is a companionway on the fore deck leading down to a tiny forward cabin, in which we installed four cramped berths with sadly restricted headroom.

At the back of this fore cabin a door in a watertight bulkhead leads into the engine room, where the 120 hp Mercedes diesel is installed. A skylight relieves the gloom of this compartment, an asset rather cancelled out in our case by the sledges, inflatables and so on piled on top at sea, or the styrofoam insulating sheets affixed for the polar winter. We installed a diesel generator in the engine room and built a container for ice chunks round the exhaust pipe so that the hot exhaust could melt ice for drinking and cooking. All electric wiring was replaced (the new electrical equipment provided free of cost by General Electric). The engine room was insulated and a toilet and wash basin were added in an annexe.

The next compartment aft had been the fish hold. It was already well insulated and was to become the most popular cabin on the ship. Six bunks, with lockers for personal effects and a hanging locker, were crafted here. This centre cabin hosted three couples on the 1981–2 expedition. In 1982–4 it was chosen by everyone except Mimi and myself. Access was by way of a newly built companionway, and a skylight was added for visibility.

Aft of the fish hold centre cabin is a small hold, into which was crammed an incredible assortment, including for 1982–4 the better part of two years' food and a dismantled snowmobile.

Next towards the stern comes the wheelhouse with steps leading down into the galley. In the former was installed a Furuno radar, donated by Greenwich Marine, and a satellite navigation system (lent by AWA for the first voyage, and bought at a substantial discount from Brookes and Gatehouse for the second). The galley has a table that seats four comfortably, a kerosene pressure cooking stove and water tanks holding 350 gallons. This area too had to be insulated. Opening out from the front of the galley underneath the wheelhouse is a space, much restricted by food storage bins, which contains two bunks. Don and I shared this 'cave' on the 1981–2 voyage because we needed ready access to the wheelhouse. Mimi and I took it over for the same reason.

Installation of new equipment and alteration of accommodation apart, strong, high, all-round railings had to be made, the steering gear restructured, the rudder enlarged and an auxiliary jury rudder fitted. A whole sailing rig, masts, sails and stays had to be designed, made up and fitted. The masts were finally stepped only *three weeks* before we sailed for Antarctica. Following Herreschoff's original design, we plumped for a three-masted schooner rig. All this, and much more we have not space to mention, was more than enough to occupy twice the nine months available before the brief Antarctic weather slot would close. Despite the generous assistance of so many firms, the financial cost more than doubled the original purchase price of $90,000.

From the moment we bought *Explorer* until she sailed, preparations were never-ending. My Woy Woy locum ended in September, soon after Mimi had had to return to the States to complete her MA, and I moved aboard *Explorer* in a noisy boatyard, disconsolate, but with more than enough to do. Departure was scheduled for mid-December, yet a scant three weeks earlier the ship was still devoid of masts and sails, leaving little enough time in all conscience for sailing trials.

The New Zealand–Australian expedition team (we were 50:50), backed up by a multitude of helpers, were all in Sydney working like beavers a month before sailing date, and a magnificent team they were.

Don Richards, mate and radio operator, is an experienced ocean yacht skipper as well as being a professional engineer. On the radio side he organized an amateur 'ham network', to such effect that we were never out of contact with Australia. Gary Satherley is likewise a long-time cruising yachtsman and served as the very competent engineer on the voyage (a far cry from his civilian profession of newspaper editor).

The scientific group (known as the 'Kiwi Mafia') was led by geochemist and mountaineer Dr Harry Keys, who had five previous Antarctic seasons to his credit. He was partnered by his wife Karen, herself an Antarctic veteran and a most experienced and skilful sailor – unlike her otherwise accomplished husband, who I hope I can say without offence could never be called a born helmsman.

The biologists were Jenni Bassett and Paul Ensor, who had four Antarctic seasons between them. Dick Heffernan, a geophysical assistant, meteorological observer and mountaineer, with seven Antarctic research voyages on the research ship *Eltannin* and a stint as meteorological recorder on an Arctic ice island behind him, completed the scientific team.

Then there was the tenacious Dot Smith, who had been a key member of the 1977–8 Antarctic expedition in the yacht *Solo*, and who is only my junior by a year. In my student days, an uncomfortable number of years ago, when mountains seemed less tall and steep, we climbed together in the Southern Alps as fellow members of the New Zealand Alpine Club. Margaret Huenerbein, a long-term stalwart on the ORF Board, is a skier and sailor. Malcolm Hamilton was cameraman-director from Channel 7 TV in Sydney. He had had no sailing experience whatsoever, so I asked my son Barry to take him to sea and 'test him to destruction'. On their return Barry reported laconically, 'He doesn't destruct!' Malcolm in fact proved to be one of the strongest members of the party. Barbara Muhvich, who is Gary's wife, was a reporter assigned by the Sydney *Sun Herald* and completed the roster.

I was fortunate in having three such experienced and responsible deputies as Don the mate, Gary the engineer and the scientific leader Harry Keys. With lieutenants of this calibre my own responsibilities were largely managerial with accent on strategy and safety. I exercised them in the main by low-key discussions with my deputies, with whom I interfered as little as possible. This was in contrast to the later Frozen Sea Expedition, where, apart from Mimi, the personnel through no fault of their own were much less qualified. The reasons we will come to later.

To everyone's surprise, including our own, *Explorer* got away on schedule on 12 December 1981. Eight days later we called briefly at Hobart in Tasmania seven hundred miles on, where we were generously loaned insulated boots, tents, climbing and crevasse rescue equipment, as well as scientific equipment by the Antarctic Division. With food and fuel for four months plus ample reserves, polar gear and clothing, living quarters for the twelve of us reminded a friend of a 'better class of slave ship'. Storm or shine, decks slippery with ice or bunks soaked by storm waves sweeping the deck, nobody ever complained.

We steered south across the roaring forties, howling fifties and screaming sixties. The forties treated us well enough, as a result of an unusual high pressure zone, the fifties came up with a gale or two, but all in all the Southern Ocean let us off lightly. I won the sweepstake (no prize) when icebergs were sighted from 65°S on, but there was no pack worthy of the name. Icebergs are no menace in clear weather or with radar (which the unfortunate *Titanic* lacked); pack ice is another matter. That year it had crushed and sunk a well-found German supply ship. Another, an ice-strengthened Icelandic trawler under British charter, suffered a like fate in 1986.

The main navigational challenge was to keep direction crossing the position of the South Magnetic Pole which, unlike the geographical South Pole, changes position slowly over time, and currently lies some sixty miles off the Antarctic coastline. The magnetic compass was useless here and within a radius of 600 miles, so the best I could do was to improvise a sun 'compass' diagram. Since the sun circles the horizon near the poles in summer moving 15° each hour, I was able to construct a figure showing the bearing of the sun at each hour of the (24-hour) day. This served us well enough for direction, for a hazy sun generally peeped through the overcast every hour or two. When the sun remained hidden there were generally lines of the ocean swells to steer by, while the temperamental satellite navigation (sat. nav.) system, whose antenna later turned out to be loose, periodically updated our position at intervals varying between hours and days. Sat. nav. apart, we were back in the days of the old Polynesians or the Vikings.

It was Margaret who first sighted land, the crevasse-scored front of the Astrolabe Ice Tongue. We turned east along the coast and, after a night of storm when the deck, anchors and wheelhouse windows became sheathed in ice, we sighted the rocky Cape Denison that was our objective, dwarfed by the looming continental ice sheet behind. We motored carefully into a long narrow inlet christened by Mawson the 'Boat Harbour' and made fast securely with lines to boulders ashore.

The very first task when we landed was set by Harry Keys and Dick Heffernan. This was a training session for all hands in self-arrest with an ice-axe when sliding down a snow slope, crampon technique and crevasse rescue. In crevassed country you are of course all roped together, but when someone breaks through and his fall is arrested, there remains the problem of getting him back to the surface, especially if he has only one companion. The most useful method is for the victim to climb the rope himself using foot slings already threaded through his waist harness and Jumar clamps. These can be slid up the rope but then lock, so that with two Jumars and two loops, each foot can be raised alternately. It sounds easy, but is less so when you are spinning round and round trying to keep your balance in the foot loops. At least I found it so when Dick had me climbing up a small ice cliff.

The ice cap behind the cape was heavily crevassed in places, as we found on two one-day excursions led by Dick to prospect routes along the coast. No one fell into any of these fearsome caverns, but we were well equipped to haul him out if he had.

The name 'Home of the Blizzard' was coined for Cape Denison by Mawson, who wintered there in 1912 and 1913. The name is an apt one, for it is the windiest spot on earth, with winds averaging gale force (38 knots) throughout the year and rising in extreme conditions to 150 knots.

Our arrival had coincided with a rare calm and we were fortunate in having nearly a week of perfect weather in which to complete our penguin and seal counts at the cape and the Mackellar Islands and for Harry and Karen to get geophysical samples and to duplicate Mawson's seventy-year-old photographs of the ice edge. Jenni, Paul, Margaret and Karen camped for several days on Mackellar Islands Adélie penguin rookery doing the counts. Though these islands are only a mile or two offshore, I was anxious the whole time they were away – watching the barometer and the clouds, keeping frequent radio schedules, and personally accompanying every trip to the islands in the inflatables, the sturdy Beaufort and the lighter Metzler.

Mawson's old hut proved to be in a sad state of disrepair and was mostly full of drifted snow. Gary, assisted by Barbara, patiently tunnelled his way into the living quarters, which contained such items as a jar of honey (that in the interests of science rather than greed I tasted and found perfectly preserved), *The Memoirs of Sherlock Holmes* as a serial and the *Illustrated London News*'s 'stop press' account of the loss of the *Titanic*.

The weather broke after that, nearly causing a fatality when a dinghy swamped. (I will describe this harrowing incident in a later chapter when we come to small-boat precautions.) By noon on 29 January the wind had eased enough for us to cast off the web of mooring lines we had rigged to the boulders. Despite Paul's expert handling of our home-made 'echo sounder' – a large shackle on a line – we 'charted' an unmapped submerged reef with our keel before we reached open water.

We planned an exploratory probe eastward along the coast to the Mertz Glacier Tongue, a distance of some 100 miles. There we would reverse course, following the coast back past Commonwealth Bay to the French Antarctic station Dumont d'Urville; then turn north and head back for Sydney.

Mertz Glacier, named after Mawson's unfortunate companion who died of starvation and the toxic effects of vitamin A in the sledge dog livers they had eaten in their extremity, extends forty miles out to sea in a great floating tongue of ice that rises 150 feet above the water and extends 700 feet under the surface. At 1,000 square miles it is roughly two-thirds the size of Long Island.

We came up with the Mertz ice cliffs on 1 February and followed them northward to the tip. The seaward end of the ice tongue had fragmented into a monumental array of semi-detached bergs.

Harry was pleased, for in the lee of the great ice tongue the sea was calm enough to approach the outlying bergs (that were surrounded by fields of pack ice) in reasonable safety. 'But we really need,' he told me, 'a berg we can study at close range for several days, so we can measure the exact rate of melting and erosion.'

The only problem was that both sat. nav. and echo sounder were out of commission at the moment and we were still far too close to the Magnetic Pole for the compass to work. To compound matters snow began falling steadily and blotted out the sun. You should never, says the *Antarctic Pilot*, enter pack in poor visibility.

Nevertheless I took a chance. We wound our way between the floes to a suitable berg and tied up precariously to a slowly gyrating floe nearby while Harry and company hurried off in the inflatables to take measurements. During the past week, we had been getting an hour or more of darkness each night as the brief Antarctic summer drew towards its close, and with darkness compounded by thickly falling snow there could be no thought of continuing the work on the berg that night. It continued to snow heavily all night, the floes never ceased grinding together, nor did we stop having to pole off. A radio antenna on the stern was snapped off by the ice.

Conditions had not altered by morning. It was impossible to tell which way the pack was drifting and I had no desire to be crushed against the Mertz, which was visible on radar ten miles off though there was no clue in which direction it lay. I got under way despite Harry's evident distress, which he loyally tried to hide, and was soon more than glad to have done so, for when the sun peeped through at last it became apparent that we had drifted to the dangerous windward side of the Mertz and were, indeed, in danger of entrapment. It took some hours' weaving to and fro through leads before we extricated ourselves.

We turned back in the direction of Commonwealth Bay and Dumont d'Urville sixty miles beyond, but the voyage to the glacier tongue, which had produced a useful sketch map, had been worthwhile in other ways. Paul and Jenni were particularly pleased, for in the course of a few days as we skirted the coast they had landed and made counts on several penguin islands (one of them uncharted) and logged a variety of marine life, including emperor penguins, a crab-eater seal and several pods of minke and killer whales.

One incident, apparently minor at the time, was the rupture of an oil pipe that ran alongside the engine sump. The lubricating oil drained away into the bilge and the motor was hastily shut down. Gary, the engineer, soon found the leak and, with Don's assistance, repaired the pipe with plastic tubing. The sump was refilled with oil and we continued on our way. Subsequently, to make doubly sure, Gary's temporary repair was replaced by a copper tube made up at Dumont d'Urville.

Another matter to have a bearing on the later expedition was press publicity. Harry in particular had had grave doubts as to the propriety of leaving the shelter of governmental and academic institutions for the rough and tumble of the market place to fund the expedition. His concern was not altogether unfounded. Certain press reports, over which we had little control, extolled the expedition in such extravagant terms as to make us the laughing-stock of experienced Antarctic hands. Later on the reporter became disillusioned and wrote antagonistic pieces. These did us no harm at all; it was the earlier intemperate praise and unreal claims that damaged our reputation among knowledgeable people. Harry's fears were thus partly justified, but media irresponsibility in my experience is very rare – a couple of scandal pieces, the happily unfounded report of my having been eaten by South American Indians in 1965, that has been all – all, that is, until the Frozen Sea venture.

After our two months aboard *Explorer*, the large French research station Dumont d'Urville seemed a luxury resort. It had things like hot showers, clean tablecloths, and superb French cuisine, the latter accompanied by (Australian!) wine. With barely enough room for its own staff of sixty-seven, the station very kindly made their showers available and regularly invited two of us to dinner and lunch on a rotating basis. Happily, we were able to make some return through Jenni's and Paul's work with the French biologists. We were particularly privileged to meet the base director, Robert Guillard, who had seen more polar service than the rest of us put together. He was then sixty-two years old and had spent thirty-four consecutive seasons in Greenland and the Antarctic.

Here it was that Harry finally got his chance to study in detail grounded bergs in the shelter of a glacier tongue, in this case the Astrolabe. During the next eight days his team monitored the dynamics of wind and wave action, especially the undercutting on the waterline that leads to fracturing and collapse of overhanging ice, as well as underwater melt rates.

There were two contrasting confrontations with the elements on the way home. The first was a ten-hour calm with overcast sky and flat sea, when we had to lie a-hull to await some clue as to direction. The sat. nav. told us where we were, but as to which way was north we had no idea. In the words of the old Viking saga, 'the four quarters of the sky were hidden'. Eight days later we encountered a storm with winds of sixty-five knots and waves thirty feet high. *Explorer* took a battering but came through nobly. On 15 March, just three months and three days after our departure, we sailed back into Sydney with pennants flying.

The city accorded us a heart-warming welcome and the undertaking was the subject of an article in the *National Geographic Magazine* of April 1983, a paper by Harry and Karen Keys in the *Journal of Glaciology* (reproduced in the appendix) and a documentary by Channel 7 TV of Sydney.

Karen's modest description of the detective work involved in the ice margins study is worth quoting:

To find out if significant changes in the position of the coastal ice margins had taken place in the seventy years since Cape Denison and Commonwealth Bay was first visited, we have replicated more than twenty scenes taken by Frank Hurley, photographer on the Australasian Expedition of 1912–14 led by Douglas Mawson.

Our search for these photo points took us . . . [over] an area of about two square kilometres. We also visited some small islands off the Adélie Land coast. Some sites were easy to find while others took several hours to locate. The photos have been used to compare the present-day margins of the continental ice sheet with those of seventy years ago.

Some very small changes are evident. At John O'Groats at the eastern end of Cape Denison a retreat of about two metres has exposed rock that seventy years ago was covered with glacier ice. However an ice cliff at the western end of the ice-free area has bulged forward slightly. These small changes are probably local effects and we conclude that there has been no significant change in the margin of the Antarctic ice sheet at Cape Denison.

Karen and Harry had made good use of a rare opportunity to document changes across three-quarters of a century, nearly half the span of human contact with Antarctica.

Harry's iceberg measurements, in which he, Karen and Dick worked, often at some peril from calving ice masses, at arm's length from the bergs, with Margaret and Dot vigilantly manning the support boat, were most productive. Wave action and calving were found to be of great importance in paring away the apparently indestructible monsters. But because the greater part of an iceberg is submerged, the slower process of submarine melting turned out to be twice as effective in reducing its mass.

The idea has long been canvassed of towing icebergs to arid regions to provide fresh water. Harry's results suggested that a medium-sized berg on a voyage of two or three months to Western Australia would lose approximately half its mass on the way.

2

A Dream becomes Real
March–November 1982

All men dream: but not equally. Those who dream by
night in the dusty recesses of their minds wake in the
day to find that it was vanity: but the dreamers of the
day are dangerous men, for they may act their dreams
with open eyes, to make it possible.
             T. E. Lawrence, *Seven Pillars of Wisdom*

My own dream, following the success of the Mawson Anniversary Expedition, was to mount an international mixed-sex research expedition, and freeze our small ship in for the winter as an environmentally harmless base whence we could travel far over the frozen sea. My companions had each their own dream. The following chapters relate how well or ill the dreams were translated into reality.

The venue of this venture lay far to the west-southwestward of Australia, midway to Africa across the Indian Ocean and due south of India, thus committing *Dick Smith Explorer* to a 5,500-mile approach voyage.

The ORF research projects included a sea ice study to be conducted by Mimi and myself, which turned out to involve the year-round monitoring of eighteen potential ice anchorages and the collection of data on sea ice formation, decay and breakout, as well as mastering techniques of over-ice travelling and camping. We aimed to learn as much as we could about how to use the frozen sea as a road: when it was safe and would even permit camping; when and in what circumstances it might suddenly disintegrate, as it had done several times in the past, causing the deaths of brave men. There have been some immortal over-ice journeys, that we will come to later, but not so much was known so far about the ice in our particular sector.

Perhaps the most original project was Mimi's small-group study. There were few scientifically organized studies of groups facing the stresses of real-life frontier situations. All of us volunteered for this documentation of our Antarctic life, the results of which have been found relevant to long-term ventures into space, as well as to more mundane human activities. The study was set up under the auspices of anthropology professors Victor Turner and Ed Erickson of the University of Virginia, both of whom, sadly, died while we were in the field.

There were several programmes worked out with outside institutions, in most of which Gill Cracknell and Jannik Schou were active. These included lichen and moss collecting, fish sampling, Amanda Bay emperor penguin census, seabird counts, Adélie penguin stomach contents, ocean seabird counts, seal tagging, plankton filtering at sea and seal vocalization recording, which last was Mimi's responsibility. Some of the results were destined for inclusion in the international Biomass data that should help the setting up of guidelines to prevent undue depletion of Antarctica's fauna.

As soon as I could after our return from Cape Denison I put the refitting of the ship in train. I was anxious to visit the USA, mainly to obtain a commitment from *National Geographic Magazine* for articles on the two voyages, something that could only be done personally. Articles apart, there were the cameras and film they could provide. Then there were the questions of recruiting participants and obtaining polar clothing – and lastly, seeing Mimi.

I was at my wits' end over the air fare until Mimi took the bull by the horns by selling her only assets, a windsurfer and much loved BMW car. (*National Geographic* subsequently bought the story rights and reimbursed the fare.) In the short month in the USA that followed Mimi had to finish her MA (on data she had amassed in Papua New Guinea), while I wrote the *Geographic* article on the recent trip;[1] Mimi was equipped and given instruction as *National Geographic* photographer, and she put together the small-group proposal. We set out to obtain equipment and gather recruits.

Before we go further an explanation about Mimi and myself is overdue. The other expeditioners will be introduced in due course, but she and I were in at the start. On the face of it we are a most unlikely team. Mimi was at the beginning of our expedition thirty-one years old and I was sixty-four. We will see later how our partnership came about.

Mimi George is a graduate student of anthropology at the University of Virginia. 'Tall, dark and free-ranging, mysteriously active with men,' someone called her. 'She's such a jock,' another friend remarked, a reference to her playing soccer and basketball. This is hardly fair because she has also studied art and music and is very feminine, even though it is hard to get her to wear anything more formal than running shoes and jeans.

Her university career has been long-drawn-out, being interrupted by the

[1] 'Voyage to Antarctica', April 1983.

need to make a living and pay her fees. To this end, she has been a charter boat skipper, an assistant cook in a restaurant, and a painter of high-rise buildings – work demanding a good head for heights, but appropriate since her great-grandmother was a Mohawk, a tribe which nowadays produces notable high steel erectors. Both she and I tend to rate money or conventional status rather low in our scheme of things.

The names of Mimi's uncles, Ottavio, Julio and Caesar, testify to the family's strong Italian cultural identity. Unlike me she is naturally handy, so much so that at high school she scored the highest marks possible in mechanical aptitude. On the negative side, being so practical herself, she can become impatient with others slower and less dextrous than herself.

Nautical expertise was a top consideration for an expedition that would be something like five months at sea. Here her experience is broadly based. Four summers of ocean racing apart, her experience skippering charter yachts and cruising up and down the Atlantic seaboard from Rhode Island to the West Indies has been extensive. The only cautionary note, not apparent at the time: she had generally worked with people whose standards were competitive, and had not often had to 'jolly along' those of lesser natural bent, who might resent a constant demand for excellence.

For my part, I had never previously met anyone so entirely devoid of race or colour prejudice, or so free from sexual 'hang-ups' as Mimi. She is that rare creature, even in today's open society, what the Tahitians call a 'Firebird' or a 'Free Woman'.

Competent and devoid of pretence herself, Mimi is no actress, revealing her feelings in her face more clearly than she knows, so that her perception of someone as fool or knave is unfortunately writ large on her face – not always the best recipe for popularity! Like all individualists, she attracts both life-long friends and, being a standing reproach to the timid and narrow-minded, automatic detractors as well.

The two of us originally made contact over the mutual interest in Polynesian navigation that I will come to later. But I very soon realized that she was a natural candidate for Antarctic exploration as well.

I myself was raised in New Zealand, my mother being a fifth-generation Kiwi, and though I am now an Australian I am still bound by strong ties to the country where I grew up. I cannot, indeed, get particularly worked up about a dichotomy between these two countries, that have so much in common and that must increasingly share a joint destiny. I remain, therefore, committed to both.

As a boy and young man I was shy but I was also adventurous in the sense of needing to come to grips with nature. I cared little for organized games, which I found oppressive and restricting in a land full of forests, mountains and wild rivers. At seventeen I celebrated my last days at boarding school by building a canoe and informing the headmaster that I was going home in it at the end of term – 450 miles across New Zealand by river, portage, lake and sea coast. His prompt veto was undermined by my parents' written permission – at what cost to their peace of mind, since I was an only child, I realized after becoming a parent myself. Since no one else would come with me, I set out alone.

It was on this trip that I first experienced the fulfilment of enforced self-reliance in struggling towards a goal. There were times, like a capsize in the icy Tongiriro river, that had only once before been shot, when I came close to losing heart. To haul the light craft on long portages I constructed a trailer with bicycle wheels. Correctly anticipating frequent wettings, I carried no blankets and slept wrapped in a ground sheet. But when I did reach my home in Auckland I had an empty feeling, as if an essential ingredient of endeavour were missing – left behind somewhere in the rapids of the Tongiriro.

I rediscovered it while taking part in the ascent of nineteen unclimbed peaks in the South Island, where I went to medical school. (One of these mountains I called Mt Carinna, after my mother.) But then followed a period at Leeds University Medical School in England and, after qualification, the latter part of the Second World War and adventure as a parachute medical officer of a much less pleasant sort. Indeed, the war cured me of adventurous ambitions for the time being, so after a period in Jamaica, I settled down to practise in East Ham, where I did my best to put aside thoughts of free winds and open spaces.

Yet even here restlessness intruded from time to time; lying in bed on foggy nights I could not sleep for the hooting of ships' sirens that came clear across two miles of sooty rooftops through the frosty air. I tried to ignore the message that the sea was there waiting, still untamed and free and aloof as it had always been; still beautiful and terrible in its impersonal anger. I made tentative approaches to the sea – like a sailing dinghy that I built, and a 27-foot, sixty-year-old barge yacht in which I became acquainted with most of the sandbanks of the Thames Estuary. In general, however, I did succeed in overcoming these irresponsible longings.

Eventually, self-examination forced the belated realization that the link connecting that first canoe, through mountain and forest, to the old barge was in fact the very essence of my character. The particular challenge that fascinated but also appalled me with its difficulty was the first single-handed transatlantic race of 1960. Buying the 25-foot *Cardinal Vertue* with the aid of a bank loan, I made New York in fifty-four solitary days to come third behind Francis Chichester and Hasler. The story is told in my first book, *The Ship Would Not Travel Due West*. I had begun to realize another cherished ambition, to write.

After this it was inevitable, I suppose, that the call of distant seas should become irresistible. With my then wife Fiona and our daughters, Susie aged two and one-year-old Vicky, we set off round the world via stormy Magellan Strait in the catamaran *Rehu Moana*, accompanied for two-thirds of the way by a friend, Priscilla Cairns. The circumnavigation lasted three years.

Now, ever since my school days in New Zealand and on the Pacific island of Rarotonga, where my Maori relatives had recited ancestral sea sagas, I had been fascinated by the voyages and migrations of the Polynesians who had colonized every speck of land in the Pacific – an ocean that covers a third of the earth. In an attempt to test how accurate were the old navigator-priests' methods, we used them between Tahiti, Rarotonga and New Zealand with surprisingly good results (final landfall in New Zealand was only twenty-six miles out in latitude). Later on, in Tonga and other islands we encountered sailing canoe and cutter captains who still guided their vessels by the ancient methods of their forefathers: star paths, ocean swells and birds that signpost the way to land. These encounters eventually led to a four-year research fellowship at the Australian National University, which involved going to sea as pupil of the last great pre-instrumental navigators in the world, and being instructed by them in the secrets that conferred on them the freedom of the ocean. In the ketch *Isbjorn* then, my son Barry and I spent a year among the islands, after which I wrote *We the Navigators*, the book that later brought Mimi and me together.

From exploration into the origins of man's maritime heritage it was but a short step to probing the contemporary sea frontier – the stormiest ocean on earth, that girdles the earth below Cape Horn and seals off Antarctica. So 1972 found me in 32-foot *Ice Bird* bound from Sydney towards the Antarctic peninsula 6,000 miles away. Three months and two capsizes later the gallant little ship reached her goal and the first single-handed voyage to Antarctica had been accomplished. The following equally eventful season was spent exploring the Antarctic coast and *en route* to South Africa, a destination determined by another capsize.

Lack of moral fibre ended my own voyage in Cape Town and it was left to my son Barry to sail *Ice Bird* single-handed in ninety-two solitary days to Sydney, where the battered little ship now rests in honourable retirement in the Museum of Science and Technology.

Despite the fears and discomforts I had gone through, I found myself enthralled by the stern southern continent. With like-minded friends I set up the Oceanic Research Foundation for a rather more scientific engagement with its secrets. Our first expedition was to Cape Adare and the Balleny Islands in the cramped and uncomfortable old racing yacht *Solo* in 1977–8, described here in Chapter 1.

From Mimi's cottage in Charlottesville, Virginia, we set out in May 1982, just as the dogwood and redbush were fading, to enlist support and recruit candidates. One pertinent question that gave us thought concerned our own leadership role as a couple: would it be weakened by our close relationship? Just the reverse, we concluded. Highly successful ocean cruises are very often led by husband and wife teams who are the nucleus of their ships' companies, the 'parents' of their 'family', as it were. Certain particularly isolated Alaskan stations of the US National Weather Service, notably St Lawrence Island, have likewise been manned by husband and wife teams, like that of Antarctic explorer Rudi Honkola and his wife, Barbara.

The paramount thing is, of course, the competence of the couple; each must have earned his or her position in his own right, quite apart from their mutual bond. But, however well or ill we deserved our jobs as leader and deputy, we were obviously going to need a strong team to back us up. 'Guts, flexibility and commitment', was how I summed up the qualities most needed. Experience was less vital.

Unfortunately at least eight of my former companions who possessed these attributes in full measure were not available. They were busy with their own projects, scattered from Canada to Antarctica to the high Himalaya. One had his farm to care for, another a wife and new job. We had to recruit from scratch.

At Polar Programs in Washington we were put on the track of a young man who had wintered in Antarctica. We interviewed him before we left the city, and he afterwards submitted a written application. Sad to say, his concept of Antarctic life was of being in prison – not at all the outlook we needed!

Others were not unnaturally deterred by the prospect of spending such a very lengthy period, not only without pay, but having to contribute $3,000 towards expedition expenses. Another disappointment was when a zoologist studying emperor penguins at Hubbs Sea World Research Institute in San Diego wanted to come with us but her supervisors refused her leave. Our visit to Hubbs was productive, however. Dr Jeanette Thomas, an expert in marine mammal vocalization, provided Mimi with hydrophone equipment to record the underwater sounds of Weddell seals. These sounds – 'songs' would be a more appropriate word – differed in two widely separated Antarctic locations; would there be yet a third 'dialect' where we were going?

Our final US city, Los Angeles, provided some first-rate Wilderness Experience polar clothing through the good offices of helpful West Coast climbers. Mimi was able to contact several 'human factors' researchers and we underwent our first psychological tests.

This busy month in the United States was only a foretaste of what awaited us in Australia. We landed in Sydney early in June 1982 to be met by my son Barry. An ex-Pacific trading ketch skipper and solo yachtsman, he and his wife Ros run a navigation and sailing school. Their three-year-old daughter Jacquie had obviously been carefully programmed. 'Hello Granny,' she greeted Mimi with aplomb.

My youngest daughter, eighteen-year-old Vicky, was also in Sydney at this time, back from a six-month dance tour of Japan. The sisters, Vicky and Susie, with one and a half circumnavigations accomplished at a tender age, were no strangers to the sea and its dangers. Vicky, who was soon going on tour again, took Mimi aside.

'You *will* look after Daddy, won't you?' she begged earnestly. Absurd, I thought, but how prophetic were her fears can be seen from the Prologue.

The sailing date from Sydney would be mid-November this time, a month earlier because of the added length of the approach voyage. There were just over four months to go, little enough time for all that had to be done. *Dick Smith Explorer* had proved herself in storms and ice but a lot of fine tuning was needed to improve her sailing performance; sheet winches had to be fitted, for instance, and a combined trim tab and jury rudder for better steering control and emergency back-up. Instruments such as autopilot and echosounder were in need of attention; there was a new satellite navigation system to be obtained. Closed-circuit cooling systems would be needed for both the 120 hp Mercedes diesel main engine and the diesel generator, because once the ship became icebound no outside cooling water would be available. Kerosene or diesel cabin heaters were a must. The schooner would have to be slipped for painting and for a skeg or small keel to be fitted to protect the rudder and the propeller.

There was much winter polar gear to acquire: clothing, sledges, special tents, sleeping bags, insulated boots, skis, field cookers and a snowmobile. All equipment would have to be rigorously tested. Four expeditioners were still needed since our US recruitment had been unsuccessful, ideally two men and two women; desirable skills were diesel engineer, radio operator, electronics technician, zoologist and glaciologist, and the more polar and deep-sea experience the better.

We did our best to make known the vacancies. Channel 7 screened a TV interview with us in which we invited applicants. Appropriate journals carried notices. My latest book, *The Maori*, had been chosen as New Zealand book of the month and, by courtesy of the Book of the Month Club, we were able to broadcast our message all over New Zealand in the course of a two-week book promotion tour.

There were responses aplenty to our publicity. Just over 100 people applied all told. The snag was that so very long away from home, family, and income ruled out most of the better qualified. The ones who confirmed their interest turned out to lack skills and experience. There was one gentleman, for instance, who suffered, it appeared, from every known form of allergy. He could not eat bread, biscuits, butter, margarine, most meats, sausages, tomatoes, bananas or preserved foods. We could only applaud his spirit in volunteering. Another applicant submitted a logistic scheme worthy of a super-power's resources and capped it all by a plan to circumvent pirates, manifesting, we felt, a certain lack of proportion. By now we realized that, unlike the two earlier and shorter ventures when we could take our pick of polar scientists and skilled technicians, the field this time was going to be limited.

The first person to appear on the scene and be ultimately selected was Jannik Schou, a 29-year-old Danish gamekeeper, who had heard of our need for people while he was on holiday in New Zealand and had flown to Sydney eager to take part. He was a big, powerful man, his self-image proclaimed by the Viking horned helmet that he had inked onto his rucksack and later was to use to identify all his equipment.

'I spent five years training practically on three different Danish estates to become a gamekeeper,' Jannik explained. 'This education was finished with a five-month course at the Danish school for gamekeepers. Also in this period I did nine months' military service in the Royal Queen's Guard in Copenhagen. Then I worked in deer keeping and deer stalking on the Strathspey estates in Scotland.' Jannik was a keen wildlife photographer and had had two of his illustrated articles published. He had been a handyman at the National Outdoor Training Centre at Glenmore Lodge in the Scottish Highlands, where he had learned something of snow and ice climbing techniques. He had ski'd, he said, in Scotland and Norway and had done a little sailing, mostly on his father's yacht in the Kattegat.

'Could you,' we asked, 'assist in simple maintenance procedures on the engine? We could arrange for a diesel mechanic's course for you if you like.' Jannik thought this would be beyond him. We asked him to think it over and a little later he wrote us a note: 'Have very little sense and understanding of things mechanical and electrical. I have a deep and genuine interest in joining this expedition. But even if it was to be my last straw I have little faith that a course covering the fine technology of a Mercedes Benz engine would make me an instant mechanic.'

Well, that was that, a pity we thought, since he would only have been required to assist in maintenance. But here at least was an enthusiastic strong man. He was accustomed, he told us, to working in cold, icy, windy conditions, and we had no reason to disbelieve him. He would certainly need no urging to measure his strength against the polar wilderness and seek out and observe the wildlife. Rather he might have to be restrained a little, for his prudence was yet to be tested. How well he would cope with less congenial activities was not so sure. But he was certainly a doer, and this was a very big plus indeed. Without final commitment, we accepted Jannik's offer to move his belongings into the centre cabin and to help with the preparations.

There were many volunteer helpers, with Don Richards as their general engineering and electronics supervisor, thus taking an enormous weight off my shoulders, for the preparation of the vessel was but one of our tasks, that included drumming up support: food, fuel and equipment. One major cross Don had to bear was conflicting advice from many self-proclaimed specialists. In a fit of well-justified fury, centred around the

Yanmar diesel generator that was plagued from the start with instillation and wiring problems, he penned the following lines.

The Expert

by Don Richards

After months and months of waiting
and plying them with gin
the Yanmar arrived with flute and drum
It's ready to go in!!!

After days and days of rancour
And old sores resurrected
The team from H . . . announce
The Yanmar is connected!!

'Top up the fuel – turn on the switch –
We've done it for you cheap!'
So we did all that, and would you guess
Not a bloody beep

'The wiring's wrong,' friend Roy announced
'Of this there can be no doubt – your boys
from H . . . Marine
Have got it arse about.'

So down he comes with kit of tools
And puts the wiring right
Packs up his bag and buggers off
Far into the night.

'Come back you lousy sod' we shout,
We set the dockyard ringing.
Each warning light is showing red
And every bell is ringing.

We track him down. 'I'm sorry, friends
The answer must be no –
My time is fully occupied
On my stand at the Boat Show'

So friends, the moral of these things
That all have come to pass
Is to take your bloody experts
And stick them up your arse!

This was not exaggerated. Don had no more than scratched the surface of the tale of excuses and highly expensive mistakes he was still to encounter over installation and servicing of equipment. At least he had reason to hope that the Yanmar's troubles would soon be over, and no praise could be too high for Don's efforts, upon which the success of the expedition largely depended.

Geoff Campbell, a radio and electronics enthusiast, was Don's right hand man. He worked with us every day of his six weeks' vacation; an old age pensioner named Harry spent his only two free days each week doing carpentry aboard. Tony Nelson, a schooner skipper, helped in sea trials, gave us hospitality and donated some of his own equipment. Jannik built two splendid plywood sledging boxes. Busy as we were, there was a real sense of fulfilment at each step accomplished. We worked happily, with the winter sun striking warm enough for us to go shirtless more often than not and to pad about in bare feet.

One helper, who unexpectedly was to become a member of the expedition later on, was 57-year-old Norm Linton Smith. He had driven up from Melbourne the previous year to spend three weeks working in *Explorer*'s engine room with Don and Gary. Norm had unusual ideas about diet, but there was nothing wrong with that. He seemed to love fiddling with anything mechanical, but that could be all to the good. He had a distinguished Antarctic record.

We were grateful for his help for the second year in a row when he arrived to spend a fortnight to help with the fitting out. We gladly accepted his offer of assistance and he joined Jannik in the centre cabin.

Norm's recently published comments in *Aurora* magazine (May 1985) are a good deal more negative than anything he said at the time, but he deserves his say, even in retrospect.

Speaking of the earlier Mawson Anniversary preparations, he writes:

> I lived on the boat for three weeks, helping with the conversion of the vessel from a motor fishing boat to a three-masted motor-sailer. I worked from 0730 to 1630 every day. Lewis rarely appeared at the yard to check on progress, the ORF was financially shaky and the contractors frequently went on to other jobs, such as sand-blasting and painting, presumably to get some immediate income.
>
> As a consequence, the conversion work fell behind schedule and Lewis and his crew of eleven sailed in November in an incomplete vessel. . . . In October 1982, I went to Sydney again to help in preparation for the next Antarctic voyage [the Frozen Sea Expedition of 1982–4]. This time the boat was much better prepared than at the same time in 1981, but there was still much essential mechanical and electrical work that needed to be done for a wintering rather than just a summer voyage.

All true enough, but I would like to make one comment on the earlier expedition. You are *never* completely prepared for a small-ship ocean voyage. If you wait for perfection you will never sail at all. The responsibility of leadership, and it is a very heavy one indeed, is to make sure of the essentials and get going. That no essentials were neglected in 1981 is apparent in the outcome. This cannot be said so confidently about the later venture, when I was guilty of several errors of judgement – as we shall see.

In addition to gratefully accepting Norm's help with the engines, I asked him to demonstrate crevasse rescue techniques to us all, as Harry and Dick had done at Cape Denison. 'I also trained the crew, including Lewis and George, in crevasse rescue techniques,' Norm wrote, a rather grandiloquent description of a half-hour's praiseworthy effort!

Our sleeping arrangements should now be explained, as they have a bearing on our story and because each person's private and personal living space, albeit no more than a bunk, becomes hugely important to people crowded together in the midst of vast solitudes. Mimi and I occupied the low-ceilinged 'cave' underneath the wheelhouse. It opened into the galley, thus guaranteeing minimal privacy, seeing that the galley was the ship's social centre as well as cooking area. There was just enough heardroom to sit upright and to crawl around on hands and knees. Mimi, who is tall, had to choose between sleeping curled up or stretched out, in which case her feet projected through a hole in the bulkhead and took the dregs of every icy sea that entered the wheelhouse in rough weather.

The one-time fish hold, now centre cabin, by contrast, was comparatively luxurious. Each of the four bunks had stowage space and a locker. There was a settee and a hanging locker for oilskins. The insulation was much the best on the ship.

Explorer's fore cabin had been occupied on the Mawson trip by Dot, Margaret, Dick and Malcolm. They were hardy, uncomplaining souls, who put up cheerfully with a great deal of discomfort, particularly the waves that soaked their bunks in every storm. For the new expedition this cabin, together with the lavatory-washroom that opened off the engine room, was relegated to storage, and we to the use of a sanitary bucket and the galley sink for washing.

Apart from ourselves in the 'cave', everyone shared the centre cabin for the duration of the sixteen-month expedition, though the fore cabin was free for occupation once stores had been unloaded in Antarctica.

Towards the end of his stint as helper, Norm applied to join the expedition. His credentials were impeccable: 'Radio operator in World War II bombers over Germany; mechanical engineering degree; 17 years service with the Australian Antarctic Division as training and equipment officer'. He had participated in a skidoo and sledge traverse of the Amery Ice Shelf some years earlier as well as having made a number of short visits to Antarctica and one to Arctic Canada. While he had done no serious sailing, he did know our engine room pretty well by this time. He should be able to judge exactly what was needed in the way of tools and spare parts. Norm, like me, suffers from arthritis, but reported that a specially undertaken medical check-up had given him the go-ahead for Antarctic work. A serious drawback was that he was not a ham radio operator and had no knowledge of electronics, so would be unable to service the radios, which would inevitably be subjected to not a little stress.

We turned him down, not as he has since implied in favour of a woman applicant, who had a very different potential role. We agreed to short-list him as one of the standbys, for the tally of his qualifications was impressive.

The expedition's next recruit was a youthful engineer–radio operator. He was extremely bright and functioned very well under Don's fatherly eye. Once we put to sea in real earnest, however, the true enormity of the undertaking and the weight of the responsibilities he had assumed came home to him. It is to his credit that he had the courage to acknowledge his limitations and pull out before it was too late. His action did naturally produce a first-rate crisis at Flinders, our first port of call after Sydney, as the reader will soon see.

Jamie Miller wrote to us from Melbourne asking for details of the expedition. He was, he said, '25, a science graduate of La Trobe University (B.Sc.) with majors in zoology (animal ecology) and microbiology'. He had 'studied geology to third year level'. His sailing experience had been confined to dinghies. His main recreations, he added more encouragingly, were bushwalking and ski-touring. Jamie had never managed to get a job in biology since qualifying (no discredit in the state of the job market). He had worked at assorted jobs, several of them in his father's enterprises.

After receiving our reply, Jamie wrote back on 14 July applying to join the expedition. He pointed out that 'letters can very rarely convey the character of an individual. For instance, how can a person convey his amicability? (Or lack of it?) This would be most important if 5 or 6 people were to spend 16 months in close quarters ... If necessary I will come to Sydney.' A well-expressed letter and a sensible suggestion. We asked him to visit us. But another sentence in his letter was to become significant. 'I have read the rules and conditions and am prepared to and able to meet all conditions.' These covered, among other subjects, our agreement to send all film taken to the *National Geographic*.

Jamie impressed us when he came to Sydney with his long-term enthusiasm for Antarctica and the breadth of his reading on polar exploration. His gestures were quick, his features mobile and expressive, he was an excellent and comic mimic with a fund of anecdotes and a flair for telling them. Jannik disapproved of Jamie's 'rude humour' and soon was to comment unfavourably on his untidiness, and slovenly performance during sea trials. Unfairly, as it turned out, we did not take Jannik's criticisms at face value because, with a refreshing lack of charity, he tended to be negative about *any* potential rival for a place in the crew.

After a short visit Jamie returned to Melbourne and set about busily contacting firms with requests for equipment, with some success, especially over the loan of skis. His enthusiasm in those early days knew no bounds. In one long letter after another to Mimi he outlined his plans for obtaining more equipment and for scientific research projects. There would be great opportunities for original research into seabird biology in particular, he thought. He was making out field programmes. In this, Jamie was certainly correct. The Larsemann Hills, Amanda Bay and even the Rauer Islands, which are not far from Davis station, are inaccessible to biologists in late autumn, winter and spring. Yet the area is host to innumerable breeding colonies of seabirds, including penguins, and also to Weddell seal rookeries. All this area would be accessible to us with our over-ice travel capability. Particularly important would be the spring, when exuberant life re-established itself on the Antarctic coasts.

Gill Cracknell appeared very late on at an 'open boat' fund-raising weekend. She and Mimi slipped into the centre cabin for a chat, soon joined by curious guests, who wondered audibly whether the people bunking there might not freeze solid in their sleep. Gill laughed, but listened closely to Mimi's reassuring reply.

This 24-year-old British geographer had worked since graduation for the IMCO Maritime Agency of the United Nations in London in the navigation section. She had left the agency to travel before moving into environmental research. Now on a working holiday in Australia, she had seen the Channel 7 film of the 1981–2 Mawson Anniversary Expedition on television and read newspaper reports of our plans. Gill asked about basics – what were the expedition goals and what would she be doing if she were to take part? She made clear that hard work was no obstacle and the outdoors field work was her main interest.

'Geography gives me a good grounding in field techniques and an interest in a wide variety of spheres,' she told us.

Gill loved sailing above all sports. Regular family cruises off the south coast of England might be expected to stand her in good stead, for the Channel, especially round Portland Bill, that Gill knew well, is not the world's easiest cruising ground. Her other activities included orienteering, long-distance running, skiing, squash and hiking in Britain, Norway and the USA. A thoroughly outdoor person, it was clear. I summed her up approvingly as having all the traditional English virtues – a slow starter maybe, but dogged, loyal, brave, and totally dependable once she understood a situation. There was never occasion to revise this opinion.

While still on trial as a potential expeditioner Gill burnt her boats by resigning her job to give her more time to help us get ready and give us a chance to get to know her in a working situation. She was accepted, and this was the best thing we ever did.

An essential preliminary to the expedition was a trial trip in *Explorer* to Hobart, Tasmania. The purpose was to test ship and equipment rigorously on a 700 miles each way passage, to try out candidates in two winter weeks at sea, and thirdly, to liaise with the Antarctic Division and the Australian National Antarctic Research Expeditions (ANARE), whose headquarters were at Kingston, near Hobart. Like most plans it was only partially successful.

One error on my part was to agree with the local *National Geographic* representative that Mimi should concentrate on photography. She was thus not able on this voyage to assume her duties as mate, with the result that she did not get to know the candidates 'in action', nor did they learn to work under her exacting direction. (The term 'exacting' is used without apology. Mimi, with my full backing, would be doing her best to bring the party up to the highest possible standard of competence and reliability. Nothing less would serve where we were bound.)

A second mischance was that our personnel advisor, an experienced psychiatrist with Antarctic experience, could only sail on one leg of the trip and a key candidate only on the other, so they did not meet until later. Under pressure of events I accepted Jamie's application before the subsequent psychological assessment (which all candidates underwent). This was a bad mistake because no circumstance could really justify the by-passing of rigorous selection procedures for such a demanding expedition.

Tasmania was the scene of important discussions with the Antarctic professionals. We sought information on the safest route through the pack ice and on where would be the best and most scientifically productive wintering-over site. I had had in mind the Rauer Islands, which are inaccessible from Australia's Davis base in winter by reason of unstable intervening sea ice. The then director, Clary McCue, strongly advocated the Larsemann Hills, as being near extreme helicopter range from the Australian base during the short summer and inaccessible for the rest of the year.

Most of the Ingrid Christiansen Coast of Prydz Bay where the Larsemanns are situated is poorly mapped, so aerial photographs that Clary had had prepared for us were pored over. Disappointingly, these pictures, and others that Mimi and I perused later at National Mapping in Canberra, revealed no really safe havens. There were long fjords, it is true, but these did not always unfreeze, so that getting in was no guarantee that we would get out again for years.

I agreed to try for the Larsemanns, which was obviously the site of choice for research, with the option of falling back on the security of the Rauers, which offered a host of sheltered bays, and then making use of our snowmobile to reach the main research area. But we sincerely hoped we could find a protected haven in the Larsemanns. Apart from the unknown nature of the 45-odd miles of winter ice we would have to traverse between the two areas, the proximity of the Rauers to Davis would be unsettling psychologically and scientific observations there less valuable.

The Antarctic Division biologists were eager to meet us. Many of them had for years wanted to research the sixty miles from the Sørsdal Glacier south of Davis to the Larsemanns but had been denied the opportunity except in summer by a ban on over-ice travel from Davis. They were more than anxious to set up joint projects which could capitalize on our freedom of movement over the frozen sea. Jamie and Jannik soon amassed a wealth of reprints and proposals (Gill had not yet joined us).

Equipment that would have been virtually unobtainable elsewhere was generously loaned us by Rod Ledingham, the equipment officer: a Nansen man-haul sledge, two pairs of wooden skis with bindings to fit our boots, six pairs of insulated 'Mickey Mouse' boots, ventile windproof smocks and overtrousers, alpine equipment like Jumars and two ice-axes and two Beche and one polar pyramid tent. These tents weigh 40 and 90 lb respectively, so can be dragged easily on sledges though they are overly heavy for backpacking. But they are able to stand up to blizzards when little else can.

Mimi studied social and psychological research reports in the ANARE library and consulted medical personnel. A day's snowcraft practice was enjoyable but abortive, because what little snow we found was rapidly disappearing and of the consistency of porridge.

As we set off back to Sydney we had reason to be pleased with our visit. The sea trip provided an opportunity to hone our safety procedures: making sure that everyone understood the workings of the emergency life raft release and man overboard drill, and, more especially, how to avoid falling in at all. Another safety precaution, this time to guard against the terrifying hazard of fire at sea, was a ban on all smoking below decks. Jamie, it turned out, was the only one affected. We were to be impressed at how well he stuck by the rule, even puffing away in snow storms huddled behind the forward companionway.

'You just *don't ever* fall overboard, that's the first rule,' I stressed. 'Where we are going you could be dead of cold before we could pick you up. There is no excuse for ever climbing outside our high railings without clipping on the line from your safety harness. We will always wear our safety harnesses when on watch at night and at all times when it is rough.' This rule, it is good to be able to record, was never broken.

The return trip was uneventful except for one rather disquieting incident. A candidate crew member and the psychiatrist who was making a point of working with each applicant were on night watch in a shipping lane off the New South Wales coast.

'I can't see at all well at night,' the psychiatrist confessed. 'In fact, I can't tell the red from the green ship's lights.' Now, the colour of port and starboard navigation lights is of course the key to the rules for preventing collision at sea.

'That will be all right,' the candidate assured his companion. 'You just carry on steering and do the best you can.' He thereupon retired below and went to sleep, leaving the colour-blind helmsman in sole charge of our lives.

When I was told of this incident, I chided the offender in no uncertain terms. He was apologetic, but how could we trust his judgement in the future? Eventually, it was agreed that on balance his strong points would override the weak, though he would always need close supervision. He was shortly afterwards included in the team, a decision we had no cause to regret.

Back in Sydney preparations proceeded apace. The team was now complete and all were living aboard. Lars Larsen, veteran of our 1977–8 expedition, as well as of Greenland and Mawson base, brought us the scarlet Eskimo sledge he had built us. Two American fibreglass lightweight sledges were loaned us. A second-hand snowmobile was purchased and, after dismantling, lowered with barely an inch to spare into the hold.

We were particularly indebted to Ampol Petroleum. They filled our 5,000 litre (2,000 gallon) fuel tanks free of charge with a special Antarctic mixture recommended by the Antarctic Division personnel I had consulted. In view of later events that statement needs amplifying. Special Antarctic Blend (SAB), which is about 70 per cent diesel and 30 per cent kerosene, was what they used, they told me, and Ampol agreed to make up an equivalent mixture. After we got back from Hobart Norm told us he had run primus stoves and diesel engines on the same fuel in the Antarctic, but he could not recall its name. This was impossible with our mixture, as we soon found by experiment, so I phoned the Antarctic Division from Sydney and spoke to two knowledgeable people, who both confirmed the SAB. They were right. So was Norm.

The explanation only came to light much later, and then in distressing circumstances. SAB *was* used on all the stations and in some polar vehicles, but only in electrically heated tanks. For all other diesels in the field and for primus stoves and heaters Aviation Turbo Kerosene (ATK) was the fuel. Thus, while the SAB recommendation was made in good faith in ignorance of the fact that our fuel tanks were not heated, ATK was obviously the fuel we should have had. I have one last point to add here. Someone at Hobart is alleged to have said that he recommended ATK to me during our visit. This sounds very odd, for I was there to ask advice and only too ready to follow it. I did so, and that was not the advice I was given.

Ampol also supplied lubricating oil and the kerosene for our stoves and heaters and the petrol for outboard motors and the snowmobile. They even agreed to top up our tanks at Albany, Western Australia, our point of final departure from Australia. There is no way I can adequately express our thanks.

With such generous donations as these, the ORF was making ends meet, but we crew members had little enough money to spare for our own living expenses.

'Time to go up the road for fruit and vegetables,' Mimi suggested one evening.

'But the shops will be shut now,' someone objected.

'That's the idea. The shops put out perfectly good produce in the garbage cans each night – only a little softened, maybe. David and I have been raking through the cans for weeks. Come and help us carry home the spoils.' The night's harvest of watermelons, cantaloupe, lettuce and tomatoes quite won over the doubters. I was wryly amused. In court that very morning I had been accused in a property settlement case of 'living off the backs of the business community'!

All this time Mimi was heavily engaged in sorting out still and movie photographic gear and constructing safe, dry, insulated storage places, as well as distributing questionnaires and recording interviews. It was a condition for acceptance into the expedition to participate in the study, and everyone had readily agreed. Mimi had carefully explained the methodology. Each of us would keep a structured journal that she provided, recording daily events, subjective reactions towards others and dreams and fantasies.

Questionnaires were both standardized and specially prepared. Mimi undertook to hold confidential the journal entries and questionnaire answers, which would not be looked at until after the expedition was over. These data would be reserved solely for scientific publication.

Accordingly, no confidential material has been used in this book or in Appendix 1. I doubt that the reader will miss much, however, for people freely discussed their diary entries, often reading passages aloud in the galley, joked about their answers to the questionnaires, especially the sex ones, and related with gusto the night's dreams. No sooner was all this under control, and the mate about to get systematically acquainted with the finer points of *Explorer*'s engine, generator, electrics and electronic equipment, than another blow fell. Three weeks before sailing date the food procurement arrangements, which had been in the hands of an outside helper, suddenly collapsed when the discouraged volunteer confessed that it was all too much and gave up. Things, as Mimi said, 'were in a dead stall'. She had to drop everything to concentrate on the vital task of provisioning. Gill rallied nobly to help.

It is best that Mimi tell the story in her own words.

I had to reckon on laying in basic supplies for six people, that could be supplemented by hunting, for upwards of two years should the ice trap the ship for a second unscheduled winter. We had to receive most of it free – as tax-deductible donations – and get it delivered to the wharf immediately! Quantities and ratios did not always reflect deliberate planning, but sometimes only as much as a manufacturer was able to make available or what we could not do without. We could, for instance, have done with far more chocolate than the 50 kg given us. The three dozen bottles of rum might similarly with advantage have been increased.[2] We are often asked about vitamins. Everyone was issued with 250 mg a day of ascorbic acid (vitamin C) – five times the amount necesssary to prevent scurvy. That was all. Other vitamins were present in more than adequate quantites in the general diet; no signs of vitamin deficiency ever developed. Our meals were not going to be gourmet, but we had everything we needed for good polar health.

I worked out the requirements and amounts in this fashion: I recalled what I had eaten when doing physical work in the cold – offshore winter sailing, manual work in the winter, skiing. It came out at 5,000–6,000 calories a day, with a high proportion of fats and carbohydrates. David confirmed that this was a pretty standard polar figure. Then I worked backwards to what sort of menu would provide a balanced diet with adequate supplements for an individual working in the cold for one week. I multiplied this to get the figure for six people for two years.

I separated our requirements into three sections: at sea, where snacks for night watches and items needing little or no cooking during storms would be at a premium; aboard ship at anchor or frozen in, where we could bake easily; field sledging rations, taking into account weight, limited fuel, and physical exertion in the cold.

Added complications were that everything had to keep without refrigeration (for we had none) for the first two months of warm weather, thus ruling out fresh meat, fruit and vegetables – except for oranges and onions. Then there were the limits to what we could get free or at a big discount, and the modest carrying capacity of a small ship. Finally we wanted to bring enough 'treats' to brighten birthdays and other celebrations.

The food list included: Flour ⅓ ton; yeast 15 kg; pasta 150 kg; brown rice 100 kg; muesli (granola) 3 tons; long-life bread 500 loaves; eggs 64 dozen; savoury crackers and biscuits 500 boxes; fruit bars 4,500; margarine ¼ ton; vegetable oil 300 litres; long-life milk 48 litres; condensed milk 500 cans; powdered milk 35 kg; sugar 200 kg; honey 120 kg; dried fruit and nuts 80 kg; cheese 50 kg; canned meat 340 cans; dried meat 15 kg; TVP (vegetable protein) 25 kg. For use in the field 440 five-man packs of freeze-dried meals. Tea bags 20,000; freeze-dried coffee 8 kg; pure cocoa 20 kg; salami ¾ ton – of which more later.

The food cost the ORF under $7,000, but the market value of the food was over $30,000. There was hope that some other items, mostly from New Zealand, that were not ready in time, might reach us in Albany.

---

[2] Sir Ernest Shackleton ordered 472 cases of whisky delivered at the dock side for his last expedition (Rasmussen, 1973). Men were made of sterner stuff then – and neither could we afford it!

Incredible but true, Mimi and Gill had the bulk of the stores on the dock with four days to spare. As the piles of supplies accumulated it seemed that we could never get everything stowed aboard. But pack it all in we did in the end – albeit some items did not resurface for a year or more. The ship was loaded so that she sank nine inches below her marks.

The compass was swung once everything ferrous that could affect the magnetic instrument was in place. Compass adjustment was a particularly serious matter in a steel boat with a steel wheelhouse, the more so since we would be traversing waters where the compass variation (the angle between the magnetic pole, to which the compass needle points, and the geographic pole) would sometimes exceed 90 °W, so that the magnetic compass would be pointing west when we were actually heading south.

Everyone worked with a will, without rest and with but a minimum of sleep. Even so, it was beyond logic that we could be ready on time. Yet ready we were. Right on schedule *Dick Smith Explorer* cast off from Pier One by the Harbour Bridge at midday on 14 November 1982, and one hour later lifted to the Pacific rollers as she rounded South Head. A fair northwest wind filled the sails. In twenty-four hours we were 166 nautical miles down the coast. The wearying investment of months and years had come at last to fruition. The great adventure had begun. The dream was a reality.

3

To Ile Amsterdam
15 November 1982–7 January 1983

'The wind can't read the American Pilot Charts'
attributed to Sir Francis Chichester

I laid out on the charts a dog-leg course to Antarctica, first towards the west, then south, to avoid bucking the fierce westerly winds known as the roaring forties, but properly including the fifties, that scour the Southern Ocean. The resulting wind-driven storm waves surge round the world unimpeded by large land, save only Tasmania extending down to 43°S, New Zealand to 47° and the great South American barrier that culminates in Cape Horn in 56°S.

After consulting pilot books and wind charts, I decided to skirt the strong westerly belt by keeping in the thirties. Our track would be through Bass Strait between Australia proper and Tasmania, where our first optional port of call, Flinders near Melbourne, was 550 miles from Sydney. Then we would follow a 1,350-mile slog across the Great Australian Bight to Albany in Western Australia, where we would refuel, top up water tanks and take on last-minute provisions.

Next westward again, halfway across the Indian Ocean towards Africa, 1,990 miles to be exact, to get north of Prydz Bay. The turning point could be Ile Amsterdam, Iles Kerguelen or Heard Island further south, though circumstances were to dictate the first of these. From Ile Amsterdam we could head directly towards our objective 1,860 miles to the southward. The west winds would then be on our right hand (starboard beam for purists) most of the way, but beyond about 63°S a new wind regime, the polar easterlies, prevails. We would still have a fair wind, from the left-hand side this time. The distance all told would be 5,750 nautical miles and would involve a fair proportion of head winds, storms and ultimately pack ice.

Everyone was exhausted after the demanding preparations; Jamie, Gill and the young engineer were seasick into the bargain. The fact that the toilet compartment was jam-packed with stores and gear and would remain unusable for the duration added to our problems. To have to balance on the ship's rail secured by a safety harness, or on a bucket, is less than gracious living, especially when one is feeling under the weather.

In spite of feeling and looking like death, with the ship corkscrewing and rolling, Gill showed her mettle. She was the first to spot and identify important shore lights by their timed flashes, because she was going over the charts and light list attentively so that she knew where to look and what she was looking for. She was foremost in learning to trim the sails when beating to windward while the others, like most beginners, tended to pin them in too tightly so that the ship stopped in her tracks and drifted sideways. We began to realize what an asset Gill was and hoped that Jannik and Jamie would shape up as well.

Coastal navigation, where headlands, rocks, tides, currents and shipping have to be constantly monitored, demands unceasing vigilance, far more than does the open ocean where land is far away and freighters few and far between. The 1,900 miles of coasting from Sydney to Western Australia, therefore, bade fair to be a good training ground. Mimi and I did not see much of each other because, for the time being, we each had to take charge of a separate watch.

There are numerous watch systems used at sea, the common denominator being the institution of half-length 'dog watches' which ensure that the duties rotate daily. The arrangement that we chose was six-hour watches with three-hour dog watches. Watch A comprised myself, Gill and Jamie (partly so that Gill, who had mostly worked with Mimi so far, could get used to my ways); watch B consisted of Mimi, Jannik and the engineer. These were the watch times and the first day's sequence of duties:

Afternoon watch, noon–6 p.m.	A watch
First dog watch, 6 p.m.–9 p.m.	B watch
Second dog watch, 9 p.m.–midnight	A watch
Night watch, midnight–6 a.m.	B watch
Forenoon watch, 6 a.m.–noon	A watch

One member of the afternoon watch in turn cooked the evening meal, backed up by an offsider who washed up and cleaned the galley, wheelhouse and stove. Not that there was much stomach for big dinners that first week out. Nevertheless, evening meals were planned to be communal gatherings, to socialize and talk over suggestions and problems (a weekly discussion session was also instituted). Four could sit comfortably at the galley table, while cook and assistant served or sat on plastic water cans or took turns at the wheel.

All of us made drinks at any odd time and cooked what hot snacks we wanted. From the outset the problem was to get the crew to use and maintain the pressure stove properly. The flame must burn high at all times and the burners be pricked regularly; the stove had to be cleaned meticulously. The price of neglect was sooted up burners and pipes, which wore out rapidly and leaked at the joints. The stove was essential for life support, not only for cooking, but in the Antarctic for melting ice to drink and for warmth. This stress on excellence may sound fussy, but it must be remembered that it was upon just such details of commission and omission that our very lives depended.

Noon on the second day saw *Explorer*, having rounded Gabo Island in the early hours, beating up Bass Strait close-reefed in the teeth of a rising gale. The driving chain of the autopilot snapped. The instrument had stopped twice before, once with a blown fuse, then with a faulty switch. Each time Mimi, poring over the instruction manual between watches, had dismantled the mechanism in the tossing wheelhouse and put it right. But there was no spare chain or extra links; any repair would be a harbour job. This was a blow because an autopilot is a great boon, obviating the monotony of long-term hand steering and allowing those on watch to get on with the innumerable tasks, like preventing ropes from chafing and doing minor repairs, that the sea always provides.

Navigationally the ship was well served. Day and night, storm or shine, by merely pressing buttons on our Walker Satellite Navigator and waiting a few hours at most until a suitable satellite passed over, we obtained accurate position fixes. I looked back on the 5,000 miles of the Pacific I had sailed without any instruments at all as pupil of the South Seas star path navigators and had to pinch myself to make sure I was awake and this was real. Even the familiar position fixing by sextant, so time-consuming and difficult in a storm-tossed yacht and impossible in heavy overcast, was in another dimension altogether.

The Furuno radar was another instrument that weathered successfully every abuse that ice and storm could heap upon it. How easy it was simply to read off on the radar screen the ship's distance from the coast or from an approaching ship. How welcome it was going to be later to have the assurance that some blinding snow shower did not conceal the lurking menace of an iceberg.

If these two instruments behaved impeccably, the same could not be said of the Yanmar diesel generator. It had, as we saw from Don's poetic effusion, been plagued from the start with installation and wiring problems, compounded by the conflicting advice of experts. Now it kept unaccountably stopping. It appeared to be overheating, though a faulty temperature gauge read cool, so what could be the reason? It seemed scarcely credible that yet another mistake had been made in its installation. Whatever the trouble, there was no help for it. We had no choice but to put into the delightful little harbour of Flinders to have it and the auto-pilot put right. This was hardly an auspicious start to the long approach voyage, for *Explorer* had covered less than one-eleventh of the distance in the five days since Sydney.

This time at long last we were fortunate enough to find genuine experts. The closed cooling system of the Yanmar, it turned out, was inadequate in the warm summer seas, a problem compounded by the malfunctioning of the overheating alarms. The tank through which the cooling water cir-culated, which was analogous to a car's radiator, was too small for these latitudes, though it would probably function well enough in zero tempera-tures. The solution was to restore the original sea water cooling for the time being and switch back to the closed circuit in winter quarters. A sound signal and a flashing red light were installed to give warning of impending trouble. In the event, they were never activated. It was a great relief to have a proper installation, though we could not but be bitter at the botching that had cost us so dear.

The diagnosis and cure took four days, during which the elderly auto-pilot was also put right. As if we were not busy enough, I was responsible for a ludicrous accident that wasted precious hours. When changing berths from one side of the pier to the other I swung too wide and *Explorer* went aground on a falling tide. There was no danger since the ship would, and did, float off in twelve hours when the tide came up again. But as we sunbathed on the tilted deck, our embarrassment was compounded by the sight of two helicopters from rival TV networks land-ing on the beach and their occupants descending upon us. My feelings can be imagined.

'Next time we run aground,' I promised, 'it will be in Antarctica where there are *no* TV cameras.' This was a prophetic utterance.

It was at Flinders that the young engineer's crisis surfaced with a ven-geance. His overt complaint was that Jamie's behaviour made it impossible for him to continue. 'Either Jamie goes or I go,' he insisted. While his allegations of Jamie's shortcomings had to be taken into account, it was obvious that this was a bit of a smokescreen. Something deeper underlay the complaints. Whatever else was troubling him, the only certainty was that he was looking for a way to bow out. He proposed that he continue to Albany while retaining the option of leaving us there. We well under-stood his feelings; he was a likeable young fellow to whom the realities of life at sea, the intense discomfort, uncongenial and unfamiliar sailing duties, his heavy responsibilities compounded by the refractory Yanmar and seasickness had combined to bring home how daunting was the task to which he had set his hand.

'Everyone in the party just has to be totally committed,' Mimi explained. 'There is too much at stake for us to be half-hearted. We have to be single-minded about our commitment to the expedition.'

'That is why we simply can't agree to your making up your mind at Albany,' I added. 'I'm afraid you must decide one way or another now. That will at least give us a chance to get a replacement if we have to.'

'If I withdraw now, can I carry on as far as Albany?' he asked.

'Of course. We would welcome your help.'

The conversation ranged back and forth for some time, the upshot being the young man's decision to resign. Norm Linton Smith, who of course was not there, describes the incident as follows: 'The engineer/radio op. and Lewis had had clashes and they were fed up with each other.'

Our first choice for a replacement for the young engineer came out from Melbourne that night. Things had changed, he said. He and his girl friend were going to get married. A good and sufficient reason, we had to agree, not to leave her for sixteen months. The second in line, when we telephoned his home in Sydney, proved to be away hiking in the bush for an indefinite period. We could not delay until he surfaced.

In response to a telephone call Norm Linton Smith drove out to Flinders. He was enthusiastic at the idea of joining us. Yes, he knew the engine room well from his two stints aboard. He could join the ship at Albany, which would give him time to arrange his affairs and renew his radio operator's licence.

'How about the food?' I asked, since Norm's ideas were rather unconventional.

'I will eat what everyone else does,' Norm promised, and in this he was as good as his word.

'His mechanical engineering degree is impressive.' Mimi and I were talking things over alone. 'Then there's the radio,' I added. 'He can brush that up. He's bound to be able to teach us something with all his Antarctic experience. He was very helpful doing the crevasse rescue demonstration back in Sydney. What do you think?'

'Well, it's him or no one,' Mimi replied. 'You and I could handle all the mechanical things well enough. After all, we have both looked after boats' engines and radios for years. But we have more than enough on our plates as it is and these extra chores would cut into our research time badly. All we need is someone who can take the maintenance routines off our shoulders.' We decided to take him.

This left us with the problem of Jamie in the light of the young engineer's accusations against him. While making due allowance for exaggeration, there were things that could not be ignored. He had already twice lost his temper on deck, once in Sydney harbour and again at sea, when he had shouted and sworn in a complete rage when the life raft had come adrift and had to be secured in a hurry. This was extremely unsatisfactory behaviour, even allowing for inexperience.

Our discussion with Jamie took place in a secluded corner of the pier. At first he tended to be aggressive.

'Why should I be told what to do?' I'm as intelligent as anyone,' he said.

'Intelligence has nothing to do with it. Self-control has. You have to learn to do things at sea without getting in a state. All of us must keep on learning every day. But Mimi and I have had a good deal of experience. If you resent advice and blow your top like you have done twice so far you will be no use to the expedition,' I pointed out.

'I really do want to be part of this expedition. It is my one great opportunity. Going to the Antarctic has been my dream for years. My biology and geology can be really useful – look at all the projects I've been working on since Hobart – you don't really want me to come . . .' Jamie's face crumpled and he burst into tears.

I was touched. I like a man who can cry, who feels deeply enough and isn't afraid to show emotion.

'That crying was calculated,' was Mimi's opinion.

There was another thought-provoking incident concerning Jamie. At a farewell party thrown by his family, who had arrived in full force, his brother took us aside. 'Jamie doesn't like being told what to do,' he warned us belligerently. 'He doesn't like Americans and he specially doesn't like American women. If he feels crossed he will do his best to get even and he won't ever forget a grievance.'

'Whatever problems there are, we are going to work them out,' answered Mimi temperately, for after all the brother had put away a lot of beer. Then, firmly, 'There is no changing the fact that I am a woman, I have come from America and that I am second in command of this expedition.'

'I am sure Jamie is genuinely committed to the expedition and will do his best to fit in,' I said, recalling the morning's emotional scene. 'He can't be as paranoid as you are suggesting.'

Nevertheless, the scene left a doubt as to what underlay Jamie's very real enthusiasm. I was optimistic; Mimi less so. It is only fair to add that, with one notable exception, Jamie to his credit did behave with commendable calmness while we were at sea.

Despite such misgivings, which were in any case overshadowed by the prospect of the many challenges the ocean and the ice fields would undoubtedly have in store for us, we cast off in high spirits at 7 p.m. on 24 November. Head winds and a westerly gale slowed us down until we cleared Cape Otway and the land fell away. Then the daily runs increased from a pitiable 56 miles in the first twenty-four hours to 74, to 88 and then to 144 as we gained enough sea room to make best use of the wind.

Crossing the Great Australian Bight was a good time for all of us. The days were warm and sunny, so that shirts came off and squatting over the stern to perform natural functions was no hardship. Sheerwaters in abundance and the occasional yellow nosed albatross skimmed and wheeled across the swell lines. I offered to give sextant lessons. Mimi and Jamie were the only pupils, though Jamie, overly impatient for results, soon gave up.

Explorer's three-masted rig is inefficient because of the enormous windage of the tall spars and their attendant heavy rigging, but it allows, as intended, of easy sail changing. The sails are of manageable size and any one of them can be lowered in seconds when the wind increases, far quicker than it takes to reef. The large and the small jib are hanked on to separate stays and can be readily interchanged. All in all, the schooner is extremely easy to handle and the crew were increasingly mastering the routine.

Jamie was learning well and becoming proficient at sail handling. Jannik, with a seabird identification book in hand and Jamie to help him, began systematically to make careful bird counts (which he continued to keep up whenever we were at sea). He worked hard, splicing reefing lines, bird counting, and he was generally cheerful and positive. Gill was proving herself more of a seaman every day and the seasickness that had plagued her at the outset was gone, for the moment at least.

I was surprised to find that the young engineer and Jamie had suddenly become boon companions. The former's violent antipathy had vanished without trace, nor did Jamie show any sign of resentment. It rather looked as if a game had been played. That the young engineer was capable of such was amply demonstrated several years later when he was in Wellington and *Explorer* was once again Antarctic bound. The young man was convicted in court of having sent out by radio a series of false distress calls purporting to have come from the vessel!

For the most part these were good days with generally fair winds and clear skies. For the first time in a tumultuous and hectic eighteen months Mimi and I had leisure to take stock, and to examine our personal lives, that had changed so dramatically since we met. I mentioned earlier that my book, *We the Navigators*, brought us together. Mimi had read it, reinforcing the idea already in her mind of studying an island culture whence the navigators had sprung. Her field work, however, turned out to be in New Ireland, Papua New Guinea, where voyaging was a forgotten art. But she did not lose her interest in the navigators. Early in 1979 she wrote to me through my publishers. An on-going correspondence developed.

I was increasingly intrigued by the highly individual personality revealed in Mimi's letters. Afterthoughts, amendments and additions would be scrawled along the margins and between the lines, making the epistles a challenge to decipher. In 1981 she was due to revisit New Ireland. She decided to route her flight via Sydney in June.

I was delighted, but apprehensive too on a number of counts. She was indecently young. She was much taller than me. She was very beautiful. My left hip joint, damaged in a skiing accident some years before, was due to be replaced by a stainless steel and plastic structure in May. How mobile would I be a month later? It was apparent from her letters that Mimi was an intensely physical woman.

'What is she going to think of me?' I gloomily asked my nineteen-year-old daughter Susie, who was about to depart Australia for Florence and Paris and a career in mime, acting and dance. 'After all, Mimi has six-foot athletes coming out of her ears.'

'Six-foot athletes are nice.' Susie was not being very helpful. 'But, Daddy, she knows by your picture in the book that you are a funny, rugged old sea dog. None of her friends can be all that important or she wouldn't be flying miles out of her way to meet you. Will you be all pathetic with your tin and Tupperware hip and meet her on crutches?'

'No crutches,' I insisted.

Mascot airport in Sydney, or Kingsford Smith to give it its full title, that nobody uses, is no place to meet anybody. Transpacific flights get in around 8 a.m. Then follow the interminable procedures of immigration, baggage collection and customs, which take place behind closed doors. What makes matters so awkward is that there are three exit doors from the customs area and you cannot watch them all at once, especially in the milling crowd of relatives and friends that awaits overseas arrivals.

I was not on crutches, having graduated to sticks two weeks before, and the sticks I had ceremoniously thrown into the river on the way to the airport that morning. I regretted their absence very much for I was in some discomfort as I waited in the crowd outside the arrival terminal. It did not help at all to know that I had no one to blame but myself.

Despite the photos, the tall dark girl took me by surprise with her exuberant mass of curls and her boyish stride. I had been less than frank about my height, she chided me later, for I was shorter than she expected. We embraced shyly. Despite our different generations and national backgrounds, we found we shared to an astonishing degree a common outlook and interest.

Antarctica naturally figured largely in our talks. My 32-foot sloop *Ice Bird* was still moored hard by my then home on Dangar Island in the Hawkesbury river. We set out one afternoon to bring the yacht some forty miles to a slipway in Sydney. It promised to be an overnight passage in the prevailing light airs without an engine. By nightfall sure enough the sloop was wallowing becalmed in the long Pacific swells two miles off Barranjoey Light. Then the lightest of breezes wafted us southward through the night.

Dawn found us slipping past the towering cliffs of North Head to open up the magnificent panorama of Sydney Harbour. Antarctica, so far removed from this sparkling sunny scene, where yachts and hydrofoils criss-crossed and bush-clad promontories alternated with golden beaches and massed white buildings, was still much in our thoughts. Mimi mused on some implications of the Frozen Sea Expedition. Where else, save in outer space, could you find issues so dramatically intensified? It was apparent that she had fallen under the spell of the Antarctic wilderness she had not yet seen; despite the disruptive change in her academic timetable that would ensue, wild horses were not going to drag her away from the Frozen Sea venture.

Back now to *Explorer* on her way across the Great Australian Bight. Mimi provided everyone a set of questionnaires to fill in, the sex ones in particular causing a good deal of hilarity. The earlier discomforts had pretty well banished sex from our minds, but now the subject re-surfaced in an atmosphere of light-hearted banter.

'Are you going to be like Eskimo Nell in the poem?' I asked Mimi. 'Do you remember Jim Caffin, the editor of *Antarctic* reciting it in Christchurch?

> "Back to the land of the frozen stand
> Where the nights are six months long,
> Where even the dead sleep two in a bed . . .'

We could call our book "Eskimo Nell in the Antarctic" after you and it will be a best seller.'

'That's not the idea at all,' Mimi replied haughtily.

We had made it clear to all applicants, or rather Mimi had since she did most of the interviewing, that, the good of the expedition apart, sexual mores would be everyone's own affair. Their private lives, what arrangements they came to, conventional or no, would be their own business. Celibacy would be a likely option, we both felt, but other possibilities would be same-sex or group-sex activities. Should anyone prefer some unconventional set-up it would be all right by us, provided only that the expedition was not harmed in any way.

'Haven't we found unconventional arrangements fun sometimes?' Mimi reminded me.

'You know more about that than me,' I interposed, grinning.

'Maybe,' she conceded, 'but I did make it clear to applicants I was perfectly happy with you. In fact, not one of them is appealing. It will be very interesting to see how the party's relationships work out. I wouldn't be at all surprised if we actually arranged ourselves very conventionally.'

There were not so many opportunities for the two of us to talk over plans and problems in depth, for, though we would have liked to have seen more of each other and have shared the same watch, to do so just yet would be premature. The rest of the ship's company, however, we kept swapping round to give everyone a chance to work together.

Weekly policy and criticism sessions became established, but were rather disappointing as the majority did not contribute very much, seeming to prefer to wait passively for leads from me. I could only hope that, as experience grew, so would responsibility and initiative.

It is worth saying something about the decision-making process in small groups like ours who were at grips with a formidable environment. Various strategies have been tried in cruising yachts, trans-oceanic rafts and Himalayan expeditions, to name but a few situations. They have ranged from the dictatorial to the democratic, each approach having had its successes and its failures. Elite climbing parties share much the same standards of expertise, so consensus can generally be arrived at through democratic discussion. Thus, in the mixed-sex American K2 expedition (the second highest mountain in the world), when tensions arose they were over degrees of skill rather than sex. Other things being equal, a large group needs more structuring than a small one. Some studies have suggested five to be the maximum number that can function effectively without defined leadership, no matter how evenly matched the group. The six-person Frozen Sea party was large enough to require organized management, and was far from homogeneous in experience, skills or interests, which limited effective group participation in decision-making far more than I would have liked.

This subject and its ramifications will continue to crop up in all sorts of ways in the course of the narrative. The Antarctic tradition has been to blandly cover up the reality of expeditions under the cloak of 'all jolly good chaps', so that the real story only surfaces a generation and more later. This seems to me morally unjustified and absurd. All of us make mistakes; none of us behaves like Superman under stress. That is nothing to be ashamed of, and goodness knows the most serious errors on this expedition were mine. Hopefully, the record of our trials and mistakes will help others do better if only the story is told frankly.

Many Antarctic 'old boys' would strongly disagree with this, feeling it 'lets the side down'. Australians particularly (is it some lack of national self-confidence that we should have overcome?) are oversensitive to implied criticism. Why are they ashamed to admit that explorers are human? Neither would some old hands agree that organized leadership may be essential. Norm puts forward this view: 'Lewis was very conscious of the little empire of five that he headed, and when angry placed great emphasis on his position as *leader*, George's as *deputy leader*, and Gill's as *deputy, deputy leader* and *scientific coordinator*.'

Oh dear! I was criticized after the Mawson Anniversary Expedition by our reporter for just the opposite fault – being virtually invisible behind my active deputies!

To return to the voyage once more. On 4 December the compass variation changed from east to west. In Sydney it had been 13°E that is, the magnetic compass needle pointed 13° to the left of the true direction (the mathematically minded reader can work this out for himself). We find it simpler to apply the old sailors' rhyme: 'variation east, compass least; variation west, compass best'. By 1 a.m. on 4 December the magnetic lines on the chart showed that easterly variation was down to 1°, and for most of the day there was no variation at all. This happy state of affairs was too good to last, however, and before midnight the sat. nav. confirmed that we had moved to an area where the variation was 1° *west*. By Albany the westerly variation had increased to 4°.

An hour before dawn on 7 December *Explorer* ghosted across King George Sound past the disused whaling station and hove-to to await daylight. It was still only 5 a.m. when we made fast alongside the Old Town Jetty at Albany, having averaged a creditable 110 miles a day from Flinders.

Sunny, windy Albany, with its wheeling gulls and white houses shimmering in the bright light, represented for us the end of the beginning, the jumping-off point from civilization.

Norm was waiting and duly took his place on board. Like the rest of us he signed the ORF legal document that defined, among other things, our media obligations, which included the agreement to return all exposed film direct to the *National Geographic* for processing.

Mimi, as official photographer and the one who had signed for the expensive photographic equipment and film, was responsible for seeing that the exposed cassettes were labelled and forwarded to Washington whenever opportunity offered. She had also been directed to advise us on standard procedures for exposure bracketing, preferred subjects, and so on. I labour this point because the use of film later became the focus for artificially fanned resentments.

Unfortunately, a shipment of additional film, cameras and exposure meters that should have been in Albany had not arrived. Telephone enquiries brought the assurance that they would be shipped to Davis base to await our arrival. They did, indeed, reach Davis, but only *fourteen months later* and on our very last day in Antarctica. Even so, we had enough film, but only if we used it with discretion.

The three-quarters of a ton of salami, that had of necessity been close-packed in the fore cabin, showed unmistakable signs of deterioration in the summer heat, despite the maker's assurances that it would be immune to such conditions. A delicatessen owner, called into consultation, confirmed that the curing had been inadequate. It was edible now but it might or might not remain so until we got south into the cold. There was nothing we could do but repack it and hope for the best. Fortunately, the freeze-dried meals and some dried meat that had been shipped late from New Zealand had caught us up. So, to our relief, had three out of four cases of CSR Inner Circle rum.

Ampol, again free of charge, filled the fuel tanks to their 2,000-gallon

(5,000 litres) capacity and the 350-gallon water tanks were topped up. This was little enough drinking water for six people for up to two months before we could replenish with melted-down ice. In the meantime we would have to wash ourselves and our clothes in sea water, lathering with washing-up detergent and accepting the feeling of stickiness familiar to anyone who has had to get dressed without a shower after swimming in the ocean. Washing up would always be with salt water. For cooking, a 1 to 5 ratio of salt to fresh water was generally acceptable.

There was little enough free time for any of us. What there was was devoted to writing letters, enjoying final restaurant meals and a visit by all hands to the Australian film, *The Man From Snowy River*. A sudden storm disrupted our activities and pounded our right-hand guard rail against the pier, leaving a radical S-shaped curve in one section. This highly visible sign of damage brought us much sympathy when we got back to Sydney. 'Look what those icebergs did to them – the poor things!' There was worse damage than a bent rail, however. A spreader had been torn adrift, which was re-attached by the young engineer using a special clamp made for us by ex-Antarctican Gary Clark.

The rigging was checked over by a yachtsman friend who had specially driven down from Perth; I swung the compass again out in the sound and telephoned Melbourne for the latest pack ice report; custom and im-. migration formalities were attended to. A technician was employed to look at our radios, which were not giving of their best. He had little success, and I sighed for Don Richards, now the width of a continent away.

No permission is required for a ship to sail to Antarctica, the country of registry simply notifying the Antarctic Treaty powers of the vessel's destination. The question of whether *Explorer* was 'bound foreign' or not exercised the authorities a good deal. Rather surprisingly, they ultimately decided that we were going abroad despite the fact that our destination was in Australian-claimed Antarctic territory.

Goodbye to Australia

Explorer put to sea on 13 December 1983 one week behind schedule. This was the jumping-off place into a world of an earlier time, beyond the pale of the full civilized support systems we had come to take for granted, and where we would be increasingly on our own. Whatever happened, there would be no turning back and we would all be constant companions for at least the next year.

Despite our high hopes that expected southerly and easterly winds would help us make up for lost time, these expectations were not to be realized. The four days that it took to clear Cape Leewin at the tip of Western Australia were 'motor-sailed' the whole time.

ı

This was particularly upsetting to Norm, who was miserable with sea sickness into the bargain. 'I questioned viability of voyage if engine was to be run for days on end as I do not believe engine preparation has been thorough enough,' he wrote.

'It's a horrible rusty old boat with a rusty old engine!' he put it more expressively at the time. The main trouble seemed to be the poor state of the hoses, an oversight for which I was ultimately to blame – as were those, including Norm, who had been specifically responsible for engine room spares.

The Indian Ocean proved no kinder once we had cleared Australia. Unseasonable head winds continued to plague us right into the New Year, prompting the lines at the chapter heading. So we perforce had to keep chugging along, motor-sailing much of the time, and using more fuel than I liked, though there was still a good margin. I was allowing one third of the fuel for the approach voyage; another third in Antarctica, and a third for the return. The trip back would be direct and with a fair wind, so there should be a margin over. I would have preferred to save fuel here because we would need to motor a lot in the pack. On the other hand, if we dawdled, we might miss the short summer altogether. I recalled that Drygalski's ship *Gauss* was unexpectedly frozen in for the winter on 22 February 1902 not all that far from Prydz Bay and a good deal further north. We had no time to waste.

Norm was proving conscientious, spending long and uncomfortable hours in the gloomy engine room, where his long-sightedness (he did not believe in glasses) was a serious handicap. I was concerned that he tended to resist suggestions and offers of help and seemed to be developing a tendency to regard this part of the ship as his private preserve. He was certainly trying hard on the stormy open sea where everything is about four times as hard to do as on land.

Norm's breakfasts were a source of some amusement to the crew. Everyone else was satisfied with cereal or perhaps a fried slice or two of long-life bread and a cup of coffee. He, by contrast, had an elaborate routine, which varied in detail but generally worked out something like this: Day 1, oatmeal, raisins and cracked wheat; day 2, toasted granola, buckwheat and rice polishings; day 3, apple granola, bran and sunflower seeds. All were cooked breakfasts and preparation was a major production with ingredients laid out all over the working surfaces for an hour or more.

There is nothing to criticize about these excellent concoctions, except that Norm rather cornered the ship's supply of oatmeal, and his running commentaries palled after a while. It was only when one had work to do and got behind him in the line for the stove for a cup of coffee that one chafed a little. But, after all, individual idiosyncrasies and quirks of personality are the stuff of humanity and give character to an expedition. Furthermore, familiar routines are comforting in strange surroundings.

Since leaving Albany a new watch system had been in force, three six-hour watches made up as follows: Mimi and I with Mimi watch captain; Jannik and Jamie; Gill and Norm. Mimi or myself made a point of being available at changes of watch to monitor the handover and to help with the reefing or sail changing that were timed when possible to take advantage of extra manpower. The purpose of the new watch system, which was persevered with, except in storms and ice, was to help the crew develop more responsibility and self-confidence. After all, everyone save Norm had nearly 2,000 sea miles behind them and there was ample sea room now, with no nearby shipping lanes.

I wrote in my log, 'I feel a responsible team is developing slowly, though every day someone forgets something that you really thought they had grasped. They have to be taught the same things repeatedly. Jamie's butterfly mind flits all over the place, which makes in-depth discussion with him very difficult, both person to person, and at our weekly sessions.' Nevertheless, Jamie and Jannik *were* getting the hang of sailing.

About the same time Mimi wrote in similar vein, 'It is scary how the crew break down at any degree of difficulty, like having to decide which tack will be best when it is dead obvious. In the long term, the effort expended in *training them to make decisions themselves* must pay off – but I wish we could learn a little quicker!'

A calm developed on the 21st, giving promise of a changed weather pattern to follow. The VHF antenna at the mast head had become loose. The sturdy Jannik hauled up Jamie to inspect it, then Norm, who brought the whole lot down. It was set up again by Norm at Davis when the ship was at anchor and no longer rolling. All hands took the opportunity of the calm to have a swim.

To everyone's disgust, the head winds were back again next day, blowing at gale force on the 24th and leaving an ugly sea behind the next day. In the gale's aftermath, the 1982 Christmas dinner was a bit subdued. Mimi and I officiated, though as I am the world's worst cook, my contributions to our efforts were mostly unskilled. We served tongue, dehydrated potatoes and canned vegetables, followed by fruitcake (donated by Woolworths) and rice pudding – Jannik's contribution. Champagne was broached.

New Year's Eve was more cheerful, for the sea was calmer. Mimi and I were the cooks again: corned beef this time plus the trimmings, with Bristol Cream from Jannik's personal bottle. Jamie's hypermanic jumping from subject to subject became too much for Norm. He burst out. 'Cut out that incessant chatter!' All to the good, we thought, to have people speaking up spontaneously.

Gill, who was developing into a real blue-water seaman under Mimi's guidance, still had less self-confidence than her ability warranted. It was true that we each had to be tolerant of others and avoid unnecessary conflicts, but there were times when speaking out was important. Gill tended to be a friend to all by slurring over problems which she was capable of resolving. We were confident that time would cure this – and it did.

A disturbing happening took place on 3 January. It should be explained that a ship's logbook, or 'captain's log', is an official document with legal status, in which is recorded navigational and other data. In addition, the skipper may 'log someone' for a dangerous lapse in performance. Something of the sort had happened to Jannik, for instance. He had been required for a time to enter his positions in pencil because of repeated careless errors that took others hours to sort out. On the day in question Jannik and Jamie, whose turn it was to cook, left the stove in an indescribable mess – covered in spilt food, grease and soot and with burners clogged. How often had we stressed how vital to our very lives was the stove's proper maintenance; this mess was a major fire hazard to boot! If they had still been awake I would have handled the matter verbally. They were asleep so I logged them in no uncertain terms. 'Cleaned filthy stove left behind by Jannik and Jamie. Please never repeat this pigsty. David.'

Was I unduly harsh or insensitive towards tender feelings? It is up to the reader to judge. Mimi's diary account is more objective than mine:

When Jannik and Jamie came back on watch, Jamie in a temper took it upon himself to write in the ship's log: 'Go stuff yourself. If you can't put it nicely than you're a cunt! We all make mistakes! Should you maintain such an attitude I'll do it again at leisure. Jamie.'

David was furious. 'I'm not having this,' he shouted at Jamie, who replied with a string of irrelevant accusations: David had wasted time looking for an untoward source of magnetism in the wheelhouse when swinging the compass off Albany; he, Jamie, had once heard David and me 'quarrelling'; I was fussy and did not know what I was doing. David answered each point patiently, but he stated adamantly. 'The leadership will continue to exercise its duty to make judgements decisively in matters of safety, even if it means speaking harshly when necessary.'

Many more discussions ensued, with Jamie gradually altering his perspective as he brought out some of his deeper concerns. A very big plus, he verbalized his resentments towards me. At first, he admitted, he had had doubts about my competence, then he had felt competitive towards me, though he was not sure over what. He now realized that his reasons for wanting to go to Antarctica were romantic ones. This new insight was a wonderful step forward, if only he could keep it up, even though his understanding of what the expedition was about remained questionable. Jamie apologized for writing his note and agreed it was wrong. David, generously I thought, let him cut out the page and re-enter the day's legitimate navigation data. (The incident would have remained unrecorded had it not been the precursor of a pattern of later outbursts).

Our weekly meeting had been postponed because Norm had dismantled the stove in a well-meaning effort to clean it, so that the galley was uninhabitable all day long while he struggled blindly to put it back together again (he rejected the loan of my reading glasses). At the meeting, Jamie acknowledged that he had not understood the implications of his behaviour, nor realized what the log was really for, or the leadership set-up at sea. He now perceived that the discarding of the log page had been a charitable gesture and grasped at last how much faith we had placed in him at Flinders when we had discounted the young engineer's criticisms.

'Though it is easy for Jamie to feel remorseful after the event,' Mimi wrote, 'and to revise perspectives late in the day, I do feel we are progressing. Morale is high. David pointed out that "Morale is based on competence and integration of a team." I believe this is beginning to sink in.'

Another part of this discussion was devoted to Ile Amsterdam. Because of the poor anchorage, at least two prople would have to be on board at all times, but I promised to try to give everyone a 'fair go' ashore. It was important for our credibility as an independent expedition not to cadge from any bases we might visit, I stressed. We had all the necessities we needed, except for some new hose pipe for the engine's cooling system that Norm rightly considered essential.

Ile Amsterdam

There is always something a shade uncanny and very exciting, no matter how sophisticated one's navigational aids, when a mid-ocean island rises up out of the sea ahead. The weather was hazy on 5 January so the conical silhouette of Ile Amsterdam materialized no more than seventeen miles off. The island is circular, five miles or so across and 3,000 feet high. Its grassy slopes are devoid of vegetation larger than bushes and it is the home of some 1,500 wild cattle, a legacy of early attempts at settlement. There is no all-weather anchorage.

By 6 p.m. we were off the base, whose buildings were surprisingly elaborate and numerous. A large supply ship was lying at anchor a mile down the coast with a bevy of launches fussing mysteriously around her. The vessel's name, we soon learned, was Marion du Fresne. One of the launches broke off its activities, motored towards us and throttled down, pitching and rolling a few metres off.

'Monsieur David, Monsieur David, 'ello!' Who on earth could know my name here? It turned out to be the previous year's expedition leader from the French Antarctic base of Dumont d'Urville. It was there that we had met on our last trip. What were they doing in their launches, we wanted to know? Obviously some project in marine biology. Not at all!

'*Langouste!*' was the reply. With a fine sense of proportion the ship's company were busily engaged in hauling up wickerwork traps full of succulent southern rock lobsters.

Leaving Mimi in charge, I motored ashore in the Beaufort inflatable (the rubber duck) with Gill and Jannik to pay our respects to the base leader. He was hospitality itself and invited us all to make free with his mess hall. Since we could not all go, I returned aboard and sent Jamie to join the other two ashore, while Mimi, Norm and I moved the ship to a reasonable anchorage near *Marion du Fresne*.

Even here in the lee of the island *Explorer* rolled heavily. The wind sang in the rigging, while from the rocky shore a quarter of a mile away came a chorus of barks, coughs and grunts, all part of the varied repertoire of the fur seals that were lying among the boulders. Some cows were mooing and bellowing near the shore too, we thought, though we had failed to spot them before daylight faded. It was only later that the French biologists told us that the fur seals were adept at mimicking the lowing of cattle no less than the clatter of outboard motors.

Next morning it was Mimi's and my turn to go ashore, followed later by Norm, who had volunteered to change the engine oil with Jannik's help before landing.

'I will shoot for you a cow,' offered Peter the Gypsy, the supply officer.

'We have no fridge or deep freeze, thank you all the same,' we explained hastily.

'O.K. then. There are some out of date cans I will give you. I have spoken with the little lady who stamps your letters [Gill, who had brought ashore the philatelic mail] about it. Is no trouble. Are you *sure* you don't want a cow?'

There were nine meteorologists and biologists out of a total complement of thirty on the island, a very high proportion of scientific to support personnel. Fur seals, penguins and seabirds were the main objects of study for the biologists. The bird people were all agog over finding a breeding pair of royal albatross, the first so far reported outside New Zealand.

Friendly as were the people at the base and on board *Marion du Fresne*, and charming as were the little yellow-crested rock hopper penguins, two of which were pets at the base, our abiding memory of Ile Amsterdam will always be of the fur seals. These beautiful animals were hunted to near extinction last century. Now they are staging a comeback, nowhere more dramatically than on Amsterdam. Half-grown yearlings and graceful females frolicked in the surf among the kelp; magnificently maned males roared defiance at their rivals, or perhaps it was in frustration as they tried to keep order among their flirtatious wives. The youngest pups were ashore with their parents, wriggling about like furry grubs. A Frenchman handed one to Mimi and she cradled the little creature, rocking it like a baby.

On our last evening we were royally entertained to dinner aboard *Marion du Fresne*. This was a memorable occasion indeed. We would dearly have liked to have lingered longer in this hospitable spot, but a sharply falling barometer and heavy swells making up from the northwest, which burst high over the landing place, were broad hints for us to be gone. We reluctantly got under way at 8 a.m. on 7 January after a stay of only thirty-seven hours.

4

Beset in the Polar Pack
7 January 1983–4 February 1983

The course was now due south and we drove along with a fair wind. The island receded rapidly and we regretfully hauled the French courtesy flag down from the starboard yardarm. Soon a northwest gale was making up on our starboard quarter. Sixty miles on, the uninhabited St Paul's Island was glimpsed briefly between rain showers. This island, unlike Amsterdam, does have a sheltered anchorage inside its flooded crater, but the tortuous approach channel is only six feet deep, so few ocean-going yachts can enter. Given fine southerly weather we would have loved to have tarried there and landed in the rubber duck. In present circumstances it would have been suicide to approach that lee shore.

Explorer became progressively harder to steer as the wind increased and the seas grew steeper and taller. By dusk she was running under big jib alone and even then kept broaching – swinging uncontrollably sideways across the face of the waves. Neither Mimi nor I could hold the ship steady for long. The next step was to stream the small kedge anchor astern on fifty metres of nylon warp in an attempt to keep the bow pointing down wind. This did not work either. Still the gale kept increasing, to force 10, then to storm force 11, when the wind tore the wave crests off bodily and turned the sea white with foam. The schooner was labouring badly and the reason was not far to seek. She was grossly overloaded. The seabirds had long since departed, save only the absurdly fragile-looking tiny storm petrels, that danced through the tumult with feet flicking the foam. How aptly did the seamen of long ago name them Mother Carey's Chickens, for who else but *Mater Carissima* – Mother Carey – herself, they believed, could guard such frail creatures in the heart of the tempest!

The time had come to heave-to, to head the ship up into the wind with just enough steadying sail to keep her inching forwards while drifting sideways. This procedure is not very practicable in small yachts, which get spun about by the waves so that their sails flog to pieces; for vessels the size of *Explorer* it is an ideal way to ride out a storm. On this occasion matters went awry. The storm jib went up all right, but someone prematurely let go the foresail halyard, which snarled round the climbing rungs on the foremast. Mimi went aloft in the howling darkness in a vain attempt to disentangle the mess. The best we could do was to hoist the mizzen. This worked very well indeed, the sail at the rear tending to drive the schooner up into the wind, while the storm jib held her away from it, so that she lay in dynamic balance steady and snug with her head about 50° off the wind, rising buoyant as a duck, with occasional seas crashing aboard just forward of the wheelhouse.

The ship now headed roughly north with the wind and seas on the port bow. There was good reason for lying-to on the port tack in this manner. Southern Ocean gales typically begin as warm fronts with the wind from the northwest,[1] a falling barometer, overcast and rain. When the cold front arrives after some hours, often as a violent line squall, the wind backs rapidly to south of west and strengthens, while the glass starts to rise and the sky to clear. A ship on the port tack at the outset will, when the wind backs, be facing into the old seas. If she had been on the starboard tack these waves would come abeam, the most dangerous angle, since they could roll her over.

Our storm duly followed the text-book pattern. After fifteen hours hove-to, during which time we lost ground sixteen miles to the northward, we were able to get under way again, bruised and shaken but with renewed respect for the sea. One crew member, who shall be nameless, understood nothing of this despite my explanations. 'David turned the boat the wrong way round and wasted sixteen miles,' I overheard him complain!

Progress was erratic through the forties and fifties, with wind strength varying with disconcerting rapidity from gale to calm and back again. There seemed always to be too much wind or too little. Almost imperceptibly it grew colder. The sun was rarely out for long, so that wet clothes were hard to dry, the engine room being as cold as anywhere else now that the motor was run less often.

Gill was still troubled with recurring sickness whenever the sea was rough, which was often. This did not prevent a close relationship from developing between her and Jannik. From the outset the three unattached men had courted Gill. Now she made her choice known and the couple moved into one bunk and draped a blanket across their portion of the centre cabin. This gave a good deal less than complete privacy, but once we were in winter quarters and the stores filling the fore cabin had been unloaded and put ashore, there was nothing to prevent them from taking over that spare cabin for themselves. They preferred, however, to remain in the centre cabin with the other two.

[1] The corresponding northern hemisphere sequence is a warm front from the southwest and a cold front from the northwest.

Did the formation of the new couple polarize the party? This is an important question that the reader must answer for himself as the story unfolds. In watchkeeping, we had found that Gill and Norm worked well together, as did Jamie and Jannik, and this changed not at all. The differences between various groupings in the party, that were increasingly becoming apparent to Mimi and me, were not sudden developments, nor were they to be so simply explained. One night at dinner, shortly before Ile Amsterdam, Norm had broached the subject of friendship.

'I am disappointed,' he said, 'that we have not all become firm friends.' Mimi was the only one to take this up.

'I think it's really too early to judge. Strong friendships usually build up slowly, as each learns to have confidence in the other.' She refrained from adding that we might have few interests in common save for the joint enterprise which locked us together as a team, fearing that this might sound derogatory. It should not have been: Mimi and I share an amazing spectrum of ideas and there is no implied criticism of Gill and Jannik, Jamie and Norm in acknowledging that, the expedition apart, their enthusiasms and interests were different from ours – neither worse nor better, simply different. That being said, although not the most sociable of persons, I should have striven harder to become involved in their individual concerns.

Norm and Jamie were, in fact, drawing closer. They tended to find more common ground during the next few months and increasingly spent time together, often deep in conversation about their home city, thus, incidentally, effectively excluding the rest of the crew.

We had hoped that Jamie's growing friendship with the older man would steady him down. I spoke to Norm about this, appealing for him to use his influence, and he did in the early months express a desire to help in just this way. But before long it became apparent that Jamie's was the dominant influence rather than the other way round.

Unfortunately, Norm had a bad spell of his own at sea. His arthritis was troubling him, as well it might in the prevailing damp, but he refused any treatment, insisting that he 'didn't believe in medicines'. To make matters worse, circumstances conspired to confront him with challenges to his self-image as an engineer who was on top of the job. These were issues that he found it hard to face up to, compounded by the fact that he had difficulty seeing clearly in poor light.

By 12 January the stove, that the engineer had recently worked on extensively, was leaking fumes and kerosene, with burners flaring and smoking. It had to be fixed. Mimi, with Gill to assist her, stripped it down, and I was forced to insist that only those two must service the stove in the future. It was too vital a piece of equipment to be trifled with, regardless of anyone's feelings.

Yet neither must we impair anyone's dignity by devaluing their hard work and good intentions, we felt. So I presented my decision in a positive light, as a measure, which indeed it was, meant to relieve our engineer of some of his many time-consuming jobs. Everyone fully appreciated the fact that he was always eager to work for long hours and was only too anxious to tackle anything mechanical.

Mimi and I kept the true extent of his difficulties to ourselves as much as possible, with the result that, while Gill had some idea of the position, neither Jannik nor Jamie ever had an inkling of what were Norm's problems or his strengths.

The most practical contribution, we felt, was for Mimi to offer to help in the engine room when any mishap occurred beyond routine maintenance. She would, she realized, have to be extremely tactful and defer as much as possible to Norm's technical training and his position as ship's engineer.

This tactic was an initial success when the dynamo on the generator stopped producing current and Norm was unwilling to fix it. He could not see the place where the casing came apart and assumed that it had to be sawn open, and he was afraid that he would be unable to get it back together again. Since the generator was to be our major power source through the winter, not to mention our needing it now, I insisted that the engineer accept Mimi's help. She saw where it came apart, and the problem, a loose brush, was fixed in no time, for which Mimi gave the credit to Norm. Both remarked on how well they had worked together.

Yet Norm's hostile feelings, negligible at the time of this success, increased during the ensuing weeks, a circumstance not helped by Jamie, who in many an aside at the galley table, all too audible in our 'cave', encouraged him to stand up for his dignity and not be pushed around by a woman.

Alienation was thus developing in just the way that we were trying to avoid. Some commentators have seen this beginning of polarization as a reaction to Gill's and Jannik's closer relationship, but to attribute such a problem to any single cause would be to accept an overly simplistic solution.

The oceanic limits of what may be termed 'Greater Antarctica' are best defined as the Antarctic Convergence, where chilled north-moving Antarctic water sinks down beneath the warmer temperate sea surface to continue flowing along the bottom to the Equator and beyond. The boundary is so well defined that we crossed it in one day under sail, in 52°S on 17 January, the ocean's temperature dropping from 8°C to 4°C and the air temperature from 5°C to 2°C in the process.

The position of the Convergence changes very little with the seasons but is different from one ocean to another. In the Indian Ocean, where we were, it lies in 52° or 53°S and runs between Iles Kerguelen to the north, which are vegetated, and Heard Island 150 miles to the south, which is pure Antarctic. The line of the Convergence dips south across the Pacific, so that Cape Horn off Tierra del Fuego in 56°S remains north of it, with its beech forests, guanacos and humming birds. Then, in the Atlantic, the line moves further north again so that South Georgia, in much the same latitude as Cape Horn, is sub-Antarctic. Not the climate only, but the dominant species of birds and marine life are different on each side of this invisible division.

Explorer was not the only expedition yacht afloat on those waters that summer. Two separate parties were bound for Heard Island. Heard is almost completely covered by crevassed ice and is dominated by the 2,746-metre Big Ben, whose crest is an ice-choked crater surrounded by blizzard-shrouded peaks. The mountain was first climbed in 1965 by an independent expedition in the schooner *Patanella* led by Warwick Deacock, the ship being skippered by the legendary Bill Tilman. A true Renaissance man born out of time, Tilman won distinction in arms in both world wars; his humour was dry, his writings scholarly. He led the British Everest attempt in 1938 and subsequently sailed his Bristol Channel pilot cutters far into the Arctic and Antarctic seas, climbing remote peaks wherever he went. He was hoping to celebrate his eightieth birthday in Antarctica when he was lost at sea off the Falklands in 1977–8. A digression, maybe, but men like Tilman should never be forgotten.

To return to the current year. An Australian party led by Ross Vining in the yacht *Anaconda* made a successful second ascent of Big Ben during their month's stay on the island from 21 January. Meanwhile, an ex-whale chaser, *Cheynes 11*, was heading for the island with another party. This did not fare so well. Bad weather frustrated their endeavours on shore and the chaser's fuel consumption was far more than expected so that, on the way back to Western Australia, the ship ran out of fuel. Makeshift sails were rigged and the voyage continued at a speed reported to have been two knots, a record, said one wag, for a motor vessel under sail. *Cheynes 11* arrived in Albany in mid March, under tow. All these stirring events were still in the making when we passed 100 miles to the eastward of Heard Island.

Cold was now a real problem, for at near zero Celsius we had entered the true Antarctic seas. The transition across the Convergence was sudden. Just a week before, jeans, wool shirts, a sweater and gumboots or sneakers, with perhaps a canvas jacket or a parka and Marlin waterproof foul weather gear when necessary, had been enough. From now on, there would be no deck work, especially involving metal, without gloves.

Selecting clothing for a wet-cold environment is in many ways more difficult than finding protection against much lower dry cold temperatures, for wetness destroys insulation so that the body chills as quickly as if naked. In this connection down garments are a danger, especially at sea, for when soaked they insulate like wet blotting paper and do not dry readily. Synthetic fibres are much better. However, our gear on this and the last expedition served us admirably, particularly the float suits. These Canadian garments were wind- and spray-proof nylon overalls lined with buoyant insulating foam, that were originally designed for workers on Arctic and North Sea oil rigs. As they were not completely waterproof, additional foul-weather gear, like our Marlin smocks and overtrousers, was needed in bad weather. The only disadvantage of the float suits was that the fabric was impervious to vapour, it did not 'breathe', so that one became wet with sweat during heavy work. This was rarely a problem at sea, but was a real disadvantage in autumn sledging. The buoyant and insulating properties of the float suits could be life-saving – as we will come to later.

Insulated rubber boots, like the 'Mickey Mouse' variety loaned us by the Antarctic Division, were bulky but waterproof and kept our feet warm even in far lower temperatures than these summer ones. Hats were a matter for individual choice, woollen balaclavas or beanies being favourites.

The greatest problem was how to protect our hands, while at the same time retaining the capacity to tie knots, cleat sheets and halyards and handle tools. It was never completely solved. The best we could come up with was Damart or thin wool gloves worn inside industrial plastic or rubber gloves. The combination was clumsy and finger ends tended to be cleated in with the halyards, but it kept our fingers from freezing. When the wheelhouse was dry inside, which was not so very often, one could wear big clumsy polar mitts for steering. But they were extremely ·vulnerable to damp and once wet became soggy and useless and were difficult to dry.

The log on 22 January reads: 'Wind southerly, force 4, light flurries of snow, Sat. Nav. position 59°.15′S, 78°.59′E, over eastern edge of Banzare Bank', then in capital letters 'ICEBERG, 7 miles off on the starboard bow' – our first iceberg. There was very little darkness now, and what there was that night was relieved by a bow-shaped aurora that arched from horizon to horizon athwart our path, lighting up the seascape with a pulsing yellow and green radiance that revealed the ghostly berg silhouettes. Forty, in all, we counted. They were small and weather-sculpted, obviously destined to melt away altogether before the summer was out. The bergs were not dangerous because they were in plain sight or else would have been visible on radar. The smaller bergy bits could be easily spotted too. It was otherwise with growlers. These are the central cores of icebergs, the last stage of their melting, and are made up of green compressed ice. Polished smooth by the waves, they wallow awash, very hard to see when whitecaps are on the water and solid enough to discourage collision.

We threaded this extensive berg field for twenty-four hours. Such a heavy concentration so far north was probably, we thought, the legacy of the break-up of large bergs that had grounded on Banzare Bank the previous summer. From then on icebergs were more widely scattered, but we anticipated meeting more of them when we came to the pack 300 or 400 miles ahead.

These first bergs were mostly remnants of the tabular bergs that are spawned by the Antarctic ice shelves. They float about two-thirds submerged. Glacier bergs, extruded from valley glaciers much like those of the Alps, are smaller, more irregular in shape and more compressed, so that they float deeper, with five-sixths of their mass under water. Medium-sized bergs of both types commonly ground on the 100-fathom line, that is, in 600 feet of water.

Bergs often weather into fantastic spires, arches, pinnacles and caverns. They frequently tilt over, exposing past water lines. Sooner or later most capsize. Their colour varies according to contained impurities and light effects under the low sun, from emerald green to blues and purples, pink, white and chocolate. Words cannot well convey their awesome grandeur and majestic beauty.

The polar pack

Five days and 350 miles south of the first iceberg, *Explorer* entered the fairyland of the polar pack on 27 January in 65°.50′S, 79°.29′E at four o'clock in the morning. The sea and air temperatures were both −1° Celsius. We were 165 miles north and 60 miles east of the Australian Antarctic base of Davis. Of my reasons for entering the pack at just this point, more anon. For the moment Mimi and I, who were on watch, were wholly enthralled by the vista of variegated floes glistening under the red and gold of the sunrise. Gill glanced out of the companionway, cried out with excitement, and ran barefoot to the rail. A bevy of Adélie penguins sleeping on a floe jumped up in alarm, scurried round in a circle, then tobogganed away to the far side of the floe and dived into the water. Farther on, a somnolent crab-eater seal raised its pointed snout, peered at us myopically and flopped back into the floe again. Far down a lead a minke whale surfaced and blew. Snow petrels were circling around.

The Antarctic winter pack extends a variable distance out from the coast, in many places 600 miles or more. At this time of year, in mid summer, the pack had broken up into individual floes; some had drifted north and melted, others were jammed close together, even sometimes rafted and compressed, others still were scattered into open pack and threaded by wide leads of ice-free water.

The pack was open, the weather fine and the barometer steady. I decided to probe south directly towards Davis. Progresss was excellent at first, though from time to time we had to retrace our course to find better leads, which usually turned out to be ones to the westward. Mostly we

were able to con the ship from the deck. Only now and then did someone
have to go aloft to the crow's-nest or the lower spreaders for a wider view. I
took the helm for the time being whenever the going was hard, being the only
one yet accustomed to manoeuvring in ice. This is a tricky business. You
have to be aware of the more distant leads towards which you are aiming,
while being for ever alert for underwater spurs that can hole a ship; you must
know when to crawl dead slow through massed brash ice, and be ready to
swing round sharply at a moment's notice, or to go into reverse, not always
an easy matter with our cumbersome gear lever. There are times when you
must nose ahead between two floes and push them apart. *Explorer* is able to
move ahead, however slowly, through pack up to about seven or eight tenths
concentration (fraction of the sea covered in ice). That is, she can push
obstructing floes aside, always provided there is somewhere for them to go.
She has not the power of an ice-strengthened merchant ship to crunch
through floes ten feet thick or hurl them out of the way one on top of another.

Everyone learned to steer through ice and to con the ship in the days
that followed, some more efficiently than others. Jamie proved excellent in
the crow's-nest at directing us through the nearer leads. Jannik's, Gill's
and Norm's reactions were rather slower. Mimi was the strategist, the one
able to chart a course for a long distance ahead from aloft. She became
adept at sorting out the run of the leads in the context of wind, current
and the sky signs. I was less often in the crow's-nest, rarely climbing above
the spreaders, for my sense of balance was still impaired from a retinal
detachment six years earlier, a result of my rough treatment in *Ice Bird*,
the surgeons thought. My left and dominant eye had remained in bad
shape, so that for a year or two I saw double. Persistent re-education in
coordination by tackling activities like driving, hiking and skiing paid off
handsomely, but I am still chary of situations where putting a hand or
foot wrong could lead to a tumble.

The Antarctic Circle, 66°.33′S, was crossed the following day, 28
January, and duly celebrated. Fifty miles into the pack now and mostly
good going, except for back tracking now and again, each time edging
further west towards where 'water sky' indicated a clearer passage. 'Water
sky' and 'ice blink' are the reflection up onto the clouds of the sea and ice
respectively. In ideal meteorological conditions with low stratus and good
light a veritable overhead map of ice pack (or snow covered land) and
open water is projected. Nevertheless, I was anxious to obtain satellite ice
reports from Davis and I asked Norm to scan the frequencies.

His effort was rewarded.

'VLZ Davis, VLZ Davis, this is VJ 3348 *Dick Smith Explorer*, calling
you on 4040 kilohertz, listening for you on 4040 kHz. Do you read me?
Come in please. Over.'

'Hello *Dick Smith Explorer*, this is VLZ Davis. Yes, we read you loud
and clear. What is your position and when can we expect to see you?'

Welcome words indeed! Not so encouraging was the news that Davis had no ice information whatsoever and did not know how to obtain any. For some technical reason they felt unable to contact the Americans at McMurdo or the Russians at Molodezhnaya, both of whom issue monthly ice bulletins. The best they could do was to try to get in touch with the supply ship *Lady Franklin*, which was due at Davis in about ten days, and ask her to obtain reports from McMurdo and pass them on to us together with her own facsimile data.

This was a blow. No information was available just when we needed it most – all the more since the leads were closing around us, mile-wide channels shrinking in an hour to a fraction of their former size. We looked like being beset and very shortly. At least we now had a daily radio schedule with the outside world.

To make communications simpler, we altered our clocks to 'Davis time', an artificial convention they had adopted for communicating with other stations and Australia. They were on what is termed zone − 7 hours time, that is their zone time − 7 hours was Greenwich Mean time (GMT). To put it the other way round, Davis was seven hours in advance of GMT. Now since the sun 'moves' westward at 15° each hour, longitude 78°E, where we were to spend the winter, is, properly speaking, less than six hours fast of Greenwich, not seven. We continued to keep Davis time for the next year, but we had to remember, especially when the autumn days drew in, that our true local midday by the sun was about 1.15 p.m. not 12.

My fears of entrapment by the ice were realized. There was time only to lay *Explorer* alongside the slightly concave edge of a large floe and then make fast to it with the kedge anchor, when the last of our lead was obliterated. A short time before Mimi had put out on a small ice pan that she had tethered to the ship to take photographs. Half an hour later she could simply step 'ashore' onto the floes on either side. For all our data on winds and currents, I must admit that there is something profoundly mysterious to me about the movement of pack ice. One day it is there, close set about your ship. The next it has gone, none knows whither. In our case it chose to stay put. There was no pressure against the hull, I was relieved to note. On the other hand, we could not go anywhere. There was nothing for it but to wait, and make the best of our holiday. All hands gladly took the opportunity to stretch their legs. We even jumped across the adjacent floes to talk to a crab-eater seal who, true to his kind, was surly and would have none of us. We sunbathed in shirtsleeves on carrymats spread out on the floe, cheerfully broaching a couple of bottles of wine. After the Southern Ocean this was bliss.

All the party were in high spirits now that the weary ocean crossing was behind us. Everyone, including Jamie, had nice things to say about my leadership (how ironically undeserved this was, we will see very soon). We had got over the worst part, I told the crew at our meeting that night.

From now on there would be the real thing, what we had come for, high Antarctica. Less praise was lavished on Mimi. As mate she had had to exercise the sharp edge of executive command, to supervise and ensure performance. Her authority weighed particularly heavily with the men; Mimi spoke her mind 'man-to-man' – an unfamiliar 'American aberration' from a woman.

Several bergs were our spectacular neighbours, some of them probably grounded, because the water hereabouts was in places less than 100 fathoms deep. The pack that enclosed us, we found by our sat. nav. fixes, was drifting bodily westward, eight miles in the twenty-eight hours that we were beset that first time.

In the early afternoon of 30 January the pack opened up as mysteriously as it had closed in. There were about 100 miles still to go to reach Davis. I decided to press on southwards down the now wide open leads. This was a bad error of judgement that I cannot justify. I will explain how it happened.

In Hobart Mimi and I met with experienced polar personnel who, with the best will in the world, advised us that Prydz Bay could become a trap. The westward drifting pack (for this was in the zone of the polar easterly winds and west-going currents) fetched up against Fram Bank at the western side of the bay in a lethal 'log jam' that must be avoided at all costs. Keep well to the east, they reiterated, as far east as you can get.

We afterwards learned from the Danish captains that the best route skirted the western side of the main pack. Yes, there were dangers in getting *too far west*, true enough. But it was perfectly safe to sail as far west as 71°E. This was over 200 miles west of where I had entered the pack. Given that I had not these facts at the time and that I was obsessed with the dire warnings against excessive westing, were there not clues to suggest that we might be heading straight into the heaviest pack while a clear road might lie to the west? There were such clues.

There is a difference between scratching and tearing yourself to pieces, as the old New Zealand saying goes. In other words, I could have sailed 100 miles further west and still have been well clear of the dreaded Fram Bank. The shoal area we were traversing and Four Ladies Bank further south might be expected to trap grounded bergs which would tend to anchor and consolidate the pack, perhaps thick multi-year pack. A course further west would skirt these banks in deeper water.

Mimi pointed out more than once that water sky was invariably more in evidence to the west, while ice blink was worse to the southward. 'I don't like the look of these floes here,' said Mimi uneasily. 'They are massive and seem to have been around a long time. Twice at least we only got anywhere by following leads that led to the west. Now there are no more of these escape leads, just southgoing ones that run deeper into this old ice.'

The sensible course would have been to turn back north again and work our way westward as Mimi was suggesting. But I stubbornly insisted that we continue south.

At first all went well. The sea temperature was down to $-1.3°C$, a normal figure in the pack ice. The veteran ice pilot Bill Tilman had impressed upon me long since that when the sea temperature dropped below $-1°C$ the pack was close at hand. Snow petrels too, he added. Snow petrels never flew far from the ice, no more than twenty miles at most. True enough, a pair of these lovely dove-like birds had scouted us the evening before we had reached the pack.

In an anticipated repeat of last season's performance, the taps and pipes from the water tanks to the sink proceeded to freeze. For the moment they could be thawed out by the hot air from Mimi's hair drier, brought for this very purpose, but later we were reduced to siphoning out the water from the tank inlet into plastic containers.

The leads trending south were wide now, the barometer at 995 mb was high for the area though it had begun to fall. The breeze was from the southeast, light for the moment but increasing. A pod of six killer whales cruised by, the males easily distinguished by their enormous dorsal fins that projected more than a metre into the air, like the sails (conning towers, they used to be called) of small but lethal submarines. Then on 31 January, with as little warning as before, the pools of open water around us began to shrink, more rapidly this time, with the floes coming together with greater force. I picked the best indentation I could find in a substantial old floe and manoeuvred *Explorer* up against the edge, which was level with our rail. Just in time. Another floe bore down upon us with frightening rapidity. The propeller screeched briefly as we were pushed up on to an underwater ice shelf and I hurriedly shut off the motor. Firmly locked in, we swept helplessly along in the pack. The barometer had begun to fall steeply, the southeast wind was very strong now; driving mist and snow showers obscured the sun.

Storms in the pack are anomalous in their effects. On the one hand, the ice damps down the waves, so that vessels have at times found refuge from Southern Ocean storms by steaming deliberately into the pack. If the pack is open, however, so that the damping effect on the waves is limited, or the gale very severe, the floes themselves get tossed to and fro, to the imminent danger of any ship in their path. Moreover, even distant gales can cause extensive ice movements, which can lead to the dreaded rafting and pressure, eloquently known to the British Arctic trawler men as 'screw ice'.

An anxious period followed as the floes, with us as their prisoner, skirted a huge grounded berg. Behind it was a pool of relatively open water into which we struggled, thankful to have attained some shelter as the floes moved past, grinding and thumping ever faster, driven by the full gale that was now blowing.

By midnight we were hard put to it to remain in shelter. Mimi and I took the watch an hour early and, while the others retired to the centre cabin out of the way, we struggled for control. The need for judgement, experience and direct communication was so great then that another person would not have helped.

'Huge floes break up, overturn and sweep past,' I wrote in the log. 'We have to weave to and fro under power without a break to maintain contact with the sheltering berg.' Mimi had to keep racing back and forth across the snow-covered deck and up the climbing rungs on the foremast to the crow's-nest or spreaders to spot the best temporary shelter, then down again to the wheelhouse to give me directions. In our most desperate moments we had to lie right under the 130-foot, in part overhanging, icy battlements of the berg itself, which we looked up at askance. I recalled how the Russians had daringly put a party 'ashore' on an ice shelf by rigging a gangway from their mast head to the top of the ice cliffs and how, only minutes after the ship had pulled away, ten thousand tons of ice had cascaded down into the sea just where she had been lying.

Thankfully, the pale dawn found the racing clouds slowing down at last. The gyrations of the pack slackened. By 7 a.m. Gill and Jannik could take over under supervision. By midday on 1 February the immediate danger was past.

New leads opened before us and we followed them southwards until, at noon on 2 February, we were once more close beset, this time among old multi-year floes, twenty to twenty-five feet in thickness (Mimi measured one with a line and sinker, her estimate being subsequently confirmed by an icebreaker captain).

Mimi and I had been under tremendous pressure during the storm, having been continuously on duty. The others had conducted themselves well. I was especially gratified that no one had shown any sign of panic in the perilous situation just past, or, indeed, during the arduous approach voyage. This was a big plus and a tribute to the crew. Anyone who has seen people give way to unreasoning panic, as I have at sea and in combat, knows how utterly unnerving it can be. We had much to be thankful for. But though we could now rest physically and catch up on sleep, the situation was far from reassuring. We were sixty-seven miles into the pack, ninety-eight from Davis, and the days were passing. It was February already and the memory of Drygalski's *Gauss* being caught in an early 22 February freeze-up nagged at us. It is one thing to winter deliberately in a protected Antarctic bay; it is quite another to be frozen-in in the open pack. Some ships like *Belgica* have survived the experience intact. Others like *Aurora* escaped with the loss of a rudder. Others again, like Shackleton's *Endurance*, despite her massive construction – her stem was six feet thick – have been crushed into matchwood. Only last summer a modern German supply ship, many times stronger than our little *Explorer*, had been crushed and sunk by the ice in the Ross Sea. My foolhardiness was beginning to come home to me.

For the time being there was nothing to do but wait for the pack to relent. Norm had a birthday, which Jannik proposed to mark by laying out 'Happy birthday Norm 58' on a floe in pieces of salami.

'It won't work. Those two scavenging skuas that are flying around will gulp them down quicker than you can lay them down,' I objected. I was wrong. The skuas, after examining the salami intently, flew hastily away. Fortunately *we* had ham and birthday cake with which to celebrate!

Then other guests arrived. Six emperor penguins suddenly jetted up out of the water on to our floe and proceeded to take up residence. They showed mild curiosity but no fear of these odd foreign 'penguins' that had invaded their world. Their gait was rolling and dignified like very old mariners. Walking upright was interspersed with tobogganing along on their plump tummies. Every now and then they would take to the water, weaving to and fro in a graceful under-sea ballet, 'flying' through the water with their powerful rudimentary wings, which are strong enough to break a man's arm.

An unlooked-for means of escape now offered. We heard on the radio that the United States Coastguard icebreaker *Polar Star* was due to lie-to off Davis on 3 February and to pass close to our position on the 4th. Would it not be sensible to ask her to break us a way out while she was so near? There was no doubt at all in my mind that the prudent course was to ask her for assistance. Considerations like compromising our standing as an 'independent' expedition, or my own record of a quarter-century without ever calling for outside aid, were irrelevant.

At 9 p.m. on 3 February I sent off the following radio message to the commander of the *Polar Star*.

Australian research schooner *Dick Smith Explorer* 65 feet long en route Australia towards Davis beset 4 days in close pack 66°.57′S, 78°14′E, after entering pack from the northward 27 January. Request break out a channel we can follow into looser pack. David Lewis, Master.

The response was matter of fact and in the best tradition of international Antarctic cooperation. Radio schedules were established; we might expect them late next evening.

It was precisely at midnight and snowing heavily when the giant 65,000-hp vessel came up with us, steaming through the close pack at ten knots and tossing aside the twenty-foot-thick floes as if they were ping-pong balls, her powerful searchlights probing through the curtain of falling snow. As she circled us the floes began to grind and heave, our stern lifted right out of the water and our auxiliary rudder was bent over. Another circle and *Explorer* flopped back into the water again and a track of churned-up floes and swirling water was opened before us.

5

Search for a Winter Home
7 January 1983–24 February 1983

Following *Polar Star* proved anything but easy. Although the huge ship, said to be the world's most powerful non-atomic icebreaker, was using only a fraction of her power to drive a single seventeen-foot-diameter propeller, the whirlpools it created sent floes gyrating madly and spun us round too, uncontrollably, like a top. *Explorer* repeatedly crashed head on into solid ice and brought up all standing, shuddering with the shock. As Norm rightly said, I was caught out time and again. If I kept too close to the icebreaker these batterings were the price; too far behind and the newly-broken channel closed in our faces. I had to maintain maximum speed, five knots in these circumstances, to keep the schooner under control at all. At this speed the frequent collisions with the ice were exceptionally violent – far more than the hull was ever designed to stand.

Mimi handled the heavy gear lever, being ready at a moment's notice to hurl her weight on it and thrust it into neutral or reverse. Repeatedly I had the engine screaming at full throttle – goodness knows what this treatment was doing to it! The view forward from inside the wheelhouse was so limited by the masts and companionways that Mimi had to stand at the rail to direct me, always remaining within jumping distance of the gear lever. As if this were not enough, she was handling the radio contacts between us and *Polar Star* on 2182 kHz since there was no time to pass on to Norm what needed to be said.

For a time it seemed as if we would not make it at all. As we were backing out painfully for the nth time after a collision, the captain of the icebreaker came on the air with a chilling suggestion. He could not afford to delay indefinitely if we were unable to keep up. He would take us aboard, he offered, and our ship would be abandoned. No way in the world! Few words sufficed for Mimi and I to agree that we two would not leave *Explorer*. We doubted whether any of the others would go willingly either, but we were responsible for their safety and would evacuate them to *Polar Star* if our ship could not be broken out. After all, the pack would probably continue to open and close periodically so there was a very good chance of escaping under our own steam before freeze-up, especially since there would now be satellite ice data from the icebreaker to tell us where the water was more open.

'Let's give it another try,' I said to the captain, hoping that my voice did not betray my feelings. 'I think we are getting the hang of it better now.'

So we were. We had found the best compromise distance to be 80–100 yards behind our guide's massive stern. Not that it was always plain sailing from then on, for we could neither accelerate nor stop very quickly, so that at 2.30 a.m. we came too close and scraped alongside the icebreaker's towering hull. Alert coastguard crewmen fended off our spreaders lest they catch on rails and davits. We backed clear.

Gradually as we gained westing, the heavy old pack gave way to lighter and thinner floes, and Jamie could take over from Mimi. The bilges were pumped out – no inflow of water. It was a mercy the schooner was not holed and I was proud of our tough little ship. At 7.45 a.m. *Polar Star* came to a halt in two-tenths open pack twenty-three miles west of our starting point.

'This is it, folks. Tie up alongside and all come over for breakfast.' This was captain Joe Smith in a happier mood. I had the schooner moored to a small berg, not wishing to tangle the rigging with the lofty side of the icebreaker again, and we piled into the inflatable rubber duck.

Breakfast in the captain's quarters of the great vessel seemed an incursion into another world, but the most welcome sight for Mimi and me was a satellite facsimile picture that showed almost ice-free water at the western margin of the heavy pack and extending to within twenty miles of Davis.

'But that last twenty miles is ten-tenths pack,' the captain warned us. 'It might be best if you arranged to wait for *Lady Franklin* at the edge of it and then followed her through. She is due in a few days and will be on exactly the same course as you.'

Explorer had become detached from her berg and was drifting off slowly. It was time to leave. We were profoundly grateful for his unselfish help.

The sturdy Beaufort rubber duck with its 15 hp Evinrude outboard bravely shouldered the brash ice aside, taking us back to *Explorer*. Norm has rightly criticized our lack of life jackets on this occasion – more properly, of course, float suits, life jackets being singularly useless in sub-zero water, as was underlined by the tragic fate of four students in life jackets who quickly became unconscious and died while trying to swim 200 yards to shore at Jan Mayen. The reason for my not insisting on float suits was simply lack of time. Captain Joe Smith was in a hurry to be off but this was no excuse for neglecting so important a safety precaution.

The American courtesy flag was lowered as *Polar Star* dwindled rapidly towards the horizon and we followed her westward into clear water, then swung southward, confident that our troubles were over. That they were not, was because of my second major error of judgement.

In the early hours of 7 February, almost two days after our parting from *Polar Star*, a narrow belt of floes packed tight by the south-southeast wind barred our way southward. Beyond was open water. At full throttle we pushed and bumped our way through, then shut off the motor to await full daylight and better visibility.

When we came to re-start the motor the oil pressure gauge showed nil. The engine was smothered in oil, the sump was empty, its twenty-odd litres of lubricating oil having drained into the bilge.

The same accident had happened the previous year when Gary had promptly located the fractured oil pipeline responsible and he and Don had carried out emergency repairs, so I was able to tell our engineer at once the likely cause of the trouble. The conversation took place in the wheelhouse with Mimi present. Norm says he does not remember it. The three of us repaired to the engine room, where I reiterated my suggestion and pointed out the pipeline involved. It was low down towards the front of the engine. With Mimi helping, the motor was cleaned of oil and the bilges pumped out. Now, it should be explained that the bilge beneath the engine is in three separate sections and that the oil had mainly accumulated in the front two.

By noon various nuts and bolts had been tightened down, new oil had been added and Norm assured me that leakages from these sundry joints had been responsible and that the suspect pipeline was intact. The engine was started for a trial run and the oil drained away as before. Mimi pointed out that it had all run into the front compartment, with some overflow into the middle.

'The leak *must* be over this front compartment,' Mimi insisted.

'No,' Norm argued. 'I think the trouble is either a rusted sump or a cylinder head problem.'

'In that case the oil would have run into the middle and back compartment, not the front,' objected Mimi.

I asked Norm once more if he was sure that the suspect pipe was intact and he assured me that it was. Once again, Norm disputes this account of the incident. Norm expressed himself satisfied that his tightening up of the head had cured the trouble. He advocated another engine run. Mimi took me aside on deck.

'Please let me look for the leak myself,' she begged. 'I know Norm's eyes are bad though he never admits it. I can tell that the leak is somewhere around that pipe because the leaking oil ran down into the front bilge compartment right underneath it.

'He *is* the engineer,' I replied. 'We must trust his word. I don't want to undermine his self-confidence by over-ruling him.'

So I followed the advice of the engineer and, as Mimi had predicted, when the engine was restarted the last of our reserve oil poured into the front bilge.

Norm's account does not include the conversations that took place and Mimi's and my suggestions, including my telling him of the identical happening the previous year. Here it is.

> David [it was Jannik] noticed no oil pressure on the gauge when starting the engine. I donned overalls and went to the engine room, where I found no oil on the dipstick, and lots of oil in the bilge. Mimi and Jamie pumped out 20 litres of pure oil and 30 litres of oil/water mixture. . . . The entire engine was oil-covered and this had been its state since I joined the boat. As the rocker cover holding-down nuts were finger tight, I tightened these . . . suspecting there was insufficient oil aboard when I changed the oil at Albany I had saved the old oil and 17 litres of this had now to be put into the engine, which was then started and run for thirty minutes with no drop in oil pressure. Unfortunately the dipstick reading was again nil, and I had not located the leak.

It hardly seems to have been the same incident.

Outside help was needed once again. Luckily for us, the Soviet ice-strengthened ship *Kapitan Markov* was due at our position that evening. We had already been listening with some amusement to her radio banter with Davis station, to which she was sending a helicopter on a social visit.

Base leader Davis: 'I will put a bottle on ice for you.'

Soviet physicist Nick: 'One bottle! One case maybe!' The base leader hastily concurred.

We now broke in to explain our predicament and a three-way exchange was soon under way. *Markov*'s response was positive and helpful in every way. They immediately offered us a mechanic. Davis Station cut in to suggest that *Kapitan Markov*'s helicopter should bring out an Australian mechanic and some oil on its return flight from the base, the mechanic to stay on board *Explorer* to Davis. This was agreed. The ship would heave-to near us – she was due in three hours, and we would effect the transfer with the inflatable.

'Have you ice reports?' I asked the Russian operator.

'We are icebreaker. We don't need them in summer,' he replied.

'Don't mistake us for an ice floe when you come up. We are very small!'

'Is that humour?'

'Yes.'

'We don't mistake you. You are very intrepids.'

The tall dark ship with its classic icebreaker bow and the hammer and sickle on the funnel hove-to a couple of miles off. We hoisted the Soviet courtesy flag this time. The return of the helicopter found Mimi and me bobbing alongside in the Beaufort inflatable, carrying on an animated conversation with a minimum of common vocabulary liberally supplemented by gestures with *Kapitan Markov*'s crew. The fur-hatted and fur-coated women sailors were particularly interested in Mimi. How old was she? What was her job? How long would we stay in Antarctica? Their own tour of polar duty was six months. How many women in our party? There were sixteen women on their ship, most in their thirties and forties. Some were very good-looking, I noticed. Some were sailors; some laundry workers. We tied to a rope a copy of *Voyage to the Ice*, the story of my 1977–8 expedition. It was hauled up and we received in return a guide to Leningrad's Hermitage Museum.

Before long the helicopter landed, a drum of lubricating oil was lowered down the ship's side to us and the Australian mechanic Rolly climbed down a rope ladder into the rubber duck, closely followed by his mate Don, who was wearing shorts. The Russian women pointed to him in mock horror, rolling their eyes, and laughing at his bravado.

'A nice piece of Aussie gamesmanship,' I complimented him.

'It is a pleasure,' called the English-speaking Russian physicist, Nick, leaning over the side above us, 'to meet an Australian woman.'

'I'm afraid I'm American,' replied Mimi.

'Oh well, maybe is better,' replied the Russian, a born diplomat.

I had difficulty starting the outboard in the crowded inflatable, having to tug the cord left-handed. Mimi reached over and brought the motor to life with one strong pull. The Soviet women cheered.

It took no more than five minutes for Rolly the mechanic to diagnose the trouble. It was of course the same pipeline that had given way the previous year, the one I had thought to be at fault and the very place Mimi had begged to examine. We have the segment of fractured pipe still, as a salutary kind of memento. The one bright thing that stood out in the whole sorry business was that, when the crunch came, ships of the United States and the Sovet Union had unhesitatingly stood by us in the selfless Antarctic way, and for this we are grateful.

We subsequently made rendezvous with the Canadian supply ship *Lady Franklin* at the edge of the close pack and followed her to Davis without further incident. It was on 9 February that we dropped anchor in twenty feet of water and made fast a line to rocks ashore off the big Australian station, 5,750 miles and nearly three months from Sydney.

'This is the best moment of my life,' exclaimed Jamie in excitement, and turning to Mimi he added impulsively, 'Thank you very much for getting us here.' Mimi was specially touched and so was I that Jamie, for all his preconceptions, was so graciously and spontaneously acknowledging the debt we all owed her.

At Davis Station

On shore were the trappings of science, technology and housekeeping that are the hallmarks of man's contemporary presence in Antarctica. A black sandy beach was flanked by stony slopes, the beach being amicably shared between amphibious vehicles called LARCs, a landing barge, bulldozers and a clump of thirteen somnolent elephant seals. These enormous creatures do not breed in Antarctica but on sub-Antarctic islands; the young males at Davis were simply passing a summer hauled out ashore enjoying the rare luxury of an Antarctic sandy beach.

Fifty years up from the shore the buildings began – a row of dongas (insulated living quarters), meteorology building, post office cum radio shack and the biology labs. Further back lay the dining and recreation hall, a diesel powerhouse and a huge warehouse under construction, flanked by oil tanks and a mile-long plastic pipe wound round a monstrous 'cotton reel'. Behind these again was the helicopter pad. Contact with the outside world remained exclusively by sea but a possible airport site was being surveyed nearby. There were some thirty or so men at the station, though there would be fewer in winter; there were no women this year.

Vestfold Hills, where Davis stands, is the largest coastal 'dry' area in Antarctica. By 'dry' is meant an expanse of rock, gravel and sand that is not covered by permanent ice sheet. Something like 6,000 years ago, at the close of the last ice age, the continental ice retreated twenty miles behind Davis, leaving 200 square miles of low rocky hills cut by winding fjords and dotted with lakes. Blasting winds and the summer sun warming the rock prevented year-round accumulation of snow which could have consolidated into ice again, for the Antarctic snowfall is not much, only the equivalent of five inches of rain a year. The continental ice cap and the ice shelves are likewise self-perpetuating. Permanent ice and snow have such a high albedo or reflective capacity that the rays of the low sun glance off ineffectively. In this way ice begets ice and 'dry' land remains ice-free. The Rauer Islands, with their associated mainland bluffs, constitute a very small dry area, the ten-mile stretch of the Larsemanns a larger one, though smaller than the Westfolds.

The door of the officer in charge's (o/ic's) office was labelled *Haus Bilong, Kiap*, from which it could be deduced that Peter Briggs was an ex-patrol officer in Papua New Guinea.

'*Hapinun nau! Olsem wonem long yupela bilong ples i kol tumas?*' (Happy noon! How is it going with you among the people of this cold place?), Mimi greeted him.

'Gidday,' he replied in Australian, taken aback and forgetting his rusty pidgin. Peter was strong on protocol, but no worse for that. A recent unauthorized radio call from one of our party enquiring about time-expired canned food had earned me a sharp rejoinder about official

Explorer under sail   (*Karen Keys*)

Crew in action, tacking in a Southern Ocean gale. Gill's face is just visible in the pilot house (she's steering)   *(Mimi George)*

Gill poling aside floes at the stern, as we struggle through brash filled leads in the pack ice   *(Mimi George)*

Emperor penguin and Jannik on floe. Despite our predicament we enjoyed our weeks in the pack immensely *(Mimi George)*

...ami Birthday greeting while beset.
(Mimi George)

The *Polar Star* approaching at midnight doing 10 knots, tossing aside 20-foot multiyear floes   *(Mimi George)*

View of the coast along which we would travel on the winter sea ice. Chaos Bluffs and Glacier can be seen, along with Adélie penguins and minke whale   *(Mimi George)*

Our chosen anchorage in Winterover Bay, just after the March 7 freeze-up
(Mimi George)

David unharnessed from Nansen sledge to check map during first manhaul
trip to southeast on Varyag Island. That night the ice behind us blew out
(Mimi George)

Bathing in the galley: melt the ice, sponge a bit at a time and dress again quickly *(Mimi George)*

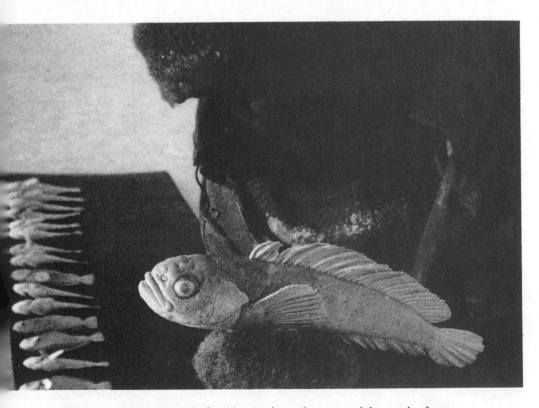

The best single day's haul. On this occasion only we tasted the surplus from the monthly specimen quota. These *Pagothenia Borchgevinki* were instantaneously quick-frozen on exposure to −20°C air. Glycopeptide (antifreeze) in their blood protects them from −0.5°C *(Mimi George)*

Weddell seal at breathing hole   *(Mimi George)*

Jannik at fishing hole. 197 specimens of six species were caught from several
locations throughout the year   *(Mimi George)*

David testing the ice thickness on the other side of a pressure ridge just south of Cape Drakon, where the ice had broken out in a storm three weeks earlier. This was on May 30, the last day we saw the sun for five weeks   *(Mimi George)*

June midwinter, sledging of supplies to fill depot at Cape Drakon
(Gill Cracknell)

channels. There was, in fact, nothing important that we needed, we stressed. We suggested, and it was agreed, that if the ship had any requests at all they should go through me to the o/ic.

Our immediate concern, we explained, was to tie up the details of the seal and penguin research projects and for someone, perhaps Jannik and Jamie, to be shown the techniques of penguin stomach sampling and seal tagging. The helicopter pilots reported the Larsemanns to be still cut off by heavy pack, but regardless of whether our wintering place turned out to be the Larsemanns or the Rauers we would be uniquely placed to make biological observations, for we would have over-ice access to some fifty miles of coast, bluffs and islands that would be inaccessible to the Davis scientists once the helicopters were shipped out at the end of the month.

Everything seemed to be going well when an unexpected problem surfaced in which the base's help was needed – and was most generously given.

'Your header tank fuel seems to be getting waxy, I noticed,' remarked Rolly, the helpful mechanic who had come out to us by *Kapitan Markov*'s helicopter.

'You mean due to cold *already*?' Mimi asked him, puzzled and disturbed. 'Is there any way you can test it?'

'Yes, we can chill down a sample and see when it thickens and freezes.'

'Then, would you test one for us please?'

The results shocked us. The fuel began to wax out at $-6°C$ and froze solid at $-16°C$. Seeing that we could anticipate winter temperatures of $-40°C$, this was a staggering blow. What could have happened?

I have already explained the misunderstanding that had arisen at Hobart when we had been advised to have Ampol provide something equivalent to the Special Antarctic Blend (SAB). The catch, it will be recalled, was that SAB was stored in electrically heated tanks like those at the base. For tractors, helicopters, sno-cats and primus stoves Aviation Turbo Kerosene (ATK) was used. This does not wax out or freeze in the lowest winter temperatures.

Peter Briggs kindly agreed to exchange fuel. Ours would be pumped into the base's electrically heated tanks, where they could use it. In return they would supply us with ATK.

The exchange was effected from the base's landing barge, which brought us out 13 × 44-gallon drums of time-expired ATK and two of SAG dewaxed diesel fuel. The base's motor pump speeded the transfer of our old fuel into empty drums and later into the station's bulk fuel tanks ashore. It was a chilly, windy job for Rolly, Gill, Mimi, Norm and me and we envied the other two, who were off learning to collect penguin stomach samples.

Norm's account of the fuel exchange is very different. 'Rolly, however, thought it would be a good idea to test the fuel, and while at

Davis I gave him two test samples.' With all due respect to Rolly, it had been Mimi who requested the fuel tests, something I told Norm at the time.

We were indebted to Davis for more than this. Methylated spirits that we needed to start the primuses had been used rather recklessly and was in short supply. The o/ic donated a further supply, as well as fuses and washers.

Norm has made much of these deficiencies, writing in bold type of 'shortages of materials in this "shoe-string" expedition with its incomplete and/or wrongly calculated stores lists'. He ignores the fact that most of the shortages he cites were in his own department, and apart from his extensive experience of the engine room over two seasons, he had had a full week in Albany to check everything over, spares included. 'Shoe-string' or no, the ORF never stinted us for essentials. Even our most costly requests for equipment were promptly met. What on earth was he doing in Albany all that time?

I may sound irritated. I am. The motor Norm so decried has since functioned without major adjustment on a second voyage to Cape Denison in Antarctica, a four-months charter in New Guinea and a pollution survey round the stormy west Tasmanian coasts. So much for the 'rusty old engine'!

Our stay at Davis was not as negative as all this sounds. The sun, occasional clouds apart, was still shining for about twenty hours each day and we all enjoyed ourselves thoroughly. Gill, whose bright good humour immediately made her a firm favourite on the base, took the philatelic mail to the postmaster, intending to carry on the good work she had begun at Ile Amsterdam, but he insisted on franking it himself. He would have time enough during the winter, he said, smiling. The sale of the special envelopes we had brought with us was counted upon to help defray the costs of the expedition. In addition to these envelopes, more philatelic letters were waiting at Davis. By what alchemy these mostly German enthusiasts had learned of the expedition defied comprehension. The addresses were often bizarre and a tribute to Australia Post for having found us. 'Captain Dick Smith, schooner Anaconda,' read one. Another appeared to have awarded me a knighthood!

It was only on the last morning at Davis that we learned that Jamie, our zoologist, had inexplicably avoided talking with the biologists at the base. What had happened to blunt his enthusiasm? He had been so very keen in Sydney and Hobart. Nevertheless, a Davis zoologist insisted that Jamie had kept away from him. Gill and Jannik confirmed this.

Mimi ran over to the laboratory building with the chief zoologist, who gave her last-minute instructions on cooperative projects and arranged radio schedules. Jamie was found and sent to the labs to do what little he could in the two hours before we sailed. The incident was distressing, especially as joint research projects were the best way for us to repay our kind hosts.

Another circumstance gave us cause for concern. Granted that we had not exactly covered ourselves with glory in the pack, information began to filter through to us about very critical press reports, apparently emanating from an unnamed spokesman in Hobart who had been having a field day at our expense. Seeing that we were a private undertaking, functioning of necessity in the full blaze of the limelight so as to keep faith with our supporters, we were a sitting target for anti-independents. Could there possibly be some sort of organized campaign of denigration, we wondered? There was. This was later confirmed by no less a person than the new Director of the Antarctic Division. But that revelation was still far in the future.

A story about the fuel swap, embarrassing to our good friends at Ampol, and parts of which, in Norm's words, 'were ludicrously distorted and sensationalized', appeared in the Sydney *Morning Herald*. The story's origin, like that of the others, was Hobart.

Another example. We had attempted to repay Davis's hospitality by issuing a general invitation to an 'open day' aboard *Explorer*. Among those who came were several who were strangely out of place with their thin town shoes and urban clothing. They shivered and were taken aback by our spartan quarters.

'You will freeze to death,' one of them exclaimed. We ourselves were perfectly comfortable, of course, in our big boots and thick jerseys (it was not nearly cold enough for quilted polar clothing). The group seemed unlike any ANARE expeditioners we had seen. Nor were they. Though they did not tell us at the time, they were a group of reporters visiting Davis as guests of the Department of Science.

Their effusions appeared in the press at a time when our only contact with the outside world was by radio, so it was left to the long-suffering ORF Board to make what little response they could. Don Richards wrote:

> Statements such as 'The boat is not insulated,' 'They had to get in-structions on how to light a Tilley lamp,' 'A poorly equipped expedi-tion, they may not be able to endure the conditions,' . . . appeared in press or on radio. The ORF Board found itself in the position of being able to make only limited comment on such statements as the facts did not come through from the expedition until much later and by then interest had subsided. The Board decided not to revive the matter or enter into arguments with the Antarctic Division, whose spokesman had made hostile comments and displayed an attitude to independent expeditions not previously made known.

Rauers and Larsemanns

Enjoyable as had been our week's stay in the comforts of civilization, we were glad to be on our way, eager to come to grips with the land we had come so far to seek. *Explorer* got under way on 16 February. The task of choosing a safe winter anchorage had overriding priority. We would have to make the right decision first time round, for once the ship was committed and the sea froze her in she could not be moved again (unless a catastrophic breakout did it for us) until spring. There would be no second chances.

Ice conditions were far from typical this particular season, as we had already found to our cost. The station weather people explained that this was an El Nino year, which might partly account for the heavy concentration of the pack. El Nino, or the Holy Child current, was formerly thought to be a purely local South American phenomenon, they said. Every five or ten years the cold nutrient-rich Peru Current is unaccountably replaced around Christmas time by a warm, lifeless stream devoid of plankton – El Nino. The fish die in millions and so do the cormorants and boobies that normally feed on them; the most productive fishery in the world collapses. Satellite imagery has revealed El Nino to be but part of a world-wide meteorological and oceanographic aberration which affects weather patterns, oceanic circulation and temperatures as far afield as Antarctica. We could well be in for an unusually long winter.

A few days earlier the Davis o/ic had taken Mimi and me with him on a helicopter trip to Cape Drakon at the southern end of the Rauers, where a pair of geologists were being moved to a new camp. We eagerly compared the map with the islands, bays and channels flitting past below, noting those fjords where last season's ice still persisted and marking likely havens for subsequent examination 'on the ground'. A long extension of pack blocked the route southwestward towards the Larsemanns, we saw. Hopefully, this might soon drift offshore, but for the moment we perforce must confine our search to the Rauers.

The heavily-crevassed Sørsdal Glacier, that juts out to sea between Davis and the Rauers, was an awesome sight from the air with its confusion of seracs and ice falls. Some winters, we knew, the sea never froze outside this glacier tongue. More often the sea did freeze temporarily but broke out unpredictably at any time of the year, usually under the immediate effect of a blizzard. The other reasons for the instability were obscure, but so dangerous was the ice fronting the Sørsdal that Davis base personnel were forbidden to go anywhere near it. In fact, they must not venture on to the ice beyond the tide-crack that bounded the Vestfolds themselves.

The morning was fine and sunny but with snow showers to seaward when the schooner moved off down the coast. We skirted a six-mile stretch of outlying Vestfold islands past isolated fields of pack and stray bergs, then the notorious Sørsdal Glacier came up to port. We inspected it with interest while motoring along its ten-mile front before turning away towards the cluster of bergs that were grounded on the windward Rauers. These massed bergs appeared impenetrable from seaward but a gap had been visible from the air.

The rationale of our quest for an anchorage can only properly be understood in the context of the prevailing Antarctic winds and currents. Where we were, in nearly 69°S, was well into the zone of the polar easterlies that blow round the continent. Down to about 63°S strong westerlies dominate the Southern Ocean, fronts and depressions moving east-southeastward to a permanent trough of low pressure in about 65°S. On the Antarctic side of this low-pressure trough the average barometric pressure rises, the winds blow from the east and the skies are clearer – the 'banana belt', as expeditioners term it. A consistent west-flowing current is produced by the easterly winds. Local topographical features may, of course, modify the pattern. Thus *all* strong and medium-strength winds at Davis, the Rauers and the Larsemanns are from the *northeast*. The current likewise flows along this portion of the coast from northeast to southwest.

Clearly, then, any bay we chose must be sheltered on the northeast and only open to leeward, for wind and current would be driving pressure ice into the windward bays and woe betide the luckless ship caught in such a lethal sandwich of rafting floes. The bay must also be shallow enough to keep out large ice.

There have, of course, been many explorers who have wintered their ships by freezing them into the ice. In fact we had a long and honourable line of predecessors who had pioneered the wintering-over technique that we hoped to revive in a modern setting with a handy little ship with up-to-date insulation, heating stoves and electrics. But many questions remained to be answered, especially for such a small ship as ours.

De Gerlache's *Belgica*, whose mate was the great Amundsen, and whose innovative ship's doctor Frederick Cook is more likely than the generally acclaimed Peary to have been first at the North Pole, was the first ship to winter in the south. They survived the 1897–8 winter in constant danger of being crushed while drifting in the offshore pack ice. But this extraordinary adventure took place in the open ocean. We are concerned here with wintering in deliberately chosen protected anchorages.

Drygalski in *Gauss* was intermediate, as it were, being caught by an early freeze-up in 1902 off the Wilhelm II Coast, which he named. He had intended to winter his ship, but not there. Grounded offshore bergs protected the ship and all was well.

Scotia of Bruce's 1904 Scottish National Expedition was one of the first to use the method successfully. The Scots were so nationalistic that they presented their South Orkneys base of Orcades to the Argentines when they left rather than let the English have it!

Then there were Charcot's two ships, *Français* and *Pourquoi pas?*, that wintered in adjacent bays on the Antarctic Peninsula in 1907 and 1909.

The Australian Rymill's schooner *Penola*, with a party of brilliant and experienced British Greenland explorers, spent two winters nearby in 1936–8 and did an amazing amount of surveying overland and in a 21-foot semi-open boat.

The latest scientific research expedition to freeze-in a ship, and like Rymill's it was a private venture, was the American Finn Ronne expedition with their three aircraft that wintered *Port of Beaumont* in Marguerite Bay in 1946–8. They drained out the fuel lines and water pipes, shut up the ship and repaired to huts ashore. Incidentally, Ronne's wife Edith (Jackie) and a pilot's wife, Jenny Darlington, were the first women to spend a winter in Antarctica. Jackie Ronne, who lives in Maryland, played an extremely active and positive role in the undertaking and deserves the accolade of 'First Lady of Antarctica'.

Lately two French yachts, Jerome and Sally Ponchet's *Damien II* and *Kim*, wintered on the Peninsula, the remarkable Ponchets in Marguerite Bay not far from Ronne's winter quarters. (I sometimes think that you soon won't be able to 'swing a penguin' in Antarctica without hitting a French yacht!)

I myself sailed past several of those Antarctic Peninsula anchorages in *Ice Bird* in 1973, and also came in sight of Port Lockroy, which is not a port at all, just a rock and ice-walled inlet where the whale chasers used to winter with a chain across the entrance to keep out the bergs.

Wintering a ship is not without dangers, as Scott found out with *Discovery* in McMurdo Sound, when she did not unfreeze for two seasons. Probably this was why Shackleton gave orders that *Aurora* was to winter further out in the Sound, where the opposite mischance had near-fatal consequences. The ship was driven out to sea in a May breakout before even the stores had been unloaded, and her rudder was torn off by the ice. Only superb seamanship brought her back safely to New Zealand, and unrivalled fortitude was shown by the ill-equipped shore party in laying their depots against all odds.

The Ross Sea, where McMurdo Sound is situated, does seem to be one part of Antarctica that offers little scope for wintering a ship. The Ross Ice Shelf that stretches east from McMurdo is one unbroken line of ice cliffs. To the east of the ice shelf the fjords never unfreeze and the coast of Victoria Land, which bounds the Ross Sea on the west, is a dangerous lee shore. Wood Bay on this coast was recommended as a winter mooring place by the Australian explorer Bernacci in 1902, and the Antarctic Pilot has repeated that advice ever since. What possessed the otherwise estimable Bernacci to give this advice I cannot imagine. I have flown over the bay twice to look it over and it was anything but inviting – jumbled pack and the bay wide open to easterly gales and bergs, and pretty deep into the bargain.

There must, however, be very many suitable bays along the enormous Antarctic coastline. The Antarctic Peninsula alone boasts innumerable sheltered havens. In addition, we know of excellent spots near every one of the three Australian bases, the French base and some of the Russian bases. It stands to reason that similar coves exist aplenty along the thousands of miles of empty and ill-mapped Antarctic shores. A careful study of aerial photographs will bear this out, and, indeed, air photos were of material assistance to us in short-listing possibles and discarding unsuitable places.

It might seem at first glance that there was nothing new to learn about polar winter anchorages, but this is far from the case where small vessels are concerned. Most over-wintering has been done in substantial deep-draught ships. Even the yacht *Kim* used *Pourquoi Pas?*'s deep-water mooring while the centreboard *Damien* was winched up on the shore. We proposed using and studying shallow bays, suitable for fishing vessels or large yachts, where the water was not deep enough to accommodate the smallest unwelcome bergy bit. Very little was recorded about the behaviour of shallow water ice as it thickened. We were to learn the hard way.

Creeping ahead cautiously, *Explorer* entered a fjord between two of the Rauer islands, Yefremov on the right and Scherbinina on the left. Beyond the latter towered the continental ice cap, mostly fronted by ice cliffs but in one place traversed by a prominent shelf of moraine that promised to be a route up on to the plateau. A nearly landlocked bay was sounded from the inflatable; it was too shallow, only 3–4 feet deep at the entrance. It began to snow, reducing visibility so much that we turned off from the wide fjord to probe a narrower channel until fast ice blocked the way. Back towards the sea again to a likely-looking little bay on the mainland opposite the glacial moraine. We hove-to while the rubber duck sounded. Depths of 15–20 feet this time, so the schooner was manoeuvred into the cove and by 8.45 p.m. was moored bow and stern to boulders on the shore.

Navigation among these islands and, indeed, round much of Antarctica is rendered difficult by the paucity of large-scale charts. The one of our area covered a distance equivalent to that from Canada to Mexico. On such a scale soundings are scanty.

There were no soundings at all for the Rauers, which, in any case, were only indicated schematically on the chart by some tiny dots.

'Did the flies make those marks or the map makers?' asked Mimi, rubbing at the Rauer Islands to see if they would come off. We did have *maps*, the Soviet map of the Rauers and Norwegian and Australian maps of the coast to Amanda Bay and the Larsemanns. But maps have the disadvantage for seafarers of not showing depth of water (soundings) or hidden hazards such as shoals and submerged reefs. Hence the caution with which we proceeded and the need for vigilant lookouts. The echo-sounder measured the depth of water amidships, it is true, but this glacier-moulded sea bed often shoaled abruptly in far less than a ship's length into reefs, fjord sills (transverse barriers of hard rock) and isolated underwater pinnacles. Even in a relatively well charted place like Commonwealth Bay we had struck with some force last season on an uncharted reef that had given no clue to its presence.

Charts apart, maps of the shores of Prydz Bay are still woefully incomplete, because exploration has been very recent. It was only in 1935 that whaling captain Klarius Mikkelsen in *Thorshavn* was the first man to discover the Vestfolds, Rauers and Larsemanns. It was his ship's dentist, Lief Sørsdal, who gave his name to the glacier. In the following year, 1936–7, the region was photographed from the air and partially mapped by the Norwegian whaling magnate Lars Christensen's expedition. We were lucky that Gill had come by xeroxed copies of these maps for Brattstrand Bluffs, Amanda Bay and the Larsemanns; they were useful despite serious latitude anomalies. The American Lincoln Ellsworth Expedition of 1939 in *Wyatt Earp* was next; Sir Hubert Wilkins, who was a member of this party, built a cairn somewhere on the Rauers which nobody has been able to find since.

In the post-war period the area was photographed from the air in the course of the United States Operation High Jump of 1946–7. ANARE expeditions led by Philip Law further explored the Vestfolds and Larsemanns in 1954–5. A Soviet expedition in 1956 made much the best map of the Rauer Islands to date, and we were grateful to the Soviet Committee for Antarctic Research for sending us this and other maps, by return mail and free of charge. Davis station was established by Dr Law in 1957.[1]

The night in moraine anchorage began calm and still and remained so until about 4 a.m., when a katabatic wind got up and quickly reached gale force. These winds are the bane of East Antarctica. The cold air overlying the continental ice cap rolls downhill with ever increasing momentum like some aerial river to the sea, which, even in winter, is far warmer than the plateau. The strongest katabatics blow at Commonwealth Bay, making it the windiest spot on earth, as we could testify, but they are far from negligible elsewhere. Typically these winds begin in the early hours, blow hard through the morning and die away in the afternoon or early evening. Sometimes they may let up for days of blessed relief, or they may be intensified by lows which succeed in crossing the Antarctic low-pressure trough. Katabatics die away progressively out to sea, fifteen miles from the coast being about their limit.

By 5.30 a.m. the gale was so strong that we feared for the ship's safety,

[1] It will be noted that many of the Rauer Islands have two names. For convenience we give them both, but the Norwegians and Russians have temporal priority over the Australians.

so we hauled ourselves ashore in the rubber duck and put out two extra warps before returning to our bunks. Later that morning the wind moderated enough for everyone who wished to go ashore. Mimi and I scrambled up the hill behind the cove to inspect the moraine. It was separated from us by a ravine, the upper part of which was occupied by a bright green frozen lake and the lower, beyond a snow-covered rock barrier, by fast ice dotted with basking Weddell seals. The frozen lake, we saw, could be crossed by way of a sand bar to the foot of the moraine beyond. On the way back Mimi and I found a secluded patch of gravel among the rocks that was, we thought, sheltered from the wind. Here, for our first time in Antarctica, we made love in the chill fresh air, but, since the one below had the doubtful benefit of the permafrost and the one on top of the icy wind, we did not repeat the experiment.

Explorer did not leave moraine cove until 3 p.m., when the worst of the katabatic was over, and continued south between the islands. We had already begun the systematic monitoring of the tides that was continued right through our stay in Antarctica. In default of tide tables we had to note the times of high and low water ourselves. At first we assumed that it would be easy to deduce the tide times for succeeding days, seeing that in most places successive lows and highs follow each other at intervals of about twelve and a half hours. For instance, high water in moraine cove was 2 a.m. on 17 February, so we anticipated the next high at 2.30 p.m.

There was but little tidal regularity in the Rauers, we found later, perhaps because of the tortuous channels. Low water was often around 10 in the morning for days on end and high water around 6 p.m. The rise and fall of the tide was 4–5 feet, until the sea froze and damped down the daily excursion to almost nothing, though even then the power of the imprisoned sea was apparent at springs when it sometimes flooded the shoreline tide-cracks for a foot or more. The only consistent regularity was the familiar occurrence of spring tides at full and new moon with neaps between.

The schooner motored steadily southward down a wide sound, leaving to port the islands named Lokot or Fishook, Pchelra and Sapozhok or Little Italy, and then was diverted by pack ice into a narrow channel between off-lying islets and Little Sicily, where we crunched hard aground on underwater boulders. Since this was at 3.30 p.m., the tide should have been dropping for half an hour. Providentially it was still flooding in from seaward bearing lines of brash ice that looked for all the world like patches of foam. With alarming bumps and thumps, thanks to the still flooding tide we were able to go into reverse and pole back into deep water.

We could count ourselves lucky to have got off so lightly, and needed to be even more cautious in the future. We would have to become more adept at reading the 'lie of the land' – where to anticipate rock sills or submerged moraine obstructions across these ice-scoured firths. We needed to be on the lookout for innocent-appearing ice floes that were in reality resting upon hidden rocks just beneath the surface.

Without further incident we cleared the southern Rauers through a gap between Chubuk or Hookah and Torckler or Ranvik islands. Accompanied by Jamie, Mimi sounded in the rubber duck two likely-looking bays on the southwest side of the latter island. The results were reasonably satisfactory: the bays were shallow enough to prevent the ingress of bergs or bergy bits but a little too exposed to the open sea for our liking, since the effect of a gale on unstable new ice in these bays might be to snap the moorings and set the ship hopelessly adrift still locked in its icy casing.

The anchorage we came to that evening was a tiny but well sheltered cove on Shleyf or Veil Island. Here we stayed for three days, exploring Shleyf itself and the adjacent Flag and Hop islands, which we reached by means of the inflatable boat. This interlude provided a welcome opportunity to stretch our legs and begin to get into trim, since nearly three months at sea had exercised our arm and trunk muscles, but had done nothing for the heart-lung respiratory capacity that is the basis of physical fitness.

Buoyant insulated overall float suits were obligatory for all rubber-duck excursions. The ruling was a nuisance because we had to take them off again when we landed; they were much too hot to wear when walking in summer. But Mimi and I insisted that they be worn in the boat because survival time in $-1.5°C$ water may be short, and because they had proved their efficacy at Cape Denison the previous season.

Anyone who may one day be at hazard in ice-cold water should be aware of the danger of sudden unconsciousness from shock and chill. On the other hand, I consider that tables of so-called 'survival times' in cold water of various temperatures are perfectly designed to stifle the will to live and kill by despair. If you have been told authoritatively that you can only survive for five minutes at a certain temperature, say, you will stop fighting well before ten.

Yet circumstances and stubborn determination have led to remarkable feats of survival. My friend Ian Smith of the British Antarctic Survey, for instance, is a massive man, fat but also heavily muscled. He broke through the spring ice in the South Orkneys on skis wearing normal Antarctic clothing. He struggled towards firmer ice, smashing a way with his skis for *over an hour* until he dragged himself unaided out on to the fast ice. Very few could match this feat. A Chinese scientist at Davis, who had narrowly survived immersion in a boating accident on one of the Vestfold lakes, suffered the effects for a full twelve months.

Only a year earlier at Commonwealth Bay we had had a lesson on the perils of sub-zero water that I will never forget. *Explorer* was moored in the 'boat harbour' at Cape Denison. The weather had broken three days earlier with a gale whose winds peaked at 70 knots (80 miles an hour), before slackening off in mid-afternoon. At 10 p.m., with plenty of daylight still left, Harry, Karen, Margaret and Jenni started ashore in our fibreglass catamaran. Jenni and Margaret wore their float suits, but Harry and Karen had on only windproof parkas over layers of woollen clothing. The catamaran was attached to one of the mooring lines with a rope and snap link to enable the passengers to haul themselves hand over hand along the line a distance of fifty yards between ship and shore.

When the catamaran reached the halfway point, waves whipped up by a savage gust swamped it and threw all four occupants into the water, whose temperature was just below freezing. Buoyed by their float suits, Jeni and Margaret quickly popped to the surface, but Harry and Karen were barely afloat, being drenched with driving water and freezing spray.

With no time to don gloves or extra clothing, Dick and I jumped into the rubber duck and hauled ourselves towards the scene of the accident. For one awful moment we thought one of them was under water, then we counted heads and realized that the submerged orange shape was one hull of the catamaran. Jenni had caught hold of the mooring line and pulled herself back to the ship, where she was lifted aboard. Dick and I dragged Margaret into the dinghy so as to be able to reach the others. Karen was unconscious and a helpless dead weight. Somehow, I really don't know how, we got her in, then Harry, who was on the verge of sinking from the paralysing cold and the weight of his sodden clothing. Desperately we hauled the dinghy back to the ship.

Once aboard *Explorer* Jenni and Margaret, who had been wearing float suits, showed no ill effects, but Karen and Harry had lost dangerous amounts of body heat. They had been immersed in below-freezing water for about four minutes, time enough for hypothermia to set in. We quickly poured hot drinks down them and took them below to their bunks, where each was bundled into heavy blankets with a fellow crew member beside them. Within hours both had been restored to health.

No wonder I was particular over float suits! My healthy respect for polar seas in small boats was also the reason why no one was allowed out alone in the inflatable and why, on any but ship-to-shore shuttles, Mimi or I were always the boat drivers.

On the evening of 21 February, from a forty-metre hill on Hop Island, we saw that the pack to the south had at long last moved out to sea. The glass was steady and the night clear with a splendid aurora, but we were reluctant to chance these semi-charted waters in any but the best visibility, so we did not get under way until next morning. Our aim was to look for possible winter anchorages in the Larsemanns and places *en route*. Brattstrand Bluffs, we found, were steep-to and offered no shelter. Massed bergs offshore forced us to close the southernmost of these red rock buttresses to within a quarter of a mile. This was unfortunate because the only really hopeful anchorage south of the Rauers that we had spotted on an air photograph was an island called Inner Brattstrandoyane that was tucked away in the middle of these bergs and was invisible from the ship. Indeed, so thickly were the bergs massed that we assumed it to be inaccessible.

Amanda Bay opened up at 5 p.m. and by sunset, at 10 p.m., we were motoring up and down hunting for a break in the wall of grounded bergs and consolidated heaped-up floes that barred our way to the Larsemanns, whose rugged brown hill tops peeped tantalizingly over the barrier of ice. A large whale blew out to sea, then a pod of twenty-five killer whales cruised by. We had come forty-two miles in an almost direct line from the Rauers and there was no more we could do before morning. The water was much too deep to anchor so we motored to the windward side of a relatively ice-free bay off the Dalk Glacier and allowed *Explorer* to drift with the light northeast wind. The barometer was steady, the sky still clear, the air temperature $-5°C$. All that night we alternately motored to windward and drifted down wind.

We managed to put Gill and Norm ashore through a field of brash ice in the morning, on Vikroy Island a mile off Vestodden Peninsula, the northeasternmost promontory of the Larsemanns. The latitude was 69°.21'S, *Explorer*'s furthest south. Gill collected lichens and mosses which she found in abundance on the island, but, less happily, reported Vikroy and the Larsemanns to be completely hemmed in by ice. And since it was the lee side of Vikroy that sported the only possible Larsemanns anchorages seen on the air photographs, that was that. There would be no winter quarters here.

On the way back we attempted to dredge up bottom samples, but all that came up from 40 fathoms (240 feet) was a spoonful of watery sediment. The schooner was back in her old berth at Shleyf by 10 that night.

Mimi and I went prospecting for further anchorages in the rubber duck next day. After coming up against a dead end, a channel choked with ice, and trying vainly to keep our hands dry and warm as we bucked wind-driven spray showers, we tried another channel that came out opposite Filla Island. The name in Norwegian means 'tallest'. At two miles in length it is, in fact, the largest of the Rauers but it is not the highest. A hill in the northeast is 82 metres high and one in the southwest, crowned by a beacon, is 81 metres. The highest island is actually Torckler towards the south of the group.

'There's a killer whale fifty feet from the dinghy!' exclaimed Mimi, just as we were reaching the middle of the wide firth.

'Which way is it going?'

'That way,' she gestured.

'Then we'll go *this* way -- the *opposite*!' I gunned the motor and headed at full speed for the shelter of Filla. Few definite killer whale attacks on small boats have been recorded but we had no wish to add to their number.

There was a roomy, well-sheltered bay near the southwest corner of Filla, we discovered, with even depths of fifteen feet. This was by far the best winter anchorage yet, and next day found *Explorer* moored bow and stern to boulders on each side of the bay and fifty yards out from the northern shore. We christened the anchorage 'Winterover Bay'. It was located in latitude 68°.49′S and longitude 77°.50′E. The date was 24 February 1983.

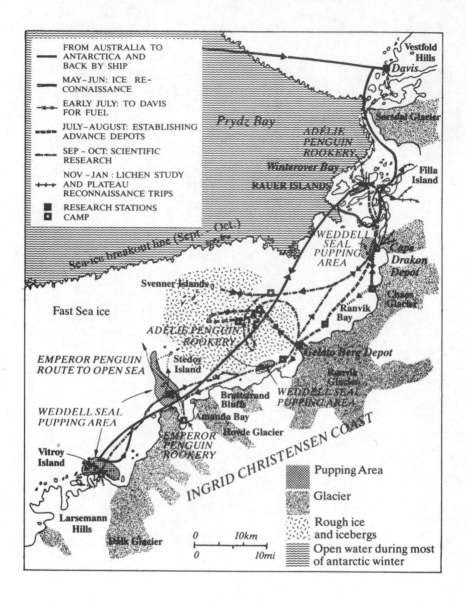

FROM AUSTRALIA TO ANTARCTICA AND BACK BY SHIP

MAY–JUN: ICE RECONNAISSANCE

EARLY JULY: TO DAVIS FOR FUEL

JULY–AUGUST: ESTABLISHING ADVANCE DEPOTS

SEP – OCT: SCIENTIFIC RESEARCH

NOV – JAN : LICHEN STUDY AND PLATEAU RECONNAISSANCE TRIPS

■ RESEARCH STATIONS
□ CAMP

Vestfold Hills
Davis
Sorsdal Glacier
Prydz Bay
ADÉLIE PENGUIN ROOKERY
Winterover Bay
Filla Island
RAUER ISLANDS
Sea ice breakout line (Sept – Oct.)
WEDDELL SEAL PUPPING AREA
Cape Drakon Depot
Svenner Islands
Chaos Glacier
Ranvik Bay
Fast Sea ice
ADÉLIE PENGUIN ROOKERY
Geddo Berg Depot
EMPEROR PENGUIN ROUTE TO OPEN SEA
Stedoy Island
Ranvik Glacier
WEDDELL SEAL PUPPING AREA
Brattstrand Bluff
WEDDELL SEAL PUPPING AREA
Amanda Bay
Vitroy Island
Hovde Glacier
EMPEROR PENGUIN ROOKERY
INGRID CHRISTENSEN COAST
Larsemann Hills
Dålk Glacier

Pupping Area
Glacier
Rough ice and icebergs
Open water during most of antarctic winter

0   10km
0   10mi

6

Frozen in for the Winter
24 February 1983–8 April 1983

Unsafe young ice . . . is saturated with water and is sufficiently translucent to reveal the dark color of the sea below. As the ice thickens . . . the color becomes grey.
R. K. Nelson, *Hunters of the Northern Ice*, University of Chicago Press, 1969

The sum of our research efforts so far had been oceanic seabird and whale counts, plankton sampling across the Convergence and daily meteorological observations, which last had been hampered by a faulty anemometer and the breaking of the wet bulb thermometer. For the rest, our energies had latterly been taken up with our search for a winter home. Antarctic research projects proper were now on the agenda. Jamie collected an impressive number of field notebooks from our stationery 'store' in the centre cabin and labelled them with his seagull logo and such warnings as: 'This belongs to Jamie, don't touch, keep away'. Jannik's and Gill's less impressive notebooks rapidly filled up with bird notes.

The southwestern extremity of Filla Island beyond the 81-metre beacon-crowned hill is an elongated peninsula. Here are located the bird cliffs where fulmars, antarctic petrels, cape pigeons and snow petrels nest. In the sheltered lee valleys beyond the cliffs are Adélie penguin rookeries, each few hundred birds having their attendant skuas, predators of eggs and chicks. The young penguins were big enough now to be safe from the skuas, the delicate snow petrels having become the victims. All the avian young were growing up; in another month or so they would have to be off to the outer fringes of the pack, which would ultimately come to extend 600 miles offshore.

Penguin stomach samples (chucks) were first on our Antarctic research agenda. You grab a squawking penguin and pinion its flippers while your companion pours a stomach full of warm salt water down its throat via a funnel and tube. The bird is upended over a bucket, into which it promptly vomits up its dinner and is released, to take off like a projectile, swearing volubly and no doubt vowing to keep clear of people in future. Meanwhile the sample is bottled and labelled and eventually returned to Australia. For most of our stay much the most popular penguin meal was krill. A less scientific way to judge what Adélies are eating is to look at their droppings, which are squirted out from their stony nests, radially, like the spokes of a wheel. A krill diet stains the rocks red, fish white and an empty stomach green. The main purpose of this proceeding, as of bird and seal counts generally, was to contribute to the Biomass programme of collecting data on which to calculate the mass of living things that subsist on krill, fish and ultimately on vegetable plankton. Such knowledge is urgently needed before commercial harvesting of krill depletes the breeding stocks and threatens all Antarctic wildlife with starvation.

At first Mimi and I transported the chuck parties to the rookeries in the rubber duck – Jannik and Jamie or Gill, with a beach cooler full of hot salt water containers, sample bottles, funnel and tube. Later on, overland short cuts were found and the boat was dispensed with. This was just as well because we wanted to save as much of our limited petrol as possible for the snowmobile, now that we were committed to wintering so far from our main target areas around the Larsemanns and Amanda Bay, the first a probable pupping place for seals, the second the site of an emperor penguin rookery.

On the return from our first penguin 'chuck' excursion we discovered that a bulky old floe had drifted into Winterover Bay and was nudging *Explorer*'s stern. When I slackened off the stern warp to let the floe go by I miscalculated and allowed the schooner to swing too close in to the shore. We woke early next morning to find the ship ominously tilted; she was hard aground and the tide this time was indubitably falling.

'Flinders again!' I groaned. 'All we need are the choppers.' We did not have long to wait. The friendly pilots, who were transporting zoologists from Davis, put down for a chat and coffee. They grinned at our predicament.

'Are you going to paint the boat's bottom?' they asked derisively.

Since the schooner would not float off until high tide that evening, Mimi and I decided to make the best of the shore's proximity to begin getting stores and gear ashore. We had already selected the site for our dump on the north side of the bay, where it was sheltered by a hill, but not so close under its lee as to be buried under the winter snowdrift that would form there, and up against a line of rocks that would stop things blowing away.

The reason for our setting up the dump was not just to make space aboard and lighten the ship, but to store at a safe distance at least half the food plus tents, fuel and survival equipment so that, if anything should happen to the schooner, such as fire or being crushed by the ice, there would be alternative food and shelter ashore. The same principle is followed at all Antarctic bases, where a hut well stocked with emergency food and survival equipment is established some way off in case of fire.

All hands turned to with a will for the unloading. *Explorer* duly floated off on the evening tide and next morning the unloading was continued. It took three days in all. With the aid of the main halyard and a sheet winch the snowmobile was carefully winched out of the hold and put down on deck to await the transformation of the bay's waters into a frozen road.

Oil cans, our precious 44-gallon drum of petrol, outboard fuel tanks filled with the same, drums of ATK (kerosene), skis, tents, tinned food, plastic sacks of salami and much else were ferried ashore in the rubber duck and stacked against the wall of rocks. Plastic sheets held down with stones were spread over the more vulnerable items – muesli, margarine, biscuits, long-life bread, and the like. Rusting of tins from the salt sea air would cease to be a problem once the sea froze. For the rest, there would be no rain and the temperature already matched that of a fridge; it would soon be down to deep-freeze levels. The plastic sheets were more to protect against blown sand and grit than anything else.

Near the water's edge we built our rubbish tip, a crude rock fireplace where we soaked our garbage in kerosene and burned it. Empty cans were raked out of the ashes and crushed by Jannik with a sledge hammer. Special attention had to be paid to burning egg shells thoroughly lest they transmit Newcastle chicken virus to penguins. This was a pristine land, we had to remember. The birds, marine mammals and simple plants had more than enough to contend with in this harshest of environments without our adding introduced diseases to their problems.

The fresh water tanks, thanks to our restraint at sea, were still half full. Water had to be siphoned out, and it would be spring before the taps unfroze; plastic water cans would shortly be taking their place for the winter. There were small lakes on Filla but, without exception, they were so alkaline as to be undrinkable and caustic enough to burn one's tongue. Ice was hacked off from old floes grounded outside the bay or else ice chunks washed up along the shore were collected and melted either on the stove or more often in the circular tank that had been constructed round the main engine exhaust pipe for the purpose. Norm was to run the motor for an hour every three days, mainly to make sure that everything was in order, but also to melt ice by the hot exhaust and, as a spin off, to warm up the engine compartment for use as a drying room. The generator was usually run beforehand to charge up the bank of starting batteries. The generator's internal cooling system, that had proved so inadequate in the

warm weather between Sydney and Flinders and had caused such disastrous overheating, was now reconnected and the Yanmar run cautiously.
All went well in the low Antarctic temperatures.

The three Hawkins Heat Wave Kerosene pressure heaters, with fuel tanks
that were pressured with a bicycle pump and had primus burners connected
to the tanks by venturi openings, had already been installed off the Larsemanns, one each in the galley, engine room and centre cabin. They
warmed the living spaces nicely and were a welcome innovation now that
the air temperature was down to –6°C and dropping daily. Unfortunately,
by 28 February, only a week after they had first been lit, the heaters began
to flare and smoke and soon gave up the ghost. It emerged that someone
had neglected to thoroughly swill out the heater fuel tanks with kerosene
as had been requested so that metal manufacturing debris repeatedly
blocked the pin-hole venturi openings. Moreover, guidelines for regularly
pricking the burners had been ignored so that they had sooted up. One of
the party was all for boring out the venturi holes and even brought a drill
into the galley for the purpose. This would have finished the heaters for
good and all and they were items of equipment that we could not spare.

Because of the heater crisis and for other reasons the weekly meeting on
the morning of 28 February promised to be an important one. Mimi and I
had been holding long, concerned and sometimes acrimonious discussions
prior to the meeting. We had not slept. A new world of opportunity was
about to open up before us, the exciting world we had come so far to seek.
Yet the Antarctic reality was obviously affecting individuals in different
ways. Jannick was frantic to be up and doing. He was away over the hills
each morning, the earlier the better; to the penguin rookeries, the bird
cliffs, and sites for fish traps. As the zoologist, Jamie was Jannik's
nominal companion, but Jamie was getting up later and later nowadays,
delaying the fuming Jannik and, as Jannik told us later, making few if any
field notes during their outings. Gill was as active as her friend, ranging
far and wide over the hills in search of lichens and special geographical
features – wind sculpted rocks like those in deserts and on Mars, as well
as embryo sea beaches that she planned to monitor.

We were at the threshold of the real thing, I reminded the meeting.
What we had already done in bringing our little ship to Antarctica against
all odds was no mean achievement, an achievement to which everyone had
contributed. The first steps towards wintering had gone well, for it would
be hard to find a more suitable bay than this one. (Indeed Norm wrote
later that 'Lewis' selection of our winter quarters would have been difficult
to better'.) The preliminaries were past, I said, and what lay ahead was
what we had come for – the exciting challenges of sledging, camping and
moving freely once the sea froze hard.

I proposed that Mimi should take sole charge of heaters, the snowmobile
and the preparation and allocation of field rations and equipment, in

addition to the galley stove, the outboard motors and the ship's navigational instruments and appliances that were already in her care. Gill would
assist her. Mimi or I must be told of any mechanical malfunctions *before*
anyone tried to tackle them. Everyone agreed with these suggestions and I
could only pray they were sincere. Mimi was taking on a lot, but, if only
everyone played their part according to their abilities, the world would be
at our collective feet.

Suiting the action to the word, Mimi set to and worked all the rest of
the day putting the heaters in order. Now that things had been put into
perspective and some practical decisions had been taken, she relaxed
visibly, to my great relief, for she had been under great strain striving to
mould a reliable team, and in default of anyone else had been venting her
irritability on me when we were alone.

It is easy to see in retrospect that the high standards Mimi demanded
were beyond the reach of this particular party, but we were still hoping
that those who were lagging in responsibility would yet rise to the occasion.
To varying degrees, everyone eventually did.

3 March was the date of the first field trip away from the ship. Freeze-
up could not be very far off but there was no sign of ice forming yet. Gill
and Norm were to camp in a valley below the moraine not far from our
first overnight anchorage so that Gill could prospect the area for lichens.
It was already apparent that these tiny tenacious plants were unexpectedly
more plentiful in the shadow of the great ice cap than on the islands
offshore. The previous day Gill had been rather overwhelmed at receiving
a 390-word radio telegram from a lichen expert at one of the Australian
universities. The message could be summed up, Mimi pointed out, as:
'Return all specimens to Australia before June.'

'Your reply should be "please expand",' Mimi suggested to Gill. 'You
had better hurry and send off those specimens – that university will soon
be bankrupt!'

Mimi and I ferried the party of two with their Beche tent and gear in
the inflatable, a cold, wet trip, I noted in my diary. The three miles took
all of forty-five minutes because the choppy seas set up by the katabatic
wind off the plateau would have soaked us with spray had we not throttled
down.

Leaving the others setting up their tent, Mimi and I headed for the
moraine itself, scrambled down the rocks to the green frozen lake and
cautiously crossed the ice-covered sand bar to the other side. There we
strapped on crampons and set off up the frozen snow of the ramp at a
great pace until the slope eased and the whole Rauer archipelago was
spread out below us and the Vestfold Hills peeped up over the intervening
Sørsdal.

'The crampons were fantastic,' Mimi wrote in her diary. 'It was a glori-
ous experience.' And more prosaically, 'I felt sluggish, needed Polaroid

glasses rather than yellow ski visor goggles and couldn't stand still to take photos without stiff and painful hands from the bitter wind.'

The way up to the plateau had proved easy enough on crampons but we were prospecting a possible 'overland' route to Davis, 130 miles or so away around the head of the Sørsdal, and it was apparent that a skidoo with standard rubber tracks would slide helplessly on the glassy surface and would have to be manhandled laboriously with ropes, blocks and belays. A possible way, we concluded, but for emergencies only.

The campers were hunting for lichens on a distant seaward ridge, tiny figures in that vast loneliness. We waved to them on the way down, then continued to the rubber duck and returned to *Explorer*.

Next morning, 4 March. there was no wind and the temperature was $-8.5°C$. The head of the bay was covered with a half-inch sheet of soft grey ice that had formed during the night. Jannik and Jamie were ferried ashore and went off on a penguin count, after which Mimi and I spent several hours hauling the ship through the new ice, so that we could get in the anchor, which had served its purpose, and reposition the four shore warps. The motor could have been used to push us through the ice, and, in fact, we later did the routine third-day engine run, but we wanted to find out how resistant was the new ice. It was remarkably tenacious.

The first of our two daily schedules over the field radio was at noon.

'Shore party, this is Dick Smith Explorer, do you read me? Over.'

'Dick Smith Explorer, reading you loud and clear,' Gill answered.

'Ice is forming in the bay, Gill. We have looked out from the hill and everywhere else seems clear at present. But you had better be ready to cut short the trip so that we can pick you up after our schedule this evening.'

There appeared to be no urgency at the moment. Surely there would be ample warning before ice formed in the sounds and fjords between the islands. There was no warning at all. Between 6.30 and 7 p.m. the sea froze almost instantaneously right to the horizon. Pausing only to make a hurried radio call to Gill and Norm to pack up their tent and equipment and get it down to the water's edge, we pulled on our float suits, loaded the emergency tent and food into the dinghy and set off without waiting for Jannik and Jamie to return.

The Beaufort had to plough through half an inch of soft new ice for the whole three miles. Our attempts to find open water cracks came to nothing. Would this constant ice-wear tear the dinghy cloth, we wondered anxiously? A pod of Minke whales surfaced down the sound *en route* towards the open sea, but we had little attention to spare for them. The amount of fuel being consumed was worrisome since the added resistance of ice-breaking required more of it and there was only one tank.

When we reached the moraine around 8.15 p.m. the tent was being folded; we left the food box behind and hurried the rest of the gear to the inflatable on the run in one hasty trip.

It is Mimi's story now because she was the driver. She wrote in her diary:

We were hopeful of being able to follow our already broken path back through the ice, but it had closed up completely. Suddenly the motor spluttered and died. The fuel tank hose where it connected to the motor had split. I cut off the end of the tube, pried the clamp off the motor fitting, forced the hose end back over the fitting and held it in place by hand while David drove. The chill to my fingers was agonizing. Quite apart from discomfort, the ride back was tense while we took a circuitous route that hugged the islands as closely as possible lest an emergency landing should become necessary. All of us were mightily relieved to regain *Explorer* and to find that Jannik and Jamie were safe aboard. They had been resourceful enough to use a styrofoam sheet, 6 feet long by 3 feet wide and 6 inches thick, as a raft and had pulled themselves along by a breastline. The toughness of the Beaufort inflatable was astonishing – six miles through abrasive ice all the way and the only tear was a small one in the bottom of the boat, not in the inflated tubes that formed the sides.

One bonus of this excursion was that Gill, who had been nervous and unsure at having the responsibility of being in charge of a field party – albeit of only two people for two days – had gained greatly in confidence.

For the next few days a lane was kept open to the shore down which the rubber duck could be hauled attached by a line and snap link to a breastrope. The styrofoam 'raft' proved a boon because it could be skated over the surface of ice that was still too thin to bear a person's weight and it would easily carry two people. Mimi had been sorting out and checking over our food to make sure we were reserving sufficient light and nourishing items for the field – freeze-dried meals, chocolate, biscuits and the like. The necessary restrictions on unlimited use that this entailed were irksome to some of the party, so it was a relief to be able to please everyone by doling out the first instalment of our winter ration of Sanitarium Foods' muesli bars (Granola fruit bars). There would be one a day for everyone while on board, and two extra per day for field trips. Mimi handed out a month's allocation of thirty bars each to everyone. We were a bit startled to find that Jannik and Jamie had eaten all theirs in the first two days!

Possible complications of the freezing-in process worried me, especially what would happen to us if a storm should break out the ice while it was still unstable. The anchor was no longer under the ice and the ship was connected directly to the shore, but would our mooring lines stand the strain, I fretted? A weather report for the Southern Ocean, relayed from Davis on the evening of our return from the moraine, forecast a low which, if it should come this far south, would be with us early next morning, according to my reckoning. 4 a.m., therefore, found me dressed and checking on the ice, weather and barometer. A gusty north-easter was blowing and the glass had fallen slightly. It was not a threatening picture but it was a beautiful one. The sky was clear and, beneath a half waning moon and the cold flames of an aurora that arched over the lonely hills, the ice glistened silver in the bay and far out over the frozen sea. Would our bay ice begin to separate if it did blow up, I wondered? 'There is so much I don't know,' I wrote in my journal. In the event, the morning dawned still and windless, so that the worry had all been for nothing.

Everyone was active in the days that followed. Jannik and Jamie trekked almost daily to the bird cliffs and rookeries and Jannik put down fish traps, which netted hosts of tiny sea lice and delicate elongated creatures that we christened 'Yuk worms', but no fish. Gill usually took Norm as her companion on her lichen hunts. Though the going was hard, he enjoyed it. The mate and I concentrated above all on planning and organizing for the longer excursions that would soon be possible and climbing different vantage points to note the limits and texture of the sea ice.

Skis were one problem. Because skis spread one's weight they were essential to safety on thin ice, but ours needed a lot of attention before they could be used. The Antarctic Division had lent us two pairs of old wooden touring skis that were heavy and clumsy and required waxing; parts of their bindings were missing. Jamie had obtained four pairs of modern cross-country skis with rat-trap bindings on loan from the manufacturer. He also had his own pair. These skis were excellent in every way, but, except for Norm and Jamie, who had their own cross-country ski boots, none of the rest of us had boots that fitted the bindings. Jamie had figured that we could construct suitable boot attachments or over-bindings and had brought leather sole pieces and kangaroo hide uppers for us to make up ourselves and fit to our insulated Sorrel boots so that they could be attached to the ski's rat-trap bindings. (The ideal would have been ordinary cross-country ski boots with insulated covers or spats, but we were unable to get hold of any either in Australia or the USA.)

Unfortunately, the leather fittings were hard to make and softened immediately on contact with the slushy ice surface to take on the constituency of cardboard. We had to try something else. The choice fell on motor car tyres that we carried as fenders. These were laboriously sawn up with hacksaws and shaped into boot fittings. But these were no more of a success either and, despite experiment and hard labour that lasted till the end of the month, they were never remotely satisfactory.

So, apart from Norm and Jamie with their cross-country ski boots, the rest of us fell back on the two pairs of wooden skis. Mimi and I, with ice testing in prospect, took them over, tarred and waxed them carefully and repaired their bindings as well as we could. Our rope attachments held the skis in place efficiently enough, but the snag was that there would be no way of removing them if we fell through the ice – a disturbing thought since we would be the ones reconnoitring its thickness.

Cold weather protection of the ship was now becoming necessary. Sheets of styrofoam were cut to size ready to fit over the large wheelhouse windows and over the engine room skylight, but they would block out so much light that they would not be put into place until it grew much colder. Norm hunted up the parts of the tough little wind generator that would produce two amps in fresh winds, in anticipation of the time when the sun would no longer be available to activate the solar panels on top of the wheelhouse. Tarpaulins were prepared ready to be rigged over the wheelhouse and stretched over the booms when and if heavy snow fell.

We made sledge harnesses from our sea-going safety belts by putting them on backwards and adding shoulder and breast straps of climbing tape. The safety line with its snap hook could then be clipped onto the sledge behind. These makeshift harnesses worked very well indeed, we found in due course, the pull being mainly from the waist and partly from the chest and shoulders. This was just as well since we were all except Norm to drag sledges behind us a good distance, Mimi, Gill, Jannik and I for nearly 500 miles. The one minor inconvenience of the arrangement was that the buckle of the safety belt was at the back, and hard to reach.

Mimi fought a sometimes losing battle to maintain the photographic gear. Batteries were vulnerable to damp and cold and fared particularly badly. All lubricants had been removed from the *National Geographic* cameras in Washington DC – Nikon FM's and Nikonos II's mostly – so that they would not freeze. This was a wise precaution. Unfortunately, the sound-recording movie camera loaned us by Channel 7 TV had not been similarly treated, broke down completely at this early stage, and defied all repair efforts. The silent underwater movie camera would now have to suffice. The weather grew steadily colder and we were glad of the double glazed portholes in the galley, the thick insulation in the centre cabin, and of course the heaters.

Six days after the freeze-up the ice was thick enough (three inches) for us to walk ashore and the Beaufort was hoisted out and stowed on the after deck. An unexpected visitor arrived that day, 10 March. This was Clarrie McCue, the then director of the Antarctic Division. He was leaving next day, together with the helicopters, on *Nanook S*, the last supply ship. If anyone wanted to leave with him, he would be glad to take them, he offered, publicly and privately to each of the crew.

'You must be joking!' exclaimed Jannik.

Clarrie did, however, take along our non-functioning movie camera. He also made a remark that was so startling that I did not have the wit to ask him what he meant.

'You have already cost the Antarctic Division $45,000.' It was more than a year later at Sydney that I enquired his meaning. 'Oh, someone, I think it was our spokesman, gave me the figure. It was all rubbish; there was no truth in the figure at all!'

By 12 March the ice outside the bay was firmer, two inches thick on average and elastic and springy. Mimi and I, cutting holes from time to time with an ice axe to gauge the thickness, succeeded in reaching the next island on skis. Soon we hoped to be breaking out from the confines of Filla Island, when wider horizons would open up for all of us.

While perspectives were opening up for us, they were very near closing altogether for *Nanoon S* and her distinguished passenger. We only heard the full story long afterwards and what follows is of course hearsay, so cannot be guaranteed in all detail, and naturally the incident was kept from the press. What appears to have happened is this. After leaving Davis for Australia on 11 March in sunny weather with the temperature $-11°C$, the ship was beset and drifted slowly offshore. No icebreakers were in the vicinity, and, it being so late in the season, there was every likelihood that the ship was trapped for good. Apart from Clary, the passengers included most of the team who had spent the previous winter at Davis. The emergency stores of winter clothing and equipment were opened – to reveal nothing but pyjamas (this detail from the ship's captain)! By the time the decision was taken a week later to evacuate the passengers back to Davis for another winter, the ship had drifted over seventy-two miles and was beyond the range of her small helicopters. The Russians were appealed to and readily agreed to send in their large helicopters to effect the evacuation. Happily, before they could arrive, the fickle ice opened again and released the ship. The wisdom of operating supply ships without icebreaker support so late in the season, no less than twenty days after the date Drygalski was frozen in, is open to doubt. Needless to say, in accordance with the bureaucrats' code of silence the Hobart press spokesman who had lampooned us so cruelly kept very quiet about this incident. All this high drama was, naturally, beyond our ken at the time.

The last Adélie penguins to leave, some only now shedding the last of their moult, were trudging out over the ice towards the ever-receding sea in long lines or little groups of three or four.

The first snow fell on 14 March. The equinox was lately past and the days from now on would shrink rapidly. The effect of five inches of snow cover on the still marginal new sea ice was disconcerting. A mushy layer of brine formed at the snow–ice interface; the insulating effect of the snow blanket was to warm the salty ice beneath so that it lost its elastic strength. Places we had crossed with ease the day before were now unsafe. No matter what wax we used the snow balled up under our skis. The islands in the sound were no longer accessible; all activities had to be concentrated on Filla.

It was here that my poor balance from the old detached retina showed up. I stumbled and fell over repeatedly on the slippery, snow-covered rocks during a filming trip to the bird cliffs with Mimi, Jannik and Jamie. They skipped about like mountain goats while I floundered. For some reason I dreamt that night of a polar bear. 'He won't eat you,' I reassured Mimi in the dream, 'but he may fall on you.' Perhaps he was unsteady like me.

Ever since our arrival in the Rauers an 'out and return' sheet had been posted in the wheelhouse. On it every absence from the ship was noted: names, destination, time of departure, time of return. Should anyone not be back on time a search party would go out within the hour. Certain rules were laid down. For the present at any rate no one was to leave the immediate vicinity of the boat alone. Anyone on a day outing must carry spare clothing, 'iron' rations and map and compass and at least one in every pair a sleeping bag. Float suits would always be worn on the sea ice.

Personal waste disposal became unexpectedly complicated by misplaced aesthetic feelings. The ship's head was still full of gear as it had been ever since we set out, and the outlet pipe would be frozen in any case. Mimi, Norm and I used the bucket as we had done at sea and emptied the contents onto the ice, where it would eventually float out to sea and sink. The others could not bring themselves to render the ice so unsightly. 'It will look so bad when the choppers come back in the spring,' was the way Jannik put it. They insisted on repairing modestly ashore among the rocks, regardless of repeated reminders that their leavings would still be there unaltered a hundred years hence, and that they would have to shovel them up meticulously sooner or later and place them on the ice.

'What do you want with this sort of immortality?' I asked them. 'I know I told you about finding Mawson's massive seventy-year-old leavings in the dunny at Commonwealth Bay last year, but even if his ever come to be preserved in some Australian museum ours won't be.' No argument prevailed. They still used the rocks and in the spring had no little scraping up to do.

Now that we were really on our own it seemed time to have a modest celebration. A couple of bottles of wine from the dozen we had traded for books with 'Pepsi', the cook on *Lady Franklin*, were broached and we enjoyed a sociable evening. Jamie was a born mimic, who could be very amusing indeed when the mood took him. Norm reminisced about his war-time night bomber experiences. He really did have a splendid record behind him.

'If only we had more wine,' Mimi sighed, 'we could have regular happy hours, but no one donated enough, did they?' I dreamed that night for some reason that my youngest daughter Vicky had come to visit us. Despite the ship being frozen-in and her own three years at sea at a tender age she was unaccountably seasick. Not that the others' dreams were any less fantastic. Norm never tired of recounting his dream about a sexy possum. Gill's, Mimi's and mine were generally much less spectacular, tending to be nightmarish worry dreams closely paralleling our current reality.

Food, along with shelter and warmth the basis for our survival, presented no real problems, as to essentials at any rate. The ill-starred salami was barely edible in an emergency. Canned meat was in short supply and so was only on the menu three evenings a week, but eggs, cheese, and TVP (vegetable protein) were available to fill the gaps. Freeze-dried meals and jerky (dried beef) were being held back for use in the field, when weight would be at a premium, especially when man-hauling the sledges. It was simple prudence for us to make sure of being able to supplement our supplies by hunting. Jannik, 'the Neanderthal Man', as Jamie called him, brought in sundry birds for the larder. Unexpectedly, the wily skuas tasted best. All of them, including penguins, could have benefited from hanging. None were much to our taste but we had the satisfaction of knowing we could live comfortably off the land as other explorers had done before us if the need arose. But to make quite sure of enough meat for the winter we shot an old seal, which was tough and gamy but a welcome addition to our larder.

As the ice grew steadily stronger and increased our radius of travel we were concerned to find acceptable jobs for everyone. For Gill, Jannik and ourselves, who were enjoying everything so much, it was hard to realize that others could find Antarctica boring.

A tempting explanation would be that four of us were in couples and two were not, but this misses the mark in that the divergence had been clearly apparent long before Gill and Jannik got together. Whatever the reason, two of the party were out of step, and we racked our brains for ways to help them. Norm was a keen skier and I encouraged him. Jamie, who also had the equipment and was even more skilled, could only be persuaded to go out once. Norm's enthusiasm was a good example to everyone. Jamie, unfortunately, failed to follow his friend's example and spent more and more time in his bunk.

'Perhaps I should show Jamie how to do the hydrophone recordings of seals,' Mimi suggested. He agreed to help, and Mimi demonstrated the tape recorder and the underwater hydrophone. Her own efforts at seal sound recording had so far been mainly over the side of the ship and had been unproductive. In fact the only one had been when Jannik had braved the icy water to put his lips under and bubble 'Hallo Mimi, how are you doing now?'

'I didn't know seals spoke with a Danish accent,' she commented.

It was Jamie and Gill, incidentally, who later obtained the first good seal tape.

A day or so later I asked Norm to come with me on skis for an ice recce to a nearby sound where the ice had broken out and only recently reformed. We talked about wintering ships in the Antarctic as we slid quietly along.

'Using boats the size of trawlers to supplement the permanent bases could cut costs enormously and save mucking up the few rocky coastal areas where huts can be built,' I said. 'We will be monitoring selected bays throughout the year to see just what happens to the ice in them. There are ten possibles in the Rauers and several in the Larsemanns. Mimi and I have been watching the ice from hills 81 and 82 every chance we get and the ice has been doing some funny things – breaking and reforming to seaward, though a pattern seems to be developing. As soon as the ice is safe enough the two of us are keen to get going round the outer Rauer winter mooring sites. We will head for Shelyf, Hop and Varyag first, I think – Hell! Move away from me, this ice is shaking.'

I had been carried away by my own enthusiasm and forgotten where we were. I draw the ice axe from my belt and swung it. 'Only one and a half inches, let's go back.'

'I had thought you only wanted to end your Antarctic career with a bang,' said Norm as we moved off.

'Nearly a splash,' I countered. 'Not ending, just beginning.'

The first man-haul sledging

At long last the sea ice, now mostly more than two or three inches thick and no longer waterlogged, seemed safe for cautious man-hauling on skis. (The generally recognized minimum is 10 cm thick, about 4 inches.) The snow had largely blown off the frozen waterways, leaving yellowish gritty drifts between polished glittering ice. The rocky islands were snow-free except for drifts and hollows, having been scoured by the wind and the snow evaporated (ablated is, I think, the correct term) by the warmth of the sun and the drying effect of the wind in that desert atmosphere. This phenomenon of the vanishing snow continued to surprise us in the Rauers and the Larsemanns though not in the Vestfolds, much of which lay under a heavy blanket all winter.

Mimi and I spent a day sorting and packing our food, fuel and gear, tarring and waxing skis and filming and taking photographs round the ship. A convivial dinner that night left everyone in good spirits. All the next morning was taken up with loading up the Nansen sledge and with last-minute packing, for this was our first effort. In our anxiety to be well prepared we undoubtedly carried too much; the large pressure lamp and extra pairs of boots, for instance. Routine radio schedules were arranged for 7 p.m. and 12 noon.

It was 2 p.m. on the last day of March when we leaned into the traces and the heavy sledge moved reluctantly off behind us, jerking forward with each pull and showing no marked inclination to glide. Straining with effort over the sticky drifts and with the sledge skidding wildly on the bare patches, we huffed and panted our way down a frozen sound between Shelyf and Flag islands. Our purpose was to visit prospective winter moorings we had made note of earlier, either from the sea or the air, to photograph and sketch them and to note significant points like ice thickness. The day was windless, mostly overcast, and the temperature an unseasonably warm −7″C.

The ice in the sound was thicker than expected, 3–4 inches. We trudged along happily in our float suits, sweating despite having the zips open all down the front. After resting awhile at a log jam of drifted-up floes that blocked the straight at the halfway mark, we heaved and pushed our way through the obstruction. Being at last on the road alone was wonderful. In the narrowest part of the strait between Flag and Shelyf, not far from our old Shelyf anchorage, we came upon water overlying thin ice. This was no way for us. We hauled the sledge up and over a snow-covered point of land and down to firm ice beyond, to turn aside onto a sheltered-frozen gravel bed on Flag Island, where we camped. A group of late moulting Adélie penguins watched us listlessly. They must soon head for the open sea or be fatally cut off from their fishing grounds in open water.

We were able to drive the tent pegs into the permafrost only with difficulty. The time was 6.30 p.m., so we had come three miles in four hours, no very brilliant performance compared with Scott's average with overloaded sledges in soft snow of some twelve miles a day. He was made of sterner stuff. We were tired, irritable and chilled by the time we got in. I was desperately thirsty and grabbed the thermos of coffee eagerly, only to find it was broken. But after a 7 p.m. radio schedule with *Explorer* and several mugs of coffee laced with rum and a freeze-dried meal we both felt better. 'Wonderful to be here alone with David,' Mimi wrote in her diary.

A blustery northeast wind greeted us next morning, 1 April. The temperature was down to −11°C when we set off on skis to prospect our old anchorage on Shelyf. The tide-crack complex was wider than on Filla, we found, the ice much thicker, measuring a full 15 cm, or about 6 inches. The water was about 9 feet deep where the ship's bow would have lain had *Explorer* remained there. We were later to document dramatic changes taking place in the ice of this cove, which taught us practical lessons about choosing a winter anchorage.

Next to be monitored was a fjord on the outer side of Hop Island. Leaving our skis weighted down with rocks on the shore lest they blow away, we set out on foot across the stony hills to the fjord. It was disappointing. Though we duly photographed, sketched and sounded it, it was too shallow and too wide for a useful haven. From the hills a wide open water lead could be seen out to sea and the ice beyond Varyag had clearly broken up and reformed. Both of us felt tired on the way back and we were glad to reach camp again.

We packed up the tent next morning and set out for the tip of Varyag, the southwesternmost of the Rauers, over the ice of the open coast. The temperature was down to −16°C, there was no wind and the going was smooth and made for easy sledging. Nevertheless Mimi was uncomfortable and cold and moaned a lot; she thought we were taking too great a risk sledging over 1–2-inch new ice. I disagreed, insisting that testing new ice was what we were there for. The outer islands were wind-scoured like pictures of the Sahara or

Mars and no sheltered camp site could be found. We compromised on a snow-filled hollow on an islet close to the southern tip of Varyag. It was not until 9 p.m. that we were finally settled in our sleeping bags with the primus going. A bonus was the discovery that the sleeping bags could be zipped together so that we could be warmer and closer. That night there was no wind, the thermometer was down to − 17°C and the glass steady. Nothing gave a hint as to what was coming on the morrow.

A word here about Antarctic blizzards may not be out of place. They are warm-front storms and as such associated with a plummeting barometer and temperatures which, even in winter, rise to very near freezing point. Their direction varies according to the local topography, southeast in Commonwealth Bay, northeast at our location. The blinding blown snow, so deadly on the polar plateau, is less a feature on the sea ice, which the wind soon blasts clear of snow.

As late as midday on 3 April there seemed no cause for alarm. It remained cold, the barometer had fallen only slightly and there was little wind. Within two hours everything had changed. We were on skis reconnoitring the ice when a towering cloud of snow bore down upon us from the plateau five or six miles away. Minutes later the blast struck us with sixty-knot fury (the anemometer at Davis recorded ninety knots that night and the next). Barely able to stand, we continued our recce on foot, confirming that the ice seaward of the island had some time before broken into pans which had refrozen at all angles. Back at the tent by 4 p.m. we found that the temperature had risen to − 3°C and the barometer had fallen 12 mb in three hours.

All night we lay tensely while the wild slatting of the tent competed with the thunder of the blizzard. Next morning a brief lull allowed us to crawl to the summit of the islet. We were horrified to see that the ice road we had traversed two days before was now a waste of raging whitecaps beneath driving snow squalls. Were we cut off, was the immediate question? Not entirely, it turned out. 'The connection to Varyag looks good,' Mimi wrote, 'and there are rocks and grounded bergy bits downwind to hold it in. All else is broken out and the pack ice is *gone*! The far northeastern end of long narrow Varyag is still connected by ice to Filla. Varyag will be our lifeline but we will have to portage and relay everything some distance along and across the island before we can sledge again.'

The blizzard returned after dark. 'A fearful night of tension,' she recorded. 'The tent shaking violently with frequent whiplash cracks. Temperature 0°C.' After 2 a.m. the blizzard exhausted its fury and we finally slept.

A strong wind but no blizzard greeted us when we awoke on 6 April. The ice limits had not changed materially and a check from the top of a hill on Varyag confirmed that we must cross the island diagonally to halfway along the northern coast to find intact ice again. The tent was packed up and the sledge dragged across the narrow strait to Varyag.

Loads were allocated, Mimi taking the lion's share, an awkward burden of tent, pegs and poles, together with camera gear, radio and the filled primus stove. My lighter share included some ready-use food and an unwieldy bundle of Karrymats and sleeping bags. It was snowing heavily so we could see very little and kept straying up the wrong valleys and having to double back over snowdrifts and ridges. I had strained a back muscle some days earlier cutting holes in the ice, and, despite my lighter load, my back ached and I was very tired. It was no small relief when, just at dusk, we slithered down a scree slope to find ourselves in a sheltered valley on the northeast coat, a perfect camp site at last.

An attempt to transport all the rest of our gear in one load the following day soon came to nothing. Piling everything on the sledge, and carrying it one at each end like a stretcher, we started off. The load was something like 150 lb, and we staggered about, straining ourselves to little purpose, and soon gave up. We dumped everything but the Nansen itself, the heavy sledging box and the skis and set off once more. Even so, we had to make some twenty rest stops on the way to the tent. There I was mortified to find that we had unwittingly been carrying a whole billy full of water all the way! After a brew and a rest we roused ourselves once more and went back to retrieve the rest of the cached gear. The sky was clear now so we did not hurry and it was little hardship to make our final carry in the gathering dark.

The last and ninth day of the field trip was unexpectedly exhausting. The temperature was still high and the layer of soggy snow that overlay the ice was covered with grit blown off from the land and stuck to our sledge runners like treacle. We forced the pace to the limits of our strength, or at least mine, to get through a narrow strait where we feared the ice might have broken. All this was in the teeth of a gale. Once through the gap I had to rest and curled up on a rock ledge with my back to the wind chewing muesli and space bars for energy, while a worried Mimi tried unsuccessfully to light the primus to make me a hot drink. After half an hour I felt a lot better and we pushed on to the ship, where hot cocoa, rest and a tot of rum revived me.

We were elated to have had the best possible view of the pattern and process of ice breakout (without having gone out ourselves). Though we had covered no more than twenty-three miles in nine days and had prospected only three anchorages, we had learned a lot about the tenacity of sea ice where it was well anchored and its instability off open coasts. We had discovered that our tents could stand up to a ninety-knot blizzard in the open and found out much about mitts, hats and goggles. Washing ourselves and our clothes in the galley that night was a well-earned luxury. Above all, it was apparent from the generally warmer atmosphere aboard that the success of this first sledging venture had raised morale appreciably. Gill and Jannik were particularly eager to hear the practical details of our experience. Mimi and I went to bed that might buoyed with high hopes for the future.

7

A New Beginning
8 April–6 June 1983

[Shackleton is] vacillating, erratic and a liar, easily
scared, moody and surly; a boaster.
Dr Eric Marshall, diary, 27 February 1908

Shackleton and I are pulling at least two thirds of the
load. The big hog [Marshall] does not even pull his own
food.
Frank Wild, diary, 9 December 1908

The truism that two observers may view a companion or an incident in
diametrically opposite ways is dramatically brought out by these diaries of
Marshall and Wild, two of Shackleton's three companions in 1908–9 when
they reached to within ninety-seven miles of the South Pole.

We will return to Wild and Marshall a little further on. For the moment
let us consider *National Geographic*'s guidelines for use of film as an
example of divergent perceptions. They seemed unwarranted to some; to
others they were but necessary documentation procedures and the issue
was blown up out of nothing. The undisputed facts are that extra film
we were expecting at Albany did not arrive. We were promised it at
Davis, but it was not there either, not, that is, until more than a year
later.

The film was to document all aspects of the expedition, especially our
interaction with Antarctica and its wildlife. These were wide enough terms
of reference in all conscience, as they took in everything from portraits
and animals to scientific and scenic shots; there was enough film even
without the lost shipment.

The magazine entrusted the film and equipment to Mimi and the two of
us had, in fact, signed that only we two would handle their cameras and

meters, a proviso we interpreted liberally. The simple records the magazine asked for were for the photographer to list his name, the dates, subjects and exposures on each roll. We had agreed at the outset to abide by the ORF's commitment to return exposed film direct to the magazine for processing. Everyone was given film by Mimi, with more to come when the rolls were handed in with the relevant notes.

To our bewilderment the requirement to simply document exposed rolls was felt to be an intolerable imposition.

Even Gill said: 'This junior school type of leadership [Mimi's and mine] is intensely irritating,' adding that Mimi had made a huge mistake in saying that there would be masses of film for everyone to use as they liked, ignoring the fact that Mimi had never said anything of the sort. But Gill soon came to see things in proportion and did her best to make the people who resented any sort of restrictions 'see reason', as she put it.

The whole issue was so absurd that we thought at the time it was merely a bizarre isolation-spawned aberration. It certainly was, but beyond all reason the non-issue did not go away but built up into a festering sore, if one may mix metaphors. A great deal of abuse and foul lanaguage was levelled at Mimi and me by two of the party.

Now, the point was made at the beginning of this chapter that there are two sides to every question. How then can we judge the truth? Let us return to Wild and Marshall.

Marshall was senior surgeon, photographer and cartographer on Shackleton's *Nimrod* expedition, which also included Edgeworth David, McKay and the young Douglas Mawson, a trio who made the longest unsupported man-haul journey in history, 1,260 miles to the South Magnetic Pole. Mawson went on to other achievements in his 1911–13 expedition to Commonwealth Bay and further expeditions in the 1930s. Yet Marshall characterized Mawson in his diary as 'useless and objectionable, lacking in guts and manners'.

Marshall further wrote about Shackleton: 'He seldom puts his hand to any work, save when a cinematograph is working. His spasm then lasts five minutes' (diary, 26 February). Again, a month later: 'By God he has not played the game and is not capable of doing so; he's a consummate liar and a practised hypocrite.'

Wild, on the other hand, had nothing but praise for his leader and contempt for Marshall's failure to pull his weight. 'Marshall is just as bad again. I could shoot him' (10 December). Shackleton, on the contrary, 'forced upon me his one breakfast biscuit . . . I do not suppose that anyone else in the world can thoroughly realize how much generosity and sympathy was shown in this' (31 January 1909, when the party were starving).

Wild was to distinguish himself later as leader of Mawson's innovative Western Party, which wintered in 1912–13 on what is now the Shackleton Ice Shelf some way west of the present Soviet base at Mirny. Later still he remained in charge of the crew of the wrecked *Endurance* at Elephant Island while Shackleton went for help in his unforgettable boat journey. It was due to Wild's leadership, no less than Shackleton's, that not a single man of the expedition was lost.

Shackleton, Mawson and Wild; history ranks them among the greatest polar explorers of all time. Poor Marshall was lost after the ice crushed Bob Bartlett's *Karluk* off Wrangell Island in 1917 when, headstrong as ever, he insisted on breaking away from Bartlett in an ill-conceived attempt to cross unstable sea ice.

The point I am making, which these accounts dramatically illustrate, is that the proof of the pudding is in the eating. The actual sequence of events allows us to judge between Marshall's and Wild's contradictory opinions. People's actions speak louder than words and there *is* an objective reality to any enterprise. Similarly, the objective reality of our own expedition is recorded in documents like the ship's log and the records of field work.

To go back to our own affairs. mundane as they were compared to the heroic epics of the past. Jannik, who was assembling the Eskimo sled, had sharp words with Jamie, who was not anxious to help. 'You have two books about sledge dogs with you and you are always reading about polar travel. Now is your chance. You can see what it is all about,' Jannik exclaimed.

Gill, who had been chafing at earlier postponements of sledging by reason of thin ice before our Varyag trip, appreciated our caution since the blizzard and breakout. One result of the blizzard had been to prove that the ice *inside* the islands was now secure. Float suits could be dispensed with, inside the archipelago at any rate, and there would be more than enough opportunity for everyone to be up and doing. Accordingly we held a meeting on 10 April, the second day after our return from Varyag, to discuss field work and put forward the following programme.

Jannik and Jamie would go seal tagging to the moraine, where Norm and Gill had noticed a number of seals hauled out on the ice of a frozen fjord. They would stay one or two nights depending on the number of seals and bring back the sledging box abandoned so hurriedly when the sea froze. Since no one had gone in this direction since freeze-up, Mimi and I would ski ahead to check that the ice was safe.

On their return, Mimi and I would make a circuit of the Rauer Islands from the Moraine to Cape Drakon checking the safety of the ice, monitoring potential anchorages and picking out a site for a depot near the cape, which would be our jumping-off point for the Larsemanns in the south. Gill and Jannik would go with us to tag seals, collect lichens and make bird counts.

Gill and Jamie would then go on a seal vocalization recording trip to wherever we found active seal holes.

Once the ice was firm enough for the snowmobile, which should not be very long now, we would start laying the depot at Cape Drakon. Norm would be one of this motorized party.

The Cape Drakon depot was central to our plans, being a day's man-haul ($8\frac{1}{2}$ miles) nearer some key research objectives: the emperor penguin rookery at Amanda Bay that had never been visited while the chicks were still with their parents; probable seal pupping areas on the ice off the Larsemanns; Adélie penguin rookeries on islands down the coast; lichens on exposed rock anywhere; potential ice anchorages and the fast ice itself.

The plan had something in it for everyone, who all said it suited them. Day trips would of course continue: bird counts at the fast-emptying seabird and penguin rookeries, seal tagging and inspections of potential ice anchorages on the north side of Filla and on Yefremov Island.

Our seal tagging programme was an important supplement to that at Davis. The idea is to insert one or preferably two numbered plastic tags in a seal's tail by means of a pair of tagging pliers. Re-sights are the pay-off, since they give an indication of how far the seals roam as well as some idea of their numbers, and here we would be in a better position than the zoologists at Davis, being able to cover a much longer stretch of coastline. The seals, most of them Weddells, had no liking at all for the procedure. The few crab-eaters we encountered had short tempers and liked it even less.

The technique is for someone to stand in front of the seal, distracting it and being careful to keep out of range of its teeth, while the wily operator creeps up behind with the tagging pliers and quickly clips on the tab. That is the theory. Individual seals vary enormously in temperament and those that were justifiably suspicious, nervous or aggressive were hard to cope with.

Jannik did the lion's share of the tagging, 95 per cent at least, with Gill and sometimes Jamie to distract the animals. Gill tagged others with Jamie assisting, Mimi with me and then Jamie with Norm in the spring. From time to time Jannik returned with rents torn in his ventile trousers and once or twice with sizeable bruises. He was a glutton for punishment and never tired of the work.

There was no great change in daily routine once we were ice-bound. Collecting ice for melting into drinking water was easier with a sledge than it had been with the inflatable, several old floes that were frozen-in outside the bay serving us for most of the winter. The idea was to keep the melt tank round the engine exhaust always filled up with blocks of ice; a thirty-litre plastic can of water was held in reserve as 'blizzard water'; two more were kept in the galley for current use. A container of salt water was kept by the sink for washing up, which was done in a bowl that could be emptied over the side, for the sink outlet pipe was frozen.

Norm conscientiously kept up our evening rado schedule with Davis, who kindly relayed telegrams for us to and from Australia and the USA. No praise can be adequate for the unselfish work of Graham Dadswell, the Davis radio operator, who generally transmitted our messages to and from Australia and the rest of the outside world. Reception was often atrocious, especially as the year wore on and our two little transmitters, in default of an electronics technician like Don Richards in 1982 or Lars Larsen in 1978, lost 'steam', so that hours of patient elucidation were called for. All this was in Graham's free time. At our end Norm was equally long-suffering.

The longest messages were usually our regular reports to the ORF, but there were many personal calls too. Norm had a network of supportive friends who kept up a stream of encouraging messages, while Jamie's large family was solicitous of him in much the same way. The rest of us had less personal communication with 'outside'. Our energies were now fully engaged with the Antarctic and the last thing we wanted was to be distracted. Meteorological observations were less valuable now than they had been at sea, because of the proximity of the well-instrumented Davis and also because the anemometer and the wet bulb thermometer had both been broken. Still, we did what we could to keep records. Being able to predict coming weather was naturally of more than passing interest to us. Davis passed on the Australian Meteorological Department's forecasts for Antarctica, which had a certain dreamlike quality in their divorce from reality. More than a decade's weather records attest to the extreme rarity of southeast winds at Davis and this season was no exception. Yet monotonously, day after day, southeasters were predicted. One would have thought that the forecasters would have been interested in sometimes checking how their predictions turned out. Apparently not, for they persisted 100 per cent in error!

Nevertheless, the Met people's reports on the position, speed and direction of low-pressure systems were most valuable, although not all lows crossed the Antarctic trough of low pressure to approach our latitude. By far the best indication that something unpleasant was on the way was the sight of cirrus clouds spreading over the sky some twelve hours before a front's advent, and then thickening to cirro-stratus with a falling barometer.

On 11 April Mimi and I made a day recce west of Filla and found that the new ice formed since the 3 April breakout was almost ready to bear weight, for which we could thank the −18°C temperature. This was the eve of Jannik's and Jamie's seal tagging trip to the moraine and I experienced what became a regular occurrence on the eve of any undertaking, an outburst from Jamie. The precipitating cause itself was never important; in this case it was my insistence on taking primus spares and the requirement to return in two or three days to fit in with the agreed schedule of the other parties.

Jamie launched into a tirade of abuse. 'You were really sucked in when I cried at Flinders, you fuckwit,' was his final sally.

Jannik was upset, and Mimi wrote in her diary next day, 'Jamie was horrible, threatening David, insulting both of us, defending his behaviour, accusing and attacking David to an unbelievable extent and all without rationality or meaning.'

'It was a bad night,' she continued, 'took hours to get warm. Finally David brought me an extra sleeping bag, so his restlessness wouldn't disturb me. He himself didn't sleep but an hour due to worry and anger over Jamie's behaviour. We must get Jamie as positively operative as possible and control our own distress, but I do not *ever* wish to be in the field with him, and I would not be happy about his being with anyone else in a tough situation.'

So it came about that Jamie sowed the seeds of his own exclusion, as dangerously unstable to himself and others, from the major undertakings of the expedition.

'It was all very well for Sir Vivian Fuchs to tell an exploration medicine conference I was at that it was a good thing for a leader to be the focus of resentment, but Jamie is going a bit too far!' I said wryly. 'I'm sure my blood pressure must have been hitting 200 last night!'

'Keep a sense of proportion,' Mimi urged me. 'All it was really was letting off steam because of being highly strung and nervous. It wasn't deliberate, it was a breakdown. You'll see, today he'll have forgotten all about it.'

Mimi and I now realize that we were wrong in not subsequently making more effort, whatever our feelings, to keep Jamie company in the field, where we could have tried to help. A better leader would have been strong enough to ignore the frequent profane attacks I had to put up with. Regrettably, I am no saint.

Despite our sleepless night, the two of us were away at 11 a.m. to prospect the ice towards the moraine for Jamie and Jannik. A northeast gale was blowing in our teeth and the ice was polished smooth. We could only ski up-wind by dint of 'herring-boning', which is an uphill manoeuvre, on the flat. Every now and then a gust would blow us backwards. We were both irritable and snappish from worry and lack of sleep; gloves, makeshift ski bindings and goggles perversely took the opportunity to be awkward and, to cap it all, my right side back muscles, that had been strained on the Varyag trip, went into spasm each time I bent over. It was a miserable outing and we were glad when we had satisfied ourselves that the ice was strong enough all the way. Turning back thankfully, we passed on the good news to Jannik and Jamie, who were sensibly man-hauling on foot without skis. Our own trials were not yet over because I kept speeding up out of control down-wind and was scared of falling on to the hard ice for fear of breaking my artificial hip. So, after all our trouble to get up-wind on skis, we took them off on my rather craven insistence and slipped and shuffled back on foot.

That night it blew a moderate gale, which eased next day. The campers reported over the radio that they had tagged a crab-eater, the only seal they saw, and they returned next morning. The field radio was functioning, but only by fits and starts.

Gill and Jannik got away to the moraine on 16 April. This was to be the round trip via Cape Drakon and Torckler Island for tagging seals and prospecting ice conditions and anchorages. Mimi and I followed them. We were so upset at the atmosphere aboard and exercised as to what to do about it that we arrived at the camp site minus our tent poles – much to Gill's and Jannik's amusement. Crossed skis at each end of the tent made an acceptable substitute, though it did look rather like a surrealistic wigwam and did nothing to save our faces. Next morning we trudged three miles back to the boat to retrieve our tent poles – a lesson to us on being forgetful.

Fresh initiatives – mid-April

The way things were going with the party a more realistic attempt to fit round pegs into round holes was called for. Mimi and I hammered out a strategy in broad outline during the next few days.

Briefly, we must stop banging our heads against a brick wall. We had been at fault, we realized, in expecting everyone necessarily to fit into the niche they had originally chosen. After all, they had made sacrifices to get to Antarctica and we should help them enjoy it in their own way. In default of rewarding outlets there was nowhere for morale to go but down. More accent would have to be placed on arranging satisfying field experiences while giving greater scope for the initiative of those who wanted to be up and doing.

Was all this planning and organizing necessary in such a small group as ours? Had not Himalayan climbing parties been successfully run on consensus lines? Yes, but these were people with a common level of expertise. In our case the crew's relative inexperience underlined the need for precise and defined leadership.

Gill, while still irritated by what she felt was Mimi's over-insistence on performance, was steadily gaining insight. She had already been left in charge of the schooner when Mimi and I were ashore at Davis and had been *de facto* leader during our Varyag field trip. Her integrity, reliability and loyalty were beyond doubt, her energy unbounded. She was the obvious choice to take over the job of coordinating the ANARE-related scientific projects, namely, the seal, seabird and penguin work, in which Jamie had lost interest. The change-over would be gradual.

Jannik, with his immense zest for the outdoors and for animals, would

make an excellent offsider for Gill. Mimi and I would help them in handling ANARE-related projects, and carry on with our own work on sea ice,
winter moorings and the documentation of the group. The four of us
would make up the more active portion of the expedition, and consulta-
tions between us would of necessity tend to pre-empt the general weekly
discussions.

The alternative to such a strategy as this, for there always *is* an alternative, was to give up our major research goals outside the Rauers (both
Norm and Jamie had of late several times pooh-poohed them), stop insisting on performance standards and settle down to passively enjoy the
beauty of our surroundings. Greater harmony would no doubt have
resulted. The price: negligible scientific work and a good chance of losing
our ship and our lives through thoughtless actions.

Jamie could do the 'water column sampling'. This involved the filtering
out from sea water samples of microscopic plant life (phytoanalysis). We
had been provided with the equipment at Davis and the samples could be
taken from holes in the ice near the ship. It was not Jamie's fault that this
programme that he worked on conscientiously proved abortive in the end,
owing to deterioration of the chemical reagents. Jamie and Norm might
also make daily meteorological observations. Norm must needs keep up
with the engine and radio routines, but we should try to help him, for
instance, by taking turns at cleaning out the engine room. He and Jamie
could help in bird recording and be responsible for keeping the ship
supplied with fresh water ice.

I gave up my original plan, which I had only confided to Mimi. This
was for all six of us to go into the field at the same time – we had tents,
cookers and sledges enough – leaving the securely frozen-in ship to its
own devices, with the electrics being trickle-charged by the wind generator.
It was clear now that our field strength was too limited for this.

Should these plans not work out, we had best make contingency arrangements to evacuate to Davis anyone who might seriously disrupt the
party.

'Let's be sensible,' said Mimi. 'This would mean getting to Davis. There
are two possible routes: the 130 miles or so round the head of the Sørsdal
Glacier over the crevassed plateau with only one snowmobile is no way to
evacuate anyone. The only practical way would be across the sea ice in
front of the Sørsdal snout.'

'If it ever freezes,' I objected. 'You know that some winters there is no
ice there at all and whenever it does form it promptly breaks out again?
They say that no one has ever attempted that crossing.'

'We have no choice,' answered Mimi. 'We shall have to try it, because
anyway we need more gas for the snowmobile. It's using far more than we
expected. Even a short overnight trip will give us a chance to talk to Peter
and draw up the contingency plans. The radio is too public. We will just

have to keep on monitoring that ice from hill 82 and from the furthest-out
islands and then make our dash the moment there is an ice road.'

I myself viewed the prospect of crossing in front of the glacier with a
good deal of trepidation, Mimi with more enthusiasm.

Two questions must spring to the reader's mind. What had happened to
transform the eager enthusiasm that everyone had shown in Sydney into
disillusionment for some? And had sex after all played a significant role in
the process; had becoming 'odd men out' sexually precipitated or
materially accelerated the change? We have thought long and hard about
the answers.

On the first question, the irony was that the fulfilment of certain dreams
was blocked by practical realities they could not handle. In the less demanding environment of a base they would have been all right. For it
should not be forgotten that the stresses upon us were exceptionally severe,
more akin to those experienced by Shackleton's generation than by
modern-day Antarctic personnel. And one or two people are very often
quietly evacuated from even the comfortable bases. So if some of our
party had lost momentum, they could not really be blamed; very few
people would have had the courage to undertake what they had in the
first place.

For Jamie, it seemed that the really decisive alienation came about from
our stay at Davis. It had been a turning point, perhaps *the* turning point
for him. From then on his comments about our research plans became
consistently scathing. He made no attempt whatever to play the part, which
he had so eagerly sought, of scientific coordinator.

'If you like,' he replied, totally uninterested, to my suggestion that everyone should carry note books on their walks to record bird sightings.

'There is nothing pioneering about us.' 'Why bother? We are nothing.'
He repeated such sentiments over and over again in much the same terms.
'The only things worth doing are to help ANARE in the Rauers, it's no
use going further south.' He exclaimed one day: 'Just imagine working at
Davis and being paid $30,000 a year for it – I would gladly *pay* to be able
to work there!' The centrally heated base, with its tasty meals, radio
telephone links to home, TV, social life round the complimentary bar and
well-equipped laboratories was the real Antarctica of his dreams. The
contrast with *Explorer*'s sordid, cramped and chilly quarters, uninspiring
food and the need to work in uncomfortable conditions, as well as the
potential hazards, was too much for him to accept. His long-held fantasies
of himself as an Antarctic leader could no longer be fulfilled on our expedition.

Norm's viewpoints were quite different. He too queried the need to go
beyond the Rauers and wondered what was the use of all the long-distance
penguin counting and the rest, but he had never been interested in our
research from the beginning. He had wanted to crown his Antarctic career

by wintering over, that was all. This was perfectly acceptable and had always been understood. He had been taken as a reserve for his credentials in mechanical and electrical matters. No one dreamt, Norm least of all I am sure, how wide was the gap between the administrative work in which he had been engaged for years and practical mechanics. It was his persistence in trying to sustain a role that was beyond him that caused problems. Far from accepting assistance, as we all had to at times, he took umbrage at attempts to help him.

It should be clear by now that the party was tending to divide according to their enthusiasm for the *expedition goals*. Those more actively engaged in fulfilling them were experiencing increasing satisfaction.

Did lack of sexual outlet play a significant part in this? Of course it must have aggravated stresses, but Mimi and I are convinced that it was not the prime mover, because the tendency towards polarization was already evident well before Gill expressed her preference for Jannik.

'I am a neuter,' Jamie proclaimed more than once.

Norm had other ideas.

'People shouldn't pair off,' he told Mimi at a pre-selection interview, and went on to imply that she should not remain sexually exclusive.

'Neither Gill nor I is opposed in principle to being intimate with more than one person, and I for one have enjoyed the experience. Mimi had explained. 'But that is a matter for personal choice, not a kind of duty. Anyway I am happy with David.'

Norm really appeared to feel that the expedition women had some sort of moral obligation to oblige the men 'on demand' – rather like his attitude towards *National Geographic* film, Mimi felt – for he came back to the question several times during the expedition. Shortly before the pre-freeze trip with Gill to the moraine Norm asked Mimi if she thought he had a chance with Gill now that she had teamed up with Jannik. The same day Gill told Mimi that Norm was pressuring her. 'The women should be prepared to sleep with all the men,' he had argued.

'You are a free agent, Gill. No one can pressure you,' Mimi reassured the younger woman. Nevertheless, it 'didn't seem right' to share a tent with a woman and not have sex, Norm remarked dolefully, or so Jannik told me later.

As for Mimi being an object of sexual interest, she aroused such resentment early on by her insistence on performance, that, as she put it, 'Some people are more interested in getting back at me than in soliciting my favours.'

During the previous year's expedition to Commonwealth Bay half of us were without sexual partners. There were three couples. The rest of us, two women and four men, were happy enough; we felt no upset because the centre cabin was the 'honeymoon hotel'. There were more than enough positive outlets for us all. The same applies to the bases. After all, there are generally only a few women to a lot of men or no women at all, and morale is generally high – in proportion to the amount of rewarding work there is to do.

Close companionship is a rather different matter from sex considered on its own. Gill and Jannik developed great tenderness in their relationship and both of them had the same enthusiasm and general outlook. Mimi and I shared their feeling for the enterprise.

Love undoubtedly illuminated the lives of both couples and gave meaning to everything we experienced. Loneliness had been no stranger to either Mimi or me before we met and we could readily sympathize with loneliness in others. It seems to us that it is friendship, companionship and love that most strongly sustain important human relationships. Sex, in itself, has much less meaning. Companionship and friendship based on common interests between people of the same or opposite sexes is very sustaining, and it was just such a friendship that Norm and Jamie did develop. It was undoubtedly a very great help to them and contributed to general stability; it must have gone a long way towards restoring the balance should sexual deprivation have been upsetting them.

The red cliffs of Drakon

All this was yet to be resolved when Gill and Jannik, Mimi and I packed up the tents, buckled on our harness and moved off down a majestic sound between the bold rock buttresses and crevassed ice-falls of the continental ice on our left and the crags of Lokot and Pchelra islands on the right. Flocks of snow petrels wheeled about the cliffs forty metres above our heads, looking for all the world like whirling snowflakes. These graceful birds never wholly departed during the winter, two or three being visible most days among the crags or at least their cries being audible, a sign that some open water persisted no further than twenty or thirty miles away.

Such an ice-free expanse in the heart of the pack is termed a polynia. Polynias may be any size, often hundreds of miles across, and are believed to be caused by katabatic winds keeping open a 'lake', beyond which the winter pack may extend upwards of 600 miles. There are persistent polynias in the Ross Sea and probably in the Weddell Sea. The existence of another in Prydz Bay was suggested, not only by the snow petrels, but more definitively by the persistent offshore breakout line that we were able to observe from high places. Its existence was confirmed later in Washington DC by reference to satellite microwave and radar images (ordinary satellite photography was impossible in the winter darkness).

Each one of us trudging that morning down the frozen waterway, flanked by so much grandeur, felt unbounded relief at being away from the restricted atmosphere of the boat. Our hearts were light; adventure and discovery beckoned.

The going was not altogether easy by reason of the wind-blown grit that impregnated the packed snow surface, making us throw our weight hard into the traces at every step. Mimi and I were pulling the Nansen sledge between us as we had on Varyag, while Gill and Jannik each hauled a smaller fibreglass American toboggan-type sled. They stopped to tag seals hauled out into the ice from the tide-cracks. We photographed and made notes about alternative anchorage bays along the route.

The first circumstance to dampen our ardour was a lassitude we could not name or account for, since the going was not all that bad. The weather was excellent, clear and still, and the temperature −17°. My back hurt whenever I bent over too far but it did not interfere with hauling. Surprisingly, it was Mimi who flagged most. We quite failed to realize until we melted ice for a drink that she was dehydrated. In such cold, dry air, thirst cannot be relied upon to signal lack of fluid as it can be in more temperate climates. This was a lesson. In future we made sure of forcing ourselves to drink enough regardless of not being thirsty and we never neglected again to carry bottles of water with us on the march.

Later that afternoon the others rejoined us.

'Remember that place? Can you ever forget it?" asked Jannik as we skirted Little Sicily.

'Perhaps we should put up a monument, "This is where *Explorer* went aground,"' I responded a little testily, I am afraid, for I was tired and certainly would not forget the grounding.

It was 5.30 p.m. and dusk already. No good camping places had offered so far, only steep rocky slopes, and we were not yet confident of being able to select safe camping places on the sea ice. Chubuk Island ahead presented a promising snow-filled valley, but a foot of water in the flooded tie-crack denied us access. A shingle slope further on proved more accessible and we thankfully picked our way over the uneven tide-crack and slipped off our traces. I was unable to bend down without violent back cramps and Jannik and Gill helped put up our tent for us even before raising their own, a kindness for which we were very grateful.

Cape Drakon's importance as a site for a provision dump rested on its position as the last land, and easily identified by landmarks at that, before the Brattstrand Bluffs some twenty miles to the southwest (the direction in which the Prydz Bay coast trends). In between, the coastal ice cliffs curve round in a bay whose apex is the Chaos Glacier and a group of bluffs of the same name, and then sweep out again to form the prominent Ranvik Glacier Tongue with its corona of frozen-in grounded bergs. The first of the Brattstrands lies five miles further on across what was to prove atrociously screwed-up ice.

Spectacular red rock bluffs and nunataks (rock outcrops or peaks protruding up through the polar ice) made Cape Drakon the most exciting spot in the Rauers. The ice between it and Chubuk was new since 3 April and the bordering rocks were spattered with frozen spray like spilled ice-cream, another legacy of that memorable gale. Mimi and I clambered down the ice-sheathed rocks and ventured out cautiously over the new ice, only to find that it bent and fluxed ominously under our feet and was no more than two inches thick. This was no place to linger. Scrambling back up the rocks again, we followed a roundabout route to the cape over necks of land and boulder-strewn bays, past the mummified carcasses of a seal and an emperor penguin – how long had they been dead? There was no way of telling; it could have been last year or centuries. The ice beyond the cape was very new and wide open leads were visible two or three miles beyond in line with the direct route to the Ranvik Glacier.

'Even when the sea freezes firmer it might be better if we staged at Chaos Bluffs,' I suggested in an access of unnecessary caution. Mimi reluctantly agreed.

'Those bluffs are a long way out of our way, but I guess you're right.'

While Gill and Jannik looked for seal holes and later followed an ice-filled gulley up to the plateau, Mimi and I spent the following day examining the two bays on the west coast of Torckler Island that we had sounded from the schooner's rubber duck. A 'crazy paving' pattern of floes 3–10 yards in diameter occupied both bays. The ice was 10–12 inches thick, so had not gone out on 3 April, but had only fragmented. *Explorer* would have been safe in either bay.

By evening a northeast gale was blowing and morning found the temperature up from − 17°C to − 5°C, the hallmark of a blizzard. Braving the stinging snow and the gusts that at times knocked us off our feet, we reached the summit of Chubuk on hands and knees and peered south-eastward out to sea through the driving murk. Where the leads had been the day before a mile beyond the Rauers, the ice had now broken right away, it was not possible to see how far in the intermittent visibility. It would be three or four weeks at least, we judged, before any road to the southwest would be fit to travel. We could only hope that when it did freeze over again the ice would remain intact for the winter.

There was no point in hanging about Cape Drakon any longer. When the blizzard eased the parties separated, Gill and Jannik returning to the moraine while we two checked further anchorages before returning to the ship on 24 April after a happy nine days and thirty-two miles of man-hauling. The last morning, after we had struck our tent on Lokot and moved off, the ice cap behind us was glowing a delicate pink and fluffy clouds were drifting overhead. All of us, as Gill and Jannik agreed later, had revelled in those days of harmony among ourselves and between us and the grandeur of nature, far from the petty issues that so often seemed to plague the boat.

Progress

An upsetting mishap in our absence was the shorting out and damaging of a pair of batteries, another two being less severely affected. A veil is best drawn over the well-meaning glow-plug wiring activities responsible. Fortunately, when the ship was first fitted out, I had insisted on a duplicate battery system so that a fully charged bank would always be available for starting the engine. This bank was still intact.

'You did your best,' I told the person responsible, with a measure of restraint. 'You can't make an omelette without breaking eggs.'

'You are being very charitable,' was the reply.

Mimi was less inclined to view things so philosophically. I explained: 'What could I have said? When people know they have done badly there is no sense in rubbing it in. If we keep up people's self-respect it may encourage them.'

'You're right, of course,' she replied, 'but we only have one more set of batteries.' (At considerable expense our loyal fellow-expeditioners on the ORF Board sent us replacements on the first ship in the summer.)

27 April, a few days later, was the day Gill and Jamie set off for Hop Island to count penguins and seals. It was also, I was proud to have remembered, Mimi's birthday.

'Happy birthday,' I greeted her gaily.

'How clever of you to remember, *darling*.' That 'darling' sounded a warning note. Lewis had somehow managed to put his foot in it again. 'But my birthday was on the *17th* of April not the *27th*.' Enough said: I am convinced that the major difference between men and women is ability to remember anniversaries!

The days rolled on. Jannik tended his fishing holes and lines. Mimi and I checked out anchorages within a day's march of the ship. Two of the three possibles on the northern side of Filla looked better than ever. The one on Yefremov Island, that had appeared from the air to be sheltered, was indeed so sheltered by a reef of rocks as to be cut off from the sea altogether, a mere salt water lagoon. The VHF field radio finally gave up. A faulty transmission module turned out to be the trouble. It could not be replaced until next summer, when communication with Australia was re-established, so there would be no more radio contact with field parties – a poor lookout for the more far-ranging sledging. Mimi bound up a leak in the Yanmar exhaust pipe with putty, asbestos lagging and wire in an unsightly repair that nevertheless lasted the course. She and I disconnected the propeller shaft from the gear box lest the engine be inadvertently started in gear and the propeller be damaged by ice. The fresh water tanks began to bulge and seep, and Mimi correctly diagnosed the cause as the water inside freezing and expanding. How stupid of me! I should have anticipated this. We hurriedly siphoned off what water had not yet frozen to leave the remaining contents room to expand.

Alarmingly loud explosive sounds – bangs and cracks – began to be transmitted through the ice from the region of the tide-crack zone so forcibly that they increasingly disturbed our rest. What was happening was that, for a full seventeen metres out from the shore, the ice had begun to heap up, bulge and sometimes fracture into little walls. Not only was the process noisy, but the presssure pushed the ship over a few degrees to starboard – that is, tilted it away from the shore. There was no cause for alarm yet, but how much would the pressure increase, we wondered?

Gill and Jamie returned for more supplies, then pushed off again to camp by a seal hole we had earlier spotted by Torckler Island, armed with hydrophone and recorder.

'I haven't eaten a single one of my muesli bars so far,' Jannik proclaimed proudly on 2 May, a full two days after the bars had been issued. 'I felt I owed it to my self-respect not to eat them all at once like other times.' How very human and endearing Jannik can be, we agreed.

For the past four weeks I had been studying a host of reference books and notes that I had brought about Australian Aborigines. Orbis Press had commissioned a book on the culture of this remarkable people, a sister volume to the same publisher's *Maori*, which had been the New Zealand book of the month. Whether I could possibly write a book in such conditions I had no idea but I was determined to try. This was a subject I had long wished to write about and if successful Mimi and I would be assured of at least some income when we returned to civilization.

The days were drawing in fast. With temperatures down in the $-25°$ range the ice was thickening every day and that inside the Rauers was now more than strong enough for the snowmobile. It was 4 May when, using the main halyard, we hoisted the little vehicle on to the ice alongside and Mimi, who had been studying the instruction sheets, set to work to master the unfamiliar mechanism. She kept at it most of the day, with much encouragement and consultation from the rest of us, until it burst into raucous life at 3.30 p.m. and she went skidding round the bay in a lap of honour. The weather had been bad the last two days and without radio contact we were a little anxious about Jamie and Gill, so the two of us donned our warmest gear and set off at once for Torckler six miles away with me riding pillion. All was well and we were back soon after dark after taking turns at driving.

Two days later Gill and Jamie returned in triumph bringing the best tapes yet of Weddell seals' underwater calls. Birdlike chirrups were interspersed with long musical whistles on a descending register that we later learned were male territorial calls. There were also the popping echo location signals that were vital if the seal was to find its hole again or a tide-crack or a point of weakness in the ice cover. These wonderfully well-adapted Weddells can dive deeper than 2,000 feet and can remain sub-merged for upwards of twenty minutes.

It was not only the seal tapes that were a bonus. The trip had done something for Jamie's morale and he had apparently been much relieved to surrender the scientific portfolio to Gill.

We continued with our activities. Norm took advantage of the larger snowdrifts formed by the last blizzard to ski more often. He always craved an audience, a role generally filled by me or sometimes Mimi. Jamie, though an excellent skier and well equipped, did not repeat his one effort. I typed the first four pages of my manuscript and felt this was a landmark – at least I had begun. Jannik abandoned his unproductive fish traps in favour of fishing with hook and line. On 9 May he surpassed himself at an ice hole with a catch of no less than thirty-seven small fish. Like crus-taceans, star fish, sea urchins and other Antarctic marine animals, fish only manage to exist in the sub-zero sea water by virtue of the glycol that circulates in their body fluids and acts as anti-freeze. But, while the fish survived well enough in the $-1.5°C$ sea water, when brought up into $-25°C$ air, they froze solid at once. Since this catch far exceeded his monthly quota for fish stomach samples, Jannik laboriously cleaned and cooked about eighteen small ones. They were tasty, and a welcome cause for celebration.

The following day, with Mimi driving the snowmobile and me on the pillion most of the time and a toboggan in tow with our emergency gear, we made a nineteen-mile circuit of the northern Rauers. We scrambled up to the top of one of the northernmost group of islets, which we christened the 'Lookouts', and gazed over at the Sørsdal. The breakout line was no more than a kilometre off, we saw with disappointment, and there was no sign at all yet of ice forming in front of the glacier. Another disappointment was confirmation of Mimi's hunch that the snowmobile's fuel consumption would be much higher than we had been led to expect – 5 miles a gallon, even when travelling light and fast over a good surface. This meant that we must try to obtain more petrol from Davis if we were to use the vehicle for anything more than depot laying.

The first depot-laying trip was, in fact, scheduled for the next day, to put down the Cape Drakon dump. The Eskimo sledge was heavily loaded; everything was ready for departure; the only snag was that it would not budge. Though primarily a dog sledge and so heavier, not so wide and with narrower runners than the aluminium sledges specially designed for skidoos, it should at least have moved. While a dog team would have been stronger and more versatile than our snowmobile, the little vehicle should have been able to cope with that load. Something was obviously wrong with the snowmobile's motor, but for the moment the diagnosis escaped us. We loaded the lighter Nansen sledge with as much as it could carry and, leaving behind a few man-haul loads for a future occasion, set off with Mimi driving, Jannik walking and sometimes riding pillion and Norm and me on skis. We would change places from time to time. The ice was knobbly and swept free of snow by the wind so that the skis tended to catch their edges and were no advantage at all. This was the last time they were used in the field.

The motor ran spasmodically, with intermittent bursts of power. We did not then realize that its two cylinders fired simultaneously, so that the only clue to one being out of action (which turned out to be the trouble) was loss of power. There was no change in rhythm.

Snowmobile riding is much colder than man-hauling. The Sorrel insulated boots, that did excellently down to $-20°C$ or so, and much lower still when on foot, were not nearly warm enough when astride a skidoo or riding a sledge behind it. Clumsy but heavily insulated 'Mickey Mouse' boots or mukluks were required. We each had a pair of the former and Gill and Norm of the latter as well. For the rest, quilted down trousers and quilted down or synthetic hooded parkas were a must, together with extra layers of underwear and wool jerseys. Our faces had to be muffled against the icy wind with scarfs and goggles and at least one pair of gloves inside polar mitts was the minimum. Even so, it was necessary to stop from time to time, get off and run along to warm up – more especially later when the really cold weather set in.

Already spots on my nose and cheek would freeze white when I was riding pillion behind Mimi and exposed to the wind. I was, of course, quite unconscious that anything was wrong, but Mimi kept a wary eye on me by glancing over her shoulder. The moment a frost-nip patch appeared she would brake hastily, cup my face in her hands and take the frozen part in her mouth.

'It's nice to have it kissed better. That's the advantage of travelling with a woman,' I bantered.

The eight and a half miles to Cape Drakon reeled out behind us. Mimi and I exchanged places and took different passengers on the pillion each time the snowmobile stopped to wait for those on foot to catch up. Norm looked tired.

'Come on. Take your skis off and jump up behind,' I called, for I was the current driver.

'Too cold,' Norm replied, 'my feet would get too cold.'

'No worry, there is plenty of time to change into your "Mickey Mouse" boots or mukluks. Which did you bring?'

'I didn't bring either,' Norm admitted. Nor had he brought along extra clothes, a parka or even his inner sleeping bag. We could hardly believe our ears.

Norm explained his reasoning to Jannik that night in their tent. 'Mimi will never be able to manage that snowmobile. It's bound to break down.

So I am travelling light so that I can return on my own on skis.' The devastating lack of logic was that taking adequate gear on the sledge would in no way have precluded dumping some of it and returning 'light'.

One thing was plain; we would have to be very selective indeed in choosing participants for long-range ventures.

In the weeks since our last visit to Cape Drakon the ice had frozen to a foot in thickness; what conditions were like beyond the earlier breakout line remained to be seen. The depot site we picked was very satisfactory: a reasonably sheltered stony valley in the shadow of the cape marked as 'Drakon' on the Russian maps – the Australian maps so labelled another point a mile away. Access from the sea was up a series of tide-crack ice ramps which provided good going for a snowmobile towing a loaded sledge.

While the other two set out next day to walk to Torckler Island seal hole and back, Mimi and I eagerly went off to explore the ice off the open coast to the southward. A rude shock awaited us. An ugly-looking tide-crack of a type that was new to us extended from the tip of the cape to Chubuk and barred the path of the vehicle. The fast ice had pulled and sheared apart to a width of ten feet, leaving newer ice that became progressively thinner from the margins towards the centre, which was little more than water – a half inch of mushy transparent ice that looked black from the sea visible below. The foot or so on each side of the black centre was thicker but still dubious to tread on.

Such tide-cracks as these were non-existent within the Rauers but we were to find them everywhere on the open sea fast ice, running for miles, usually between groups of frozen-in bergs and islands.[1]

Not yet knowing how to cope with these cracks, we parked the snowmobile and set out on foot, skirting the avalanche debris beneath the ice cliffs of the Cape Drakon Glacier. Here were more of the shear-line tide-cracks and it was obvious that we would need to bring planks with us next time to bridge the gaps for the snowmobile.

When we got back to camp Mimi got to work on the motor, tracing out leads and wires, and she soon located the spark plug lead that was at fault. There was never any further trouble after she had repaired the lead. That night, having lent Norm my inner sleeping bag, I shivered miserably as temperatures dropped down to $-27°C$.

Next day, glad to be up and away, we jumped the tide-crack and walked to the breakout line that had been glimpsed through the blizzard three weeks before. It was further away than expected, a full three miles, and ran by a small islet. Mimi climbed the islet as a lookout point but the

[1] The excellent *ANARE Field Manual* (Antarctic Division, Kingston, Tasmania) describes tide-cracks as being snow-bridged, so that their width is not apparent. We saw none such. The probable explanation was the virtual absence of persisting snow cover over the sea ice in our area compared with other parts of Antarctica.

dusk was gathering and she could see nothing. Coming down she narrowly escaped a wetting when she stepped off the rocks on to a thin patch and had to leap back to land. Only yards away I was wielding the pickaxe and found a satisfactory nine inches thickness.

Now that the bulk of the Drakon depot had been stocked, snowmobile use would be reduced to a minimum to conserve fuel. The remainder of the Cape Drakon stores could easily be man-hauled. Nor would the vehicle be used for the first probes southward of the islands. Furthermore, the initial route to be tried first, we confirmed our earlier decision, would be the roundabout but prudent route via the Chaos Glacier bluffs.

On our return to the schooner on 15 May after five days in the field we found the atmosphere to be more harmonious. Day trips to fishing holes, seal holes, anchorages and the ice edge west of islands became the order of the day. I got on with my book whenever opportunity offered, a more serious occupation than my usual leisure habit of light reading. Mimi and I speculated endlessly how soon it would be safe to chance long trips out over the ice to the south.

Ice avalanche

The red ball of the sun at midday was just topping the northern horizon on 30 May when the two of us set out with the toboggan sledges for Cape Drakon again. Gill and Jannik were to join us three days later for the first overnight venture south of the Rauers. After spending a night in the roomy polar pyramid tent at Cape Drakon, we got going well before dawn, leaving the tent standing for our return – a luxury beyond words in that frigid starlit darkness. The Chaos Bluffs, our objective, lay nine miles south of the Rauers along a curving coastline of ice cliffs, for the most part 120 to 160 feet high. A hovering fog, which rolled in from seaward, worried us a little so that we took compass bearings in case it thickened, but it cleared before we came to the islet where Mimi had so nearly had a ducking, and we trudged happily along towards the spectacular Chaos ice falls, taking turns to trundle our lightly laden sledge on the glassy surface.

This was the last day of May and, at local noon around 1.15 p.m., no more than the sun's upper rim peeped above the frozen sea to the north, to wash the fast ice with red and gold and magically transform the deep purple ice cliffs into rose pink. A long winding pressure wall glowed as if with internal fire as I stepped over it to test with the pickaxe the ice beyond. This was our last glimpse of the sun for five weeks.

The bluffs were steep-to and gave one the scary illusion of being overhung by the backdrop of tottering seraces. The best camp site was a cramped ledge close above the tide-crack. At two o'clock we turned back, for the four or so hours of pallid daylight would soon fade. The silence of the frozen sea and the lonely looming plateau was broken only by the soft soughing of the wind and ever and anon the distant thunder of an ice avalanche somewhere in the crevassed labyrinth of the Chaos ice fall.

'Look,' I called and pointed upwards. A tiny point of light, as bright as a planet, was moving steadily across the face of the stars that had begun to twinkle in the twilight. Long after the satellite had disappeared we stood still, awed by this evidence of the hand of modern man over this ancient changeless land.

After a pleasant day reconnoitring the approaches to the continental ice cap and longingly eyeing the highest of the magnificent red nunataks above the cape (we would climb them one day, we promised ourselves) we were joined in the evening by Gill and Jannik. In the morning we all broke camp and set off back to the Chaos, this time to camp on the ledge we had chosen earlier. The temperature was a searing $-27°C$ and the wind off the plateau struck chill. Gill and Jannik, who were very cold, chafed at any delay while Mimi and I took advantage of good visibility to scan possible future routes past areas of broken ice and to take pictures.

These two are positive people, I mused as we trudged along. They obviously disagree with Mimi and me about a lot of things, like the amount of time we spend reconnoitring, but this doesn't dampen their keenness. Nor does it matter that we don't have much to talk about save the expedition. Personality differences are irrelevant compared with dedication to the matter in hand. And Gill and Jannik are doers.

My thoughts were interrupted by our arrival at the tide-crack that bounded the bluffs. We had jumped across it last time but our heavier sledges demanded a better route. After some casting up and down we found a firm floe bridging the diagonal shear, crossed it and hauled up on to the narrow, slippery ledge where we camped.

After a chilly night we left the tents standing and set off on foot across the fast ice in hopes of finding a good route to Ranvik Glacier tongue. It was no warmer and we hurried to make the best use of the brief daylight to reach a good vantage point when the light was strongest.

The only object of interest we passed, apart from a fresh seal hole, was a nine-foot jelly-like worm frozen into the ice.

'A case of hypothermia,' someone remarked.

After ten miles it was already past local noon, 1.15 p.m. There was little point in going further, so we climbed the nearest bergy bit and surveyed the prospect ahead. No luck. We had come to the end of the smooth going; in front was a jumbled barrier that was much too rough for man-hauling, let alone a vehicle. Our serious push south would have to be made out to sea beyond the old breakout line and along the direct route from Cape Drakon to the Ranvik. This would mean camping on the sea ice, which was against all precedent, but, from what we had seen previously, we were pretty sure that once among the bergs off the Ranvik a camp site on the fast ice would be reasonably secure.

The reason we were in such a hurry to make our way down the coast was primarily to reach Amanda Bay emperor penguin rookery by late winter or very early spring, when the chicks would still be perched, wrapped in feathered folds, on their parents' feet and we would count them and observe their development.

Back again at Chaos camp after our twenty-mile round trip, we crawled into sleeping bags, which seemed particularly icy, and lit our stove. I incautiously chewed hard on a frozen space candy bar, which proved too strong for my tooth and won the contest by a knock-out. More precisely, the tooth broke off short at the gum. Setting the stage for a dental abscess, I· thought glumly. It was hours until we at last warmed up and longer still before we slept.

It was an odd chance that, for the whole two nights we were camped at Chaos, there had not been a single ice avalanche. We had warned Jannik and Gill to expect to hear them, but when all remained silent they didn't believe us, though they were too polite to say so. Perhaps the cold·spell was responsible. Gill spent the morning scouring the bluffs for lichens, assisted by a chilled and bored Jannik with the sample bags. Mimi and I looked at various ice phenomena, the most interesting being a black 'rock' that turned out, when we cut into it with an ice axe, not to be a rock at all but jet black ice all the way through.

The way back to Cape Drakon was straightforward enough, we felt, for it to be safe to make the trek in the dark. The landmarks once we reached the islands were salient ones and I was convinced that the islet three miles out from the Rauers would remain a good guide even after dark. Accordingly, having given Gill the compass course, we struck our tent at 6.30 p.m. as the last of the daylight was fading and set out. The others would have supper and follow an hour or two later. The moon soon set behind a cloud bank, and hazy starlight and a pale shimmering aurora were the only illumination.

After about an hour there came a roar from the Chaos behind us.

'They will believe us now about avalanches,' we told each other with satisfaction, little dreaming, perhaps because we were too tired to think straight, that the falling ice might have caused trouble for our companions.

My certainty about easily finding the way proved unjustified. The landmark islet remained ahead so long that what we were looking at simply had to be the wrong one. Mimi searched the dim horizon.

'There it is,' she exclaimed. It was neither ahead nor to the left as it should have been but behind us on the right. The Cape Drakon glacier was equally deceptive.

'I've just realized,' I admitted, 'that the bank of snow on our right that I have been avoiding is really the Drakon glacier two miles away!' The skyline of the Rauers ahead was visible enough but there was no way of judging distance. An apparently far-off rock wall loomed suddenly right on top of us: the prominent Russian-mapped cape which had merged invisibly into the loftier silhouette of Sapozhok Island behind it.

When the other two, who had been due to follow no more than two hours behind us, had failed to appear after three hours we recalled with foreboding the roar we had heard. Likely as not they are having trouble finding their way, we comforted each other, remembering our own poor performance. There was absolutely nothing we could do until daylight, but worry kept us wakeful and increasingly anxious. We would start back to Chaos at first light, we resolved. Gill and Jannik arrived shortly before midnight with a tale to tell.

The ice avalanche in the Chaos ice fall must have crashed down on to the sea ice, though it was too dark for them to see precisely where. Luckily for them, they were still at their tent, for the avalanche broke up the fast ice fringing the bluff on which they were camped into separate floes that were tossed about and ground together by three-foot-high waves. The situation was worrisome in the extreme, though none of the waves washed over the ledge where the tent stood.

After the tumult had subsided they ventured out over the floes by the light of a Coleman lamp, jumping from floe to floe. When they were eighty yards offshore and not yet on undisturbed ice they were alarmed by another rumble and prudently retreated. It was several hours before the ice pans had settled together edge to edge and Gill and Jannik judged it safe to strike their tent, load the Nansen sledge and, guided again by the Coleman lamp, make their way cautiously out to the intact fast ice. (It was mentioned earlier that flashlight batteries failed in the cold and we had to rely on one Coleman and kerosene hurricane lamps.)

This incident inspired all of us with a healthy respect for the lethal potential of ice cliffs, a respect that future experiences did nothing to dispel.

Even then, Jannik's and Gill's troubles were not over. If we had gone slightly astray in the dark, they had done so with a vengeance. The nearest reconstruction they could make of their probable route was that it seemed to have taken them somewhere out towards Chubuk and Torckler Islands.

Revived by cups of tea, delayed because our burner was malfunctioning, the couple resolved to push on to *Explorer* that night rather than pitch their tent at Cape Drakon. We relaxed at last, spent a lazy day at the cape, and returned to the schooner next day, 6 June, after eight rewarding days in which we had ruled out the Chaos route in favour of a direct haul to the Ranvik, that would involve camping on the fast ice of the open coast. At least we knew where we stood and could plan realistically – a worthwhile piece of knowledge worth the seventy-three miles of foot slogging.

8

Winter Sledging
6 June–15 August

'They . . . endure a long journey nearly as well as a man,
and certainly better than a horse or a bullock. Women,'
said he, 'were made for labour; one of them can carry
or haul as much as two men can do. They also pitch our
tents, make and mend our clothing and keep us warm
at night . . . Women,' he said again, 'though they do
everything, are maintained at trifling expense; for as they
always stand cook, the very licking of their fingers, in
scarce times, is sufficient for their subsistence.'
> Francis Galton, FRGS, *The Art of Travel*, 1855

This touching tribute to women on expeditions, on the part of an African
chief of an earlier day, leaves something to be desired in terms of liberated
attitudes considered 'modern' in the Western world (though held from time
immemorial in the more enlightened civilizations of Tahiti, Samoa and
Tonga which I have been lucky enough to share). Irony apart, the bitter
conditions of winter sledging, when temperatures dropped to −38°C and the
polar night was but little relieved by the three sunless daylight hours around
noon, were a test for all of us. The women were turning out to be the best of
all, both in responsibility and, often, in endurance. It is noteworthy that, while
Jannik and I frequently developed dead white frost-nip patches on nose and
cheek, neither Mimi nor Gill ever suffered from them.

Everyone on board took part in short winter journeys, mainly to seal
holes or to Cape Drakon to add to the depot and later to build an igloo to
supplement the tents. This increased participation was the result of the
programme of winter activities designed to involve everyone which we had
worked out on the Chaos trip and discussed with Gill and Jannik after
our return.

Jamie, though somewhat lacking in spontaneous initiative, was happy enough to go along with Gill, Jannik, Mimi or me now that the main responsibility for wildlife projects was off his hands. Norm was content skiing, especially now that the snow drifts were extending, and kept busy with radio schedules and engine and generator runs.

The worst periods had been when people were confined to the ship by bad weather or disinclination to do anything and when no active schedule had been devised. We must, it was clear, keep one step ahead of the winter in our planning – a lesson for me.

A positive development was an increased interest in cooking: a kind of healthy rivalry in culinary innovation. *Any* 'new dish' using the same old ingredients was met with enthusiastic appreciation. Mimi's pizzas, Norm's chapattis and Jannik's dumplings were cases in point.

Mimi and Norm were the bread-making protagonists, though Mimi's experience of professional cooking gave her an edge. She taught Gill, Jannik and me. Jamie worked out an excellent recipe for muesli biscuits.

I was far and away the worst cook. Though Mimi and I nominally took turns at cooking on our duty nights, I was generally relegated to such simple tasks as opening cans, peeling onions (which lasted until spring), cooking pasta or rice and washing up. When it came to bread making, the instructions had to be repeated to me every time, to the great exasperation of my mentor.

One of our worst failings, Mimi and I decided rather belatedly, was that we were not spending enough time individually with the others. The party was tending to divide itself up into three pairs who were happy enough but risked getting out of touch with each other. We must behave like more responsible managers.

Mimi accordingly went off with Gill to look for seal holes near Hop and later to Varyag to scan the southern ice. I spent a long day with Jamie tramping towards the Sørsdal, which inconsiderately hid itself in a snowstorm. Seal holes, whence had emanated heavy breathing that would have done credit to a steam locomotive when the ice was thinner, were found frozen over by both parties. The seals had in the main abandoned them in favour of the shear-line offshore tide-cracks outside the islands, where the ice was thin and could easily be gnawed through. Jamie, disappointingly, was no more forthcoming than the seals.

'Are you glad you came to Antarctica?'

'I suppose so. I'm enjoying it here.'

'Are there any other things you would rather be doing in the expedition?'

'No, this suits me.'

It was all rather lacklustre but at least he *was* pleased to be in Antarctica and, as far as I know, is still glad that he came. Unexpectedly, he began to flag towards the end of what was only a ten-mile walk – the price of his long hours abed.

There was something magic about these day walks through the Rauers. The way might lie along a winding, frozen sound, then overland among wind-sculpted rocks, over snowdrifts and spiny ridges and along valleys bordered by every conceivable kind of rock formation – pillars, dragon's teeth and winding volcanic dykes for all the world like pathways. Tiny lakes, some frozen, others saline beyond belief and white-capped in the wind, dotted the valleys, their sandy margins retaining unaltered last season's footprints and here and there the bedraggled corpse of a long-dead penguin. Ever and anon a group of snow petrels would swoop out from the crags above.

One day Jannik and I were walking to a nearby seal hole which lay in the well-trodden route to Cape Drakon. The wind had blasted off the snow cover from the ice, revealing, as it so often did, items we would rather keep hidden. Now Mimi had earlier been suffering from diarrhoea, which gave her no warning, but made her stop dead in the traces and squat down on the spot. The results of these dramas were remarkably modest little wormlike objects, unlike anything I had ever seen.

'What animal do you suppose made that?' I asked Jannik. I should have known he was too observant for me.

'Mimi!' he replied, without hesitation.

On this same walk we talked about women and leadership, that had been the subject of not a few remarks from the other men. His comments were to his credit. He had no desire to lead, he told me, and I knew this to be true. He had, however, regarded leadership by women as somehow reversing the natural order of things, but he now accepted it and thought that his former assumptions had been old-fashioned.

'Good for Jannik!' I remarked to Mimi later. 'When we sailed round the world in *Rehu Maona* with a female crew – two women, two little girls and me – the "he-men" were disgusted with me; I didn't fit into their stereotype of an outdoors man at all!'

'Any innovator is an affront to the unimaginative,' Mimi answered. 'You challenge their closed worlds. Look at the way that press spokesman bad-mouthed us last February, and here we are doing first-class unpaid research for the Antarctic Division!'

'That reminds me of some doctors who said about me, "That chap Lewis isn't really one of us!" I was flattered.'

'Yes, and you should have been. We have everything: no money, I know, and no home and student loan debts, but what does that matter? We are doing something important and have good friends and families – and enough exciting plans to fill ten lifetimes!'

We were talking huddled in our sleeping bags, fully clothed except for windproof outers and boots, in the tent we pitched in mid June by the last remaining active seal hole a mile and a quarter from the ship. Here we stayed three days wrestling with a faulty tape recorder and reluctant camera flashlights and relaxing together. Heavy snow had fallen and, to our chagrin, the loaded Nansen sledge stuck fast and would not budge an inch. Even when half the gear was unloaded we could do no better than jerk the sledge forward in fits and starts. Jamie generously came to our aid and threw his weight into the traces. Even with three pulling and the lightened load it was all we could do to make the short distance and return for the rest with a fibreglass toboggan.

Surprisingly, the Nansen with its comparatively narrow runners was much less effective than the fibreglass toboggans, especially in soft, deep snow, the very conditions in which we had expected the Nansen to score. This was reinforced during two soft-snow hauls to Cape Drakon about this time.

Our stay in the tent by the seal hole was made more pleasant in that a blizzard raised the temperature to a blissful $-3°C$. On the negative side, the Hubbs Sea World tape recorder was on its last legs. Despite warming the batteries with hot water bottles in a beach cooler, the tapes had to be turned by hand. Unless we could somehow adapt the underwater hydrophone to fit Mimi's ordinary tape recorder, our seal taping days were over. This conversion required a plug we did not have, but the Davis electronics technician had told us on the radio that he could rig up a plug to fit if only we could get to see him. This raised anew the question of the Sørsdal. We had high hopes. A few days earlier, braving the wind and a $-35°C$ cold snap, Mimi and I had climbed hill 82 at noon and been able to see that new ice had formed almost to the very glacier snout fifteen or so miles away. The ice shimmered and frost smoke danced above the open water. It was hard to be certain, but perhaps in another few weeks the road might be open.

Midwinter – celebration and pressure ridges

Midwinter day, 22 June, is a landmark for all Antarctic overwintering parties, for it marks the turn of the year; from then on the sun's return comes ever closer, when the days lengthen rapidly, bringing back life to the frozen world. We would celebrate with some sort of outdoor event if the weather were reasonable, a special repast and a look towards the future.

Mimi prepared a midwinter questionnaire to record what everyone thought of the last seven months now that we were nearing the mid-point. Each of us evaluated ourselves and our companions in terms of demonstrated leadership ability, initiative, sense of humour, and so on. We were asked to identify and discuss 'the most significant events' of the expedition to date, our own contributions and the prospects for the future.

Two months earlier we had been in crisis. Low morale had threatened

to sap the expedition spirit. Roles had been rearranged, research programmes initiated and field priorities set within our reach – and now we
could see it beginning to pay off. How did the others perceive this progress?

Answering the questionnaires (though the results remain unread by me)
started animated exchanges in the galley. It was clear that Jamie still felt
himself a polar leader, Norm an elder statesman and Jannik lord of the
animal kingdom – 'a Neanderthal Man', as Jamie pictured him. Gill, Mimi
and I kept our thoughts to ourselves.

The limited perspective was disappointing and I was up most of the
night preparing an overall review of our progress and plans and of the
place of expeditions like ours in Antarctic exploration. When I finished
there were no comments at all! Somehow I had failed to make contact.

The midwinter's occasion as a whole, however, was a great success and
it was obvious that, despite all setbacks, we *were* making progress as an
expedition. Messages had come in the previous day before Davis radio
had closed down for their own celebration. Particularly welcome were
greetings from Karen and Harry Keys, who were wintering at Scott Base,
the New Zealand Antarctic station. Dick Smith, who was on his solo
helicopter round-world flight, sent a message from Japan.

There were several ideas on how best to use the short midwinter daylight.
The plan to go swimming through a hole in the ice, that Jannik and Jamie
had made back in the summer, had been quietly shelved. Norm wanted a
ski race but there were not boots and fittings enough to go round. Someone
suggested building an igloo as a model for the one to go up at Cape
Drakon, but this was vetoed for lack of time. In the end snow slides on
plastic sheets and a snow sculptures 'competition' were unanimously
adopted and we trooped off to the snowdrift at the head of the bay in a
kindly $-9°C$ temperature.

The sculptures were a mixed bag. Gill's and mine were no more than
simple snowmen – or snow women, since mine was positively Victorian in
shape. Jamie's abstract was not bad at all. I rather annoyed Jannik by, in
all good faith, mistaking his Viking horned helmet for Bugs Bunny.
Norm's Rolls-Royce radiator was exact in every detail. Mimi's lifelike
figure with its somewhat explicit male anatomy recalled a fact I had
forgotten, that she had been an art student.

Gill and Mimi were the only participants in the snow slide. From far up
at the top of the drift, where they were barely visible in the half-light
against the crags behind, they came hurtling down in flurries of snow. An
ominous chain of rocks uncovered by their whirlwind passage effectively
discouraged attempts at emulation.

Mimi and I felt it to be our privilege and obligation to cook and serve
on such occasions as this, and all hands contributed to the plan for a very
special feast. Setting the menu down here, in one of the most lovely of

Virginia gardens with a glass of wine at my elbow, it does not sound much at all, but it meant luxury for us then. We served both ham and tongue – an unheard-of extravagance – together with peas, corn, dehydrated potatoes and bread hot from the oven. These were followed by Gill's trifle and fruit cake. The last two bottles of home brew given us at Davis were broached together with three bottles of wine traded for books with the Canadian supply ship *Lady Franklin*. There was port, too. David Paine's gift of whisky and balloons, and the encouraging message he sent, added to the festivity of a memorable party.

I have not yet explained about David Paine. He had been last year's 2/ic at Davis, and before leaving on *Nanook S* he had made up parcels for us to open each month and at midwinter. One month the package might contain a game, or some paperbacks, chocolate or sweets. This time it was whisky, a jigsaw puzzle and balloons. His enclosed note read: 'Things will get better from now on.'

This kindness may seem a small thing, but it was anything but that. It meant more to us in our isolation than I can easily express. We can only say: 'Thank you, David Paine (and all the others); you understood our stresses and you lightened our burdens by standing with us, though you were physically so very far away!'

After dinner was over, the festivities continued apace. Norm's love for Australia came out clearly in the emotion with which he recited lines from a famous ballad of the bush, Banjo Patterson's *Clancy of the Overflow*.

And the bush had friends to meet him, and their kindly voices greet him
In the murmur of the breezes and the river on its bars,
And he sees the vision splendid of the sunlit plains extended
And at night the wondrous glory of the everlasting stars.

Having traversed those arid plains for months on end with Aboriginal companions, I was particularly moved.

'Men like Patterson have appreciated the outback in something of the spirit of the Aboriginal Dreamtime,' I said with nostalgia. 'The features of the land are personified for them as the work of superhuman entities and are sacred throughout eternity.'

The unaccustomed wine was having a mellowing effect on us all. It would be a good idea, someone thought, to embellish a seal tape destined for analysis at the Hubbs Sea World Research Institute. We opened the recording with Jamie's convincing imitations, followed by a limerick sung in chorus. The snag was that the tape recorder, that had been ailing, was now on its very last legs, with the result that the lewd ditty of the Bishop of Buckingham was recorded in lugubrious slow time.

All in all, midwinter was not so much a turning point, for that had been two months earlier, as a reminder of how far we had come since re-organizing the expedition.

A problem that we could no longer evade forced itself upon our attention. Unexpected things were happening in the potential winter mooring
bays we were monitoring – not least in our own Winterover Bay.

June, July and August, with lowest temperatures of $-38°C$, $-35°$ and
$-34°$ respectively, were the coldest months of the year, when the ice increased most rapidly in thickness up to 4–5 feet. In September the ice
would stop increasing and thereafter would thin down progressively until
its gradual disintegration during December or January. By 10 June the
bay ice for fifty yards out from the shore had reared up into three-foot-
high ridges to within ten feet of the vessel, and in places these folds had
sheared into eighteen-inch walls; fresh rifts and tide-cracks kept appearing
daily. Across the bay where the shore was steeper the walls were six feet
high. The explosive noises in the ice were very loud now, being especially
disconcerting at night, and the schooner was being tilted further over by
the advancing pressure ridges.

Winterover Bay was fifteen feet deep and the shores were gently shelving.
Some of the other bays we were observing were deeper, thirty feet or so,
and their banks were steep-to. They exhibited similar phenomena but only
for fifteen or twenty yards out from the shore, not fifty, and clearly would
have made better anchorages, since thirty feet is much too shallow for
even the smallest berglet. The reason for what was happening was not far
to seek and should have been obvious had I but thought a little about it.
When water freezes it expands and so occupies more and more space as
the ice grows thicker. The sea outside was frozen over for miles, so, as the
ice accumulated and expanded, it had nowhere to go but up the shore past
the high water mark, bulging downwards if the water was deep enough,
bending upwards into ridges and folds, or fracturing into rifts. Every one
of these processes was in operation in our bay, except perhaps bulging
downwards, because the water was so shallow. The sea water as it expanded
into an ever thicker sheet of ice exerted formidable pressures, especially
near the sloping shores and in shallow inlets.

How was it that we had not anticipated this disturbing phenomenon?
One reason is that the ice only grows to its full mass and distorts during
winter time and the walls and ridges subside again in the spring, leaving
no trace at all of what has happened. One vertical wall in the bay of
Shelyf, where we had anchored in the autumn and very nearly wintered,
was measured in July as nine feet high (it would have come directly under
the bow had we stayed there); in December the wall had disappeared as if
it had never been.

Why, then, had our study of the logs of frozen-in ships failed to warn
us? The answer is that, with the exception of Jerome and Sally Ponchet's
Damian II, that had a retractable keel and was winched up on the shore
by its windlass, the rest had been deep-draught ships drawing 12–18 feet of
water and so were immune to shallow-water effects. Not that there was any

immediate worry, for the angle was only about 5° when checked with the inclinometer.

'It's not worrisome so far, but how much worse can it get?' Mimi wondered.

We were alone on board this 26 June, a rare luxury that gave us a welcome opportunity to think things through and do some undisturbed writing in the comfort of the warm galley (I had got to the start of chapter 3 of my Aboriginal book). The others had left for Cape Drakon the day before to build an igloo. This was meant to be to some extent a fun project but could be a very useful one, especially if we could not obtain any more petrol for the snowmobile and had to use Cape Drakon as base for man-hauling to the Ranvik Glacier tongue and beyond. I had made a mock-up of the igloo-cum-snow cave in a nearby snowdrift as a model for Gill to follow and was sure they would make a good job of it – perhaps after a false start or two. The weather was deteriorating now, which was bound to delay the work, but the party were well supplied with tents, gear and food. A working field radio would have eased our minds, but four or five days' time would be soon enough for us to walk to the well-supplied cape if the others had not returned before then.

Meanwhile, what to do about ice pressure on the ship? The obvious solution was for us to dig a trench along the port or landward side of *Explorer*, which was the direction from which the heaped-up ice was pressing. The trench need not go right through the ice, only to just below the angle of the chine, that is, the angle between the side of the ship and the vee bottom. By digging away the upper layers of ice the pressure on the vertical side of the vessel which was pushing her over would be relieved; the continuing pressure lower down on the bottom and the keel would do no harm. It would tend, if anything, to help right the schooner. Another purpose of the trench would be to relieve pressure on the vulnerable propeller and rudder.

So Mimi and I set to work with crowbar, pick and shovel – no easy job, we soon found, for the super-cooled ice had the consistency of concrete. Still, the trench progressed. The second day's digging brought an unwelcome complication. Evidently the bottom of the ice layer was uneven because in one place the crowbar broke through and the trench flooded. Try as we would, we never succeeded in stemming the leak and, from then on, had to chip away under water. This was not quite as awkward as the two-inch skin of soft new ice that covered the trench anew each morning. We did our best to retard its formation by laying down styrofoam sheets over the trench in the evening, but this was only partially successful. The new surface ice had to be laboriously cleared away every morning. Nevertheless, all hands took their turn with a will after the Cape Drakon party returned, and Jannik's strength was particularly welcome. After the first month or so the trench only needed to be maintained, rather than deepened, so the work became much easier.

The procedure was effective. Though the pressure ridges grew higher and reached to the ship itself and the ice walls sheared up taller and more formidable than ever, the rate of increase of tilt was slowed down so markedly that it only increased from its midwinter 5° to a September maximum of $8\frac{1}{2}$°.

Past the Sørsdal to Davis

When the Cape Drakon party was due back on 29 June Mimi and I set out to meet them and encountered the triumphant returning igloo builders near Little Sicily. We pressed on to admire their handiwork, a very good-looking igloo with a snow cave extension into the drift behind. Compacted snow is never plentiful in the Rauers and the party had made the best use of rather friable and scanty raw material. There had been some sniping, Gill told us next day, over her being in charge. This was not altogether bad in that it showed how resentment of leadership as such was more of an irritant than any faulty personal style of Mimi or myself.

The seventeen-mile round trip left us tired but content and ready enough to cook an evening meal for the builders. Work on the trench occupied the better part of everyone's energies in the days that followed. The engine room was much in demand in the evenings and was used alternatively by me to type my manuscript and Gill and Jannik to practise guitar and banjo. The ice fronting the Sørsdal as observed from hill 82 seemed to be extending, but poor light made judging ice conditions off the glacier's snout fifteen miles away an impossible exercise. Lookout Islands were the obvious vantage point. There were two ways to reach them: direct on foot across the rocky valleys of Filla and the islands beyond, and the longer roundabout sledge route past the southwest point of Filla. Gill, Mimi, Jamie and I set out on 5 July with the fibreglass toboggans to camp there and reconnoitre the ice up to the glacier.

The plan was this. We would drop off the tent at the Lookouts and all go on together as far as we could towards the tip of the Sørsdal. Mimi and I would set up camp at the Lookouts and Gill and Jamie would take the short way back across Filla to the ship. We could go on with the recce the next day and return to the ship when we had found out all we could, leaving the tent where it was.

If we found the ice suitable for the snowmobile, well and good. If not, Gill and Jamie would make a further recce some days later, staying in the tent and probing the ice breakout lines near the tip of the Sørsdal. The reason for this complicated procedure was to involve the others; to get Jamie into the field and give Gill a chance to learn how to exercise judgement about measuring ice thickness and laying out a skidoo route.

My health caused Mimi a good deal of worry when we harnessed up on 5 July. The anticipated dental abscess had developed in the root of the tooth that had been broken off by the frozen candy bar, so that I had latterly been living on broad spectrum antibiotics (Mysteclin V brand of tetracycline – we will say something about our medical kit later). But despite the medication the abscess 'blew up' from time to time, and this was one of those occasions. I felt ill and tired and was only too glad to hand over the toboggan to Jamie at the halfway mark. I picked up again after we had dumped our loads at the Lookouts and came up to the Sørsdal ice cliffs. We managed to get past the first 'bluff' of the snout of the Sørsdal before the light began to fail and we retreated, Gill and Jamie making a bee-line for Winterover Bay. The next day we established that the ice was strong enough for the snowmobile except for a short stretch of newly-frozen lead right off the glacier snout.

Among the distinguishing features of the glacier were two bold bluffs and a pair of monstrous caverns. Some ugly shear-line tide-cracks in the sea ice gave us pause, for they were probably lines of weakness. The ominous sheen of open water could be discerned away to seaward. The least unstable ice seemed to be that within an eighth of a mile from the ice cliffs, where there were fewer tide-cracks to be crossed.

During our second night at Lookout Islands the weather broke. A northeast gale blew up, bringing the temperature up from $-20°C$ to $-9°C$; not quite a blizzard but certainly not the time to be venturing on to dubious ice.

'Of course we can't go near the Sørsdal in this or we might find ourselves swimming,' Mimi agreed with me.

'But I wish we knew more about ice. Harry Keys, now, he had a lot of the answers. Not that he didn't sometimes hedge his bets with proper scientific caution,' I added with a chuckle. 'He once said a piece of ice we saw was either very clean or else very dirty, and again, that it was either new or old, which didn't help us much. Don Richards wrote some verses about that. I'll show them to you when we get back to the boat.'

Here is Don's poem, entitled 'Science at Sea'.

> You are young, Dr Harry, the old man said,
> And your science has just come to season,
> But this ice that we see here is really quite green.
> Pray tell me, what is the reason?
>
> You are old, Father David, the young man replied,
> And sometimes you become quite shirty.
> The ice that you see is really quite clean,
> Or else it's exceedingly dirty.
>
> You are young, Dr Harry, the old man said,
> I find it chilly here standing outdoors,
> But this iceberg we see, all creased and crevassed,
> Pray tell me, please, what is the cause?

You are old, Father David, young Harry replied,
And with you I must be patient.
That iceberg you see is really quite young,
Or else it's exceedingly ancient.

There being no point in remaining any longer at Lookout Islands until
we knew what the gale was going to do with the ice, we took down the
tent, put it in its bag and cached it among the rocks, shouldered our packs
and set off across the wind-blown ice for Filla Island. The gale was at our
backs and violent beyond expectation.

Rather than have Mimi describe my ludicrous performance, I will set it
down myself. To begin with, the pressure of the wind on my ruck-sack
spun me round and sometimes sent me sprawling, so I took it off and slid
it along the ice by my side, in part leaning on it. This was slow and
awkward but it worked well enough until the last lap, by which time Mimi
was a good way ahead. I was wearing ventile windproof trousers over
Damart long johns and jeans. The waist tie of the ventiles and the belt of
the jeans both slipped, and down came ventiles and jeans about my knees.
I could not let go of the ruck-sack to pull up my trousers, for the pack
would have blown away, so I was compelled to waddle crab-wise, gripping
the pack with my right hand and holding up ventiles and jeans as best I
could with my left, until I thankfully reached the rocky shore and a
mirthful Mimi, whose laughter did nothing to restore my temper.

Next morning the wind was still very strong, though, as far as we could
tell from hill 82, the ice was still intact off the glacier. Norm was baking
that afternoon, stripped down to his shirt sleeves as the galley was unusually warm from the oven. I had been cravenly putting off speaking
too pointedly about hygiene, in the hope that he and his friend would
wash themselves and their clothes of their own volition. It was now 9 July,
nearly five months since we had left Davis, and neither Jamie nor Norm
had washed since then. I broached the subject with diffidence.

'The human skin is self-cleansing,' Norm declared.

'Maybe so to some extent where people go naked, but not when secre-
tions clog their clothes,' I countered.

'Then I had better do something about it, hadn't I?' Norm said good-
naturedly, and that evening he did have an overall wash and changed into
new clothing. Jamie followed suit.

On 10 July the wind had dropped and the thermometer was down again
to −20°. Gill and Jamie came with us up hill 82. The Sørsdal ice seemed
to be intact. Mimi and I were perched on the summit at 1.30 p.m. just
after local noon, when a brilliant red arc flamed among the grounded
bergs on the northern horizon as the upper rim of the sun peeped between
them for a few seconds. The other two, who were fifty feet lower down the
slope, had seen nothing and hardly believed us at first. Yet that glimpse of

the returning sun was a happy augury to us all. It was with a good heart that Gill and Jamie set off for Lookout Islands and the Sørsdal and we two returned to the boat. Their written instructions that we left for them in the tent, and which they followed conscientiously, may be of interest.

The breakout line was just this side of the second glacier bluff. The lead was frozen over thinly. The breakout edge to seaward is very dangerous and unstable with fragmenting floes. The entire area beyond the first bluff is permanently dangerous. Don't go past it unless:
1. No more wind than we four had.
2. Rising or high and steady barometer.
3. Temperature reasonably cold.
4. Do not go seaward of our previous route and avoid ice edge to seaward, but keep outside avalanche debris under the cliffs.
See you back at the boat Monday. Plan on doing all your work in front of the glacier in *one go*, and not too far out.

> Good luck,
> David, Mimi

Gill and Jamie were back at the ship at 4 p.m. two days later with the exciting intelligence that the thinnest ice off the tip of the glacier snout was more than six inches thick. This was no better than marginal, but we would chance it. There was no time to waste, for the conditions were excellent, with the temperature down to $-28°C$ and the barometer high and steady. We radioed Davis that we might be seeing them the next day and arranged extra radio schedules. Then, with no more ado, Mimi set to work on the snowmobile, which had not been used (to save fuel) for nearly two months. It refused to start. There was not even a kick. We rigged a light on an extension cord from the ship and Mimi kept at it. The spark was strong; there seemed to be no lack of fuel. Jannik pulled at the starting cord until his arms ached but there was no response. Leaving the problem for the morning, we packed our spare clothing and emergency rations on the Eskimo sledge, together with two planks for bridging tide-cracks, and Mimi parcelled up exposed film and journal entries to dispatch to America and Australia respectively.

The next act was Mimi's, so let her tell the story.

July 13 dawned clear with $-20°C$, a steady glass and no wind, all ideal for the dash to Davis. Still the snowmobile would not start. To avoid prolonging the story, the trouble was simply that, in those low temperatures, we needed to pump up the fuel to the carburettor vigorously and long, unlike the two squeezes of the pressure bulb that had sufficed in the autumn.

Obvious when you knew! There was never serious trouble with the vehicle again. But the whole morning had been wasted trying to start

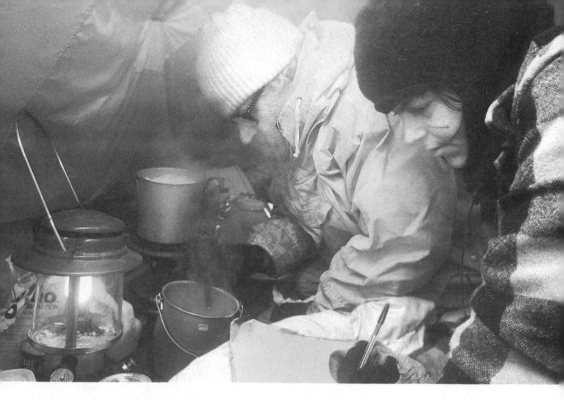

Living in tents: Mimi writing in daily journal, David melting ice for hot drinks and dinner *(Mimi George)*

Mimi driving snowmobile at speed over tide-crack 15 km to seaward off Ranvik Glacier tongue. The crack has been spread with ice chunks to help spread the weight *(David Lewis)*

David, Gill and Jannik hunting for smooth ice path in shadow of 'Gelato' berg off Ranvik Glacier tongue   *(Mimi George)*

'Sun dogs' (false suns) as we break camp on the sea ice   *(Mimi George)*

The formation of a new berg before our eyes as it calves off the Ranvik Glacier tongue less than half a mile from our camp   (*Mimi George*)

Emperor feeding chick at
Amanda Bay rookery
(Mimi George)

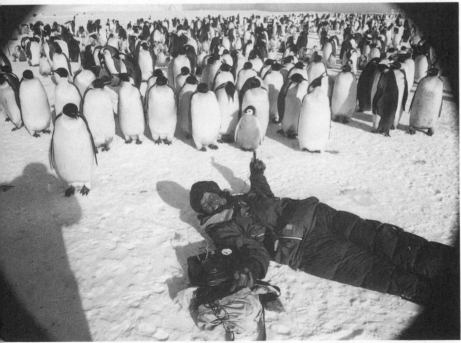

Mimi 'interviewing' emperors with vocalization recording equipment
for Hubbs Sea World Research Institute   *(David Lewis)*

David, Gill and Jannik talking, with newborn Weddell seal in foreground and line of emperors walking twenty-two miles out to sea to fish in the background *(Mimi George)*

Mimi doing hydrophone recording of Weddell seals at tide-crack hauling-out hole. Gill and Jannik tag seals in background *(David Lewis)*

In the spring Mimi clears ice from the trench which we dug through the winter to relieve the pressure from buckling tide-cracks in the shallow bay of our own anchorage. The bow has been pressured up more than a metre
(Mimi George and Gill Cracknell)

Following Adélie etiquette, this penguin peers into our tent to see if we are looking. If we look away, the penguin will immediately 'steal' the nesting-size stones we have placed in front of our tent door   *(Mimi George)*

Christmas Day portrait, 1983. Left to right (in front) Mimi, David, Jamie, Norm, (in back) Gill and Jannik *(Mimi George)*

David viewing the slow progress on sea ice break-up in December 1983. The ice deteriorated first along the shore tide-cracks and around the hull of *Explorer* as a result of solar reflection *(Mimi George)*

Portrait of David after 15 minutes in −30°C air *(Mimi George)*

the engine and we had wanted to be off the tip of the glacier tongue at
'high noon' to have the benefit of the best light. It was 2 p.m. before we
climbed onto the snowmobile with the Eskimo sledge hitched on behind,
ready and anxious to be off. Davis had radioed that skidoos would
meet us at Kazak Island, southernmost of the Vestfolds, and we had no
wish to miss the rendezvous.

So off we went, sweeping round the tip of Filla in fine style and on to
the Lookouts without incident except that we got colder all the time.
David drives the snowmobile well enough but his eyesight since his
detached retina is not perfect.

After our late start we must needs make the best possible speed between patches of bumpy ice and, the light being poor at best, there was
no question but that I must drive all the way. The sun rose fully for the
first time in five weeks and set again well before we had traversed the
wide Sørsdal front.

A tide-crack had opened a bit, barring our way near the ice cliffs, but
on inspection it looked safe enough to cross without planks provided
we took it at speed. I had been driving without ski goggles in order to
see better and my eyeballs felt stiff – as they probably were! Remounting
the snowmobile, with David riding pillion and the sledge behind, I
charged the tide-crack so fast that we hit the other side with such a
violent jolt that my contact lenses popped off my chilled eyeballs! One
lens turned up on my lap; the other was gone. There was nothing for it
but to don my glasses, which kept frosting over and reminded me of the
troubles of Cherry-Garrard, who had the same problem and made light
of it in his epic narrative *The Worst Journey In the World*, [which we will
speak of shortly].

As we neared the glacier snout I edged ever closer under the shadow
of the ice cliffs. Our attention was divided between apprehensive glances
up at the tottering battlements and ahead at the two wedges of thin new
ice that we must cross. The closer under the cliffs I went, the less thin
ice there would be to traverse; so close in we went, despite fears that the
echoing clatter of the noisy engine might bring down an avalanche about
our ears. That fear proved groundless, but our hearts were still beating
double time as I steered clear of the Sørsdal and headed out across the
frozen expanse of Crooked Fjord towards what we hoped was Kazak
Island. Had a party come to meet us, we wondered, or, more likely, had
they got tired of waiting?

'There they are!' I shouted. Two distant silhouettes with waving arms
had appeared on the summit of the island.

There remained one last obstacle between us and them, a formidable
tide-crack that we were told encircled the seaward flank of the Vestfolds.
We came to a halt on our side of the crack and the excited welcoming
committee on the other. Strict regulations forbade them from crossing.

The two planks, which we now used for the first time, proved their worth and, in a few moments, we were shaking hands, embracing, laughing and all talking at once.

We fell in behind the three skidoos that had come to meet us and, with headlight on, followed them for six miles along an intricate maze of frozen waterways until the lights of Davis showed up ahead. We then took station in line abreast and, with headlights blazing, went roaring across the frozen harbour and up the slope to the snowed-up buildings of the station. Our calculated gamble had paid off!

Mimi had reason to be proud, and the base clearly thought so too. How can I hope to describe their welcome? We were not allowed even to unload our sledge. Willing hands took care of that and bore our belongings into the vacant donga that had been reserved for us, while the snowmobile was whisked away by the mechanics to be overhauled. Meanwhile, we found ourselves in the 'Haus Bilong Kiap' being entertained by Peter, the base leader. We must bring our whole party to visit them next time, he insisted, and we gladly accepted, provided always that the Sørsdal ice remained intact.

On a more serious note, we discussed the possible evacuation to Davis and ultimately to Australia of people who might become a dangerous liability.

Now, for all the tests and interviews by which Antarctic candidates are selected, and despite high pay and comfortable surroundings far beyond the wildest dreams of nine-tenths of the world's population, never a year passes without a discreet evacuation – the accent being on the discreet – for selection of expeditioners, even given the best of facilities, is not easy. Dr Jay Shurley, one of the foremost experts in this field, considers a two-to-one success rate to be the norm, for it is generally accepted that psychological testing can do no more than exclude serious mental disorders. That being so, the possibility that anyone in our little group of unpaid, uncomfortably situated volunteers should have difficulty making the grade was not at all surprising. It certainly did not surprise Peter, who readily undertook to set up contingency spring evacuation arrangements with the Antarctic Division in Australia.

Another matter taken care of was our shooting of a seal for food. This was perfectly in order under the Antarctic Treaty, but we had an obligation to report it. Peter kindly undertook to make the necessary notification on our behalf.

The luxury of a long hot shower came next, followed by dinner where we both made pigs of ourselves; not being able to choose between steak and chicken we had both, not to mention hot bread rolls, fruit salad and ice cream. The party that developed afterwards continued long into the night. How envious the Davis people were of our freedom to travel! Most of the men were explorers at heart, especially the old hands, like technicians and engineers who had wintered over time and again. They chafed at being confined to the dull environs of the base when their own long experience highlighted how much more they could be doing. We could not help but be aware of how much their hard-won expertise was being wasted, as hair-raising anecdotes made abundantly plain.

The Australian and American practice of appointing base leaders with no previous Antarctic experience, coupled with rigid control by a distant bureaucracy, was a far cry, I told Mimi, from the British expedition philosophy – at any rate at the time of my *Ice Bird* visit ten years before. The British Antarctic Survey personnel were in the main full-time professionals, whose long experience, training and competence gave them the 'freedom of the land'.

Mimi's presence lit up the base like a beacon, both as a woman and as someone who was accomplishing things that the best of them would give anything to be doing. She quickly became a special protégée of the engineers and technicians, who were all veterans, as well as those scientists whose research interests we most shared.

'She's the best man in the party,' I told the deputy base leader. It was an assessment I was to repeat *ad nauseam*. Memorable as was our reception by these friendly and generous people, I best remember something far more personal. This was when we returned to the donga and I saw Mimi naked again after so many months swaddled in unsightly clothes. I was so emotionally affected that, even after she had fallen deeply asleep, I remained at such a high pitch of excitement that, after several unavailing attempts to rouse her, I had no choice but to lie awake reading dull magazines until she came to in the morning.

We got up dutifully at 7 a.m. feeling much the worse for wear from the celebrations of the night before, only to find that the entire 25-man base was similarly hung over.

There was so much to be done that day that we had perforce to prolong our stay until the next morning. Even this delay was a risk because the barometer had begun to fall and snow flurries drifted down from a leaden sky. A whiteout was threatening, in which shadows would disappear and the texture of the ice be blotted out, so that one could drive blindly into a snowdrift or as easily drop off an unseen ledge. Next to a blizzard that might blow out the ice, a whiteout was most to be feared. At all costs we should strive to be away by tomorrow at the latest.

There were parcels to be mailed for dispatch when the ships came back and a radphone conversation to be set up with the ORF. The electronics technician successfully adapted the hydrophone plug to fit Mimi's tape recorder, and the mechanics went over the snowmobile with her and drilled her on its maintenance and handling as well as providing extra spares.

To and fro along roadways bulldozed through the snowdrifts that reached the roof trees of the buildings (in sharp contrast to the wind-swept Rauers) we trudged, from workshop to radio shack-post office and on to the laboratories. While I conferred with the station doctor about my broken tooth, Mimi talked to the chief zoologist and others of the biological team. They were impressed at how much had been done on the ANARE-related projects, particularly by Jannik and Gill. Some 150 seals had been tagged already, mostly by this indefatigable pair. The seabird and penguin observations, penguin 'chucks', fish stomach samples and the rest came in for praise. Additional information on lichen identification was handed us for Gill.

Unfortunately Davis lacked a glaciologist that year so there was no one to give us much-needed advice about the sea ice data we were amassing in some quantity. A Chinese glaciologist, who was spending a year at Casey, another Australian station, did answer some of our questions over the radio but the exchanges were severely limited by language difficulties.

Since I had not surfaced for over an hour from my session with the doctor-dentist, Mimi, who is ever-solicitous about my welfare and con-vinced that I cannot be trusted to look after myself, came to see what was happening and found the two of us engaged in a confrontation with the X-ray machine. The station doctor had been given a crash course in den-tistry and dental radiography; I was sublimely ignorant of either. Between us, we had managed to produce excellent plates of the wrong root; we were now ready to try again. I held the plate against my gum, the machine was sighted and whirred impressively.

'That should do it,' exclaimed the doctor as he went off to develop the X-ray. He returned crestfallen.

'No luck, I'm afraid. It was another wrong tooth. Perhaps we don't really need a picture since we do know you have had a dental root abs-cess.'

'I know that right enough,' I agreed feelingly.

'I can *try* to dig the root out,' the doctor offered, 'but it will probably fragment and leave bits and pieces behind. Or else we could just leave it alone and trust to the antibiotics.'

'If you don't mind, I think we had better try the antibiotics each time it blows up,' I cravenly decided. 'Thanks all the same. I really did enjoy playing with the machine.'

'How about a scotch, then?' the doctor offered.

'Oh, no thanks,' I answered with a shudder. 'Not after last night. I know now what "the demon alcohol" means!'

This seems a convenient place to say something about our medical kit on *Explorer*, for I had been responsible as expedition doctor for getting it together. My basic philosophy is that the host of minor disorders that are self-correcting are far better left alone, and that treatment should be limited to serious or intractable conditions. These would include severe burns, soft tissue injuries, fractures, eye trauma, including imbedded foreign bodies and snow blindness, illnesses like pneumonia, appendicitis, disabling skin rashes, sea sickness and moderate and severe pain from whatever cause. It should be emphasized that on distant expeditions or in small boats at sea, one is not dealing with first aid, but medium-term management that will allow the patient to return intact or nearly so weeks or months later to where modern facilities are available.[1]

The basic stand-bys were: broad spectrum antibiotics containing an antifungal agent (Mysteclan V brand of tetracycline), which can be life-saving in infections, burns, compound fractures, pneumonia and appendicitis (which last they can control if not cure). Such antibiotics have the further advantage for lay use that you cannot overdose. For severe pain morphine by injection is still the treatment of choice. Moderate pain yields to a host of remedies; our choice was paracetamol with codeine phosphate (Dymadon). Half per cent cocaine eye drops anaesthetize the eye and allow foreign bodies to be removed painlessly. They also ease snow blindness. Eye drops containing hydrocortisone reduce inflammation, but a word of warning is called for. They are absolutely contra-indicated in persons with a history of glaucoma.

Creams containing hydrocortisone, and others with an antibiotic as well (we carried Kenacomb cream), are invaluable in irritating skin eruptions. Then there are protective sun creams, very necessary in the snow-ice glare, antifungal creams for athlete's foot, and the like.

As to fractures, inflatable splints are the thing. Silver creams for bad burns have been an enormous advance. Sea sickness 'cures' are legion and none are completely satisfactory. We carried the NASA-recommended space sickness remedies, phenergan every twenty-four hours and ephedrine hydrochloride every twelve. Then there were the necessary crepe bandages, bandaids, antiseptics, thermometers, blood pressure apparatus, and the like.

The above is not a comprehensive list. Each expedition must budget for its particular circumstances and every member's medical history and individual needs must be taken into account.

The Davis base leader looked askance at Mimi's ragged garb.

'I absolutely refuse to let you go back to the Rauers wearing those apologies for ventile trousers. They are not only indecent with the seat out but you'll likely get frostbitten too. There's a spare pair here you can have and some mukluks to wear on your skidoo. Is there anything else your party needs? We have a surplus of socks and gloves.'

'Those *would* be welcome, thanks. We never seem to have enough.' So

---

[1] D. Lewis, 'Small Boats at Sea', Chapter 13 in Edholm and Bacharach (eds), *Exploration Medicine*, Wright, Bristol, 1965. This book was from a symposium organized by the Royal Geographical Society, the Medical Research Council and the medical branches of the services.

Mimi gratefully put together a parcel of heavy wool socks, wool gloves and wristlets for each of our party.

A temporary swap had been arranged of our strong but heavy Eskimo sledge, which could easily be handled by the powerful Davis skidoos, for an Alcan skidoo sledge, which was wider and lighter and had wide runners on which people could stand.

'We'll load the sledge up for you in the morning,' the o/ic offered. 'The fifty-gallon drum of petrol will fit on all right and we will dump another at Kazak for you to pick up when you can.'

In the morning the visibility was no more than marginal, but with the barometer still falling it seemed best to be off before the weather deteriorated still further. The alternative 130-mile inland route round the head of the Sørsdal, besides being time-consuming and culminating in a descent to the sea ice either at the moraine or at Cape Drakon that would require ropes, ice pegs and crampons, would use up most of our precious petrol – all of it, if the snow were soft – so was not to be thought of unless the Sørsdal ice should actually break out.

Mimi and I were ashamed at the small return we were able to make for the gifts we had been given. The schooner's spare ensign, autographed by the crew, did, it is true, grace the wall in the bar and copies of my book, *Voyage to the Ice*, had been distributed. We felt even more beholden that morning. The Alcan sledge was being packed in the dark, but even so it was obvious that far more than petrol and some clothing was being placed aboard.

'It's nothing to do with me,' said the o/ic. 'The cook says all this is surplus.' 'All this' was steak, lamb, chicken, a 25 kg side of bacon, fruit juices, coffee and chocolate in such quantities that 'meatless dinners' would be things of the past. There were also, Norm has reminded us, biscuits, bread, matches, methylated spirits, cheese, potatoes and Ovaltine. Unfortunately there were no spares for our field radios.

'Just bury the meat in a snow drift and it will last till summer,' advised the cook when we tried to thank him. 'It would only go to waste here and be time-expired when next season's shipments come in.'

An escort of friends on skidoos came with us to Kazak, where we said a reluctant goodbye, promising to put the skidoo fuel to good use and to bring the whole *Explorer* party on a visit to Davis in the near future if only the ice held. The glacier snout was negotiated safely at exactly high noon (1.30 p.m.), but even then the ice contours and tide-cracks were very hard to see. Once over the worst stretch, Mimi handed over to me, and all went well until we hit a near-invisible ice block off the tip of Filla with enough force to badly shake up the machine and ourselves. Fortunately, there was no damage and we were back at the schooner at 3 p.m. Our headlight had been spotted two miles away and the excitement with which the Davis gifts were received can well be imagined.

The next few days were mostly spent in working on the trench and making plans for bringing everyone on a visit to Davis and, thereafter, pushing south towards Amanda Bay and the Larsemanns with Gill and Jannik. There was useful light from about 11 a.m. to 3 p.m. now; the sun was above the horizon for only an hour as yet, but the days were lengthening at the rate of twenty minutes a day, so speedy was the polar transition from sunless night to 24-hour day. Gourmet meals were the rule and life aboard was generally harmonious. To Mimi's embarrassment and my amusement, she lost the pick through a hole in the ice when digging in the trench, but fortunately crowbars and shovels were now the most useful tools.

Norm recounts what apparently seemed to him an alarming incident on 21 July: 'Lewis, sitting at dinner, became vague and almost incoherent, lost the use of his hands and fell into semi-consciousness. George and Jamie helped him into his bunk, where George attended him.'

What a splendidly dramatic rendition of someone falling asleep from sheer exhaustion! Norm continues: 'We could not find a clinical thermometer in the scanty medical kit' (no one asked Mimi for one); 'after eighteen hours in bed Lewis was up again. He attributed the event to two sleepless nights, a double dose of antibiotics, strain and exhaustion.'

Reasonable enough, I would have thought, and comprehensible to anyone with a modicum of common sense who could imagine the effects of a severe dental abscess.

Since the temperatures remained in the −35° range, we had high hopes of the Sørsdal corridor holding. These hopes were dashed on 23 July. There was no warning whatsoever. The day before the glass stood high and was rising, it was windless, the temperature was −31° and no low-pressure fronts were reported. Within a few hours a 91-knot hurricane was blowing and we could barely stand on deck, much less venture on to the slippery ice. Next day was much the same. Not until the 25th did the blizzard moderate sufficiently for us to climb hill 82 and look over at the Sørsdal. Our worst fears were realized. The ice had broken out all the way from Lookout Islands to beyond the Sørsdal snout, a distance of ten miles. The frozen road we had reconnoitred so assiduously and traversed with such circumspection had only remained intact for eight days after our return. It never reformed that winter, so no second visit to Davis was possible, nor could we recover the other fifty-gallon drum of petrol from Kazak.

Three weeks' winter journey

Two days later, on 27 July, four of us, Gill, Jannik, Mimi and myself, set off with the snowmobile for Cape Drakon and the south. Sad to say, when we reached the cape it was to find the month-old igloo beginning to sag, though still habitable for two people. Gill and Jannik slept there and spent a comfortable night. It was otherwise for Mimi and me. Upon erecting the polar pyramid tent in the dark we found it torn, and were forced to hold the flapping fabric together for a good part of a night of roaring katabatic wind. How the rent could have remained unmended was a mystery, because prompt tent repair was a top priority – a black mark for the igloo builders who had last used this tent. Had this been a blizzard instead of a strong wind the consequences could have been serious.

In the morning Gill and Jannik explained that Jamie had tugged on a guy-line as a quick way to jerk out a snowpeg, hence the rip. Gill had told him to repair it but he hadn't and she had forgotten to tell us. The hypothermia I suffered next day was certainly not helped by this sleepless night. For this was the trip, described in Mimi's Prologue, when I collapsed.

Our object was to get to Amanda Bay emperor penguin rookery at an early stage in the chicks' development. Our recce at the beginning of June had shown the ice off the Ranvik Glacier tongue to be rougher than anything we had so far encountered, but with luck there would now be enough daylight for us to find a vehicle route through the barrier.

It is not possible to speak of emperor penguins and sledging in the same breath without mention of Wilson, Bowers and Cherry-Garrard of Scott's last expedition. Emperors lay their eggs early in July on the fast ice and microscopic examination of the early embryos of these unique birds was a scientific priority back in 1911. So, between 27 June and 1 August these three man-hauled from Cape Evans to the emperor rookery at Cape Crozier and back, a distance of 134 miles all told, in temperatures down to a horrifying − 75.8°F in the most heroic bird's-nesting expedition in history. Clothing and sleeping bags became sheathed in ice, so that it often took two hours to break into the ice tubes they 'slept' in. The friction on the sledges of the super-chilled snow necessitated relaying, and one and a half miles made good in a day was often the norm. In those latitudes polar darkness was complete and time and again one or the other of the party plunged into a crevasse. A rock and snow hut they built at Cape Crozier gave dubious shelter when their tent disappeared in a blizzard and the makeshift hut's roof blew off for good measure. Only the subsequent retrieval of the tent half a mile away made survival possible. But survive they did and brought back two precious eggs. And throughout all this indescribable suffering there was no cross word spoken.

Truly, these men were giants of courage, self-control and endurance the like of which may never be seen again. Sadly, they also typified the limitations of Scott's planning. The sledges would have run easily without friction in those low temperatures had they but poured hot water onto the upturned runners to sheath them with ice as the Eskimo do. Sleeping bags and clothing need only have been tied on top of the sledges during the day for the moisture to have frozen into rime and the ice to have fragmented and sublimated so that it could have been knocked out, immeasurably relieving their discomfort. Nor was the diet of biscuit, pemmican, butter and tea adequate in quantity or in vitamin C, which it lacked completely. Amundsen made none of these mistakes, having learned from his two winters with the Eskimo, while Scott remained a prisoner of naval tradition.

Nothing, however, can detract from the saga of these brave men who brought in the emperor embryos. Two of them, Wilson and Bowers, were soon to join the immortals in another sense, when they perished in the company of Evans, Oates and Scott.

Responsibility for the two to be left behind on the ship weighed on me heavily. In the absence of field radio contact, it was essential to leave them with unequivocal instructions for any eventuality, lest they rush into hasty action, especially should our return be delayed. I prepared the following memo and had everyone read it before putting it in the log. No one made further suggestions or had adverse comments.

Procedures aboard 'Explorer' during absence of majority of the Expedition in the Field and in the event of my loss

Weather permitting, Gill, Jannik, Mimi and I will be leaving on an extended reconnaissance towards the Larsemanns on 27 July. We expect to be away four weeks but will have our own food for five, plus four weeks' food and fuel in the dumps. Our return could, of course, be delayed by weather, but a very prolonged delay would most likely be due to a breakout of the sea ice, forcing us to wait for a re-freeze to travel. Please take no action until we have been overdue 6 weeks (5 weeks recce plus 6 weeks) i.e. 12 October, when ORF should be notified and board's advice sought. I would suggest that Don Richards and/or Barry Lewis should be asked to come and take charge of the expedition, to complete programmes and to bring *Explorer* home.

In the event of anything happening to me only, Mimi will take over the leadership of the expedition and the command of the ship, with Gill as her deputy; there will be no need to bring anyone from Australia. Should Mimi and I both be lost Gill will take over the leadership of the expedition but, in this case, Don or Barry should be asked to come and take over command of *Explorer*.

On a less gloomy plane, those remaining aboard *Explorer* will be maintaining the essential infrastructure. Besides engines and electrics and fresh water, the trench alongside, especially the after part, should be kept open and the warps kept clear of ice. Ongoing observations and scientific work should be continued and a check made at roughly weekly intervals of the Sørsdal ice from hill 82.

David Lewis
Expedition Leader

We left Cape Drakon on 28 July and camped hurriedly that night in the lee of an iceberg to revive me after the event described in the Prologue.

I woke next day around noon with my mind perfectly clear but with only the haziest recollection of what had occurred. At least six hours were gone without trace and the rest was vague. Now, however, I was back to normal, so, having donned boots and ventiles, I set forth to look for the others. They must obviously have gone towards the Ranvik in search of a route. Before long they came in sight returning: three ant-like figures against the immense backdrop of the ice cliffs and the polar plateau.

A way had been found, which we followed next day as far as a strikingly weathered chocolate-streaked berg about a mile off the Ranvik, that we named 'Gelato'. The ice beyond was so very rough that our initial assessment in my field notebook was: 'very difficult even to walk; too rough for man-hauling'. Convinced that there was no easy going immediately ahead and that we would be searching for a way for quite a while, we unloaded the sledge and set up a base camp and 'dump' near Gelato. There were three possible avenues to be probed: close-in by the Ranvik, which we had already pronounced too rough for man-hauling, never mind the snowmobile; some miles out to sea inside the Svenner Islands; and an intermediate route.

The next week's field notes are full of entries like: 'Snowmobile round trip thirteen miles to near Svenners. Nothing found.' 'A day's foot recce along "roads" that small bergs had ploughed before they froze-in; all ended abruptly after a mile or so in piled ice blocks and "tank traps".' 'Blizzard-bound, Gelato camp 48 hours.'

Temperatures fluctuated from one day to another between $-12°$ and $-31°$. This was trying, but even worse was the persistent overcast which further diminished our few hours of useful light. Lines of wind hardened snowdrifts or sastrugi, tide-cracks, holes or walls were often invisible from the snowmobile driving seat, so that the way had to be charted as often as not on foot.

All four of us took a hand at driving the vehicle. My eyes were a liability though I got quite good at driving across tide-cracks. Gill was reliable though slow to react, but she could take over on easy terrain. Jannik, who had ridden motor cycles, was rather too heavy-handed for comfort or safety. The bulk of the driving, therefore, and all of it over rough ice or in near-whiteout, continued to devolve upon Mimi. This was a strain to her eyes in addition to camera work, and was made no easier by the inconvenience of having to care for her contact lenses in awkward field conditions (glasses fogged up too much to be useful). To even things up, Gill and Jannik took over the loading of the sledge, a time-consuming business, for the load had to be carefully tied and balanced.

On 7 August at about 4 o'clock in the afternoon Mimi was filming with

Jannik while Gill and I were walking past Gelato berg, when we saw a vast cloud of powdered snow erupt over the Ranvik, hiding it from view and mounting ever higher. The ice shook and trembled under our feet.

'It's smoke!' I said foolishly, without thinking.

'No, cloud!' Gill was being more sensible. But the avalanche roar that now smote our ears gave the answer; the tip of the glacier snout was breaking off. The roaring noise continued and the snow cloud swirled and eddied. Then, as it thinned a little, an ice pinnacle was revealed rising higher and higher. A new berg was being born. What a spectacle! We hurried eagerly towards it, with Mimi photographing and filming as she ran.

As the snow cleared further it could be seen that the fragmented tip of the Ranvik had up-ended, so that the former water-polished undersea surface had reared up into a sheer 200-foot-high cliff, much taller than the parent glacier behind. Avalanches of ice and snow were pouring down its sides: the snow was pink, the new berg electric blue and the Ranvik cliffs deep purple under the low sun. The sight was unforgettable. It was only as we came up with the jumble of upthrust ice blocks as big as houses round the new berg's foot that it came home to us that we had been a shade foolhardy in rushing towards it so precipitantly. Rumblings that continued off and on through the night warned us to shun the monster's close vicinity for the time being.

Two days later, when the noises had subsided, Mimi and I circumnavigated the new berg. A thirty-foot-high ramp, we found, still connected it with the ice plateau behind. It was full of great cracks and crevasses and looked most unstable. Pausing only to take photographs, we hurried away. This was no place to linger.

To anticipate a little, the end of the story came some time later. The prominent new berg, which was visible from hill 81 in the Rauers, disappeared mysteriously ten days after its formation, and when we returned in the spring we found it had capsized and split into two in what must have been an almighty cataclysm. The ice we had run across so blithely to watch the berg's birth had been splintered and fragmented and was scattered with half-ton ice blocks that had washed up over its surface.

On foot to the Brattstrands

Having been blocked so far in our attempts to find a snowmobile passage, the four of us set off on foot on 9 August to see how far the rough ice barrier extended and what lay beyond. The going was vile – glassy ice blocks separated by treacherously soft snow-drifts, into which we tumbled without warning. The temperature was −30° and our hands, through repeated contact with the snow, soon got very cold indeed.

This was particularly hard going for me, for I am rather unsteady on my feet at the best of times, and because of my vulnerable artificial hip I must do my best to avoid heavy falls. So when my balance begins to go, I never try to save myself but simply go down as gently as possible. It was comical for everyone but me! One second I would be talking at someone's elbow then, in mid-sentence, I would be subsiding gracefully on to the ice. My descent was so slow that Mimi said she could count up to five before I landed.

For the first time for over a month we found a seal hauled out beside a tide-crack close under the Ranvik, looking exactly like some great black slug. Jannik took time out to tag it. We also came upon a small fish frozen into the ice, at which Jannik peered intently, then remarked, 'I think it's dead.' I had the chance to laugh at someone else for a change.

After three hours slipping and stumbling we broke out of the jumble on-to a smooth ice plain that extended along the foot of the Brattstrand Bluffs as far as the eye could see – all the way to Amanda Bay, we hoped. Here at least was one option. We could at a pinch manhandle the two light sledges that were always carried on the Alcan over the five-mile rough stretch and man-haul on to Amanda Bay. Without the vehicle, however, we could not bring much food with us, so that our stay would be strictly limited. We would keep on searching for a skidoo route, we decided.

Gill and Jannik went off lichen hunting to an islet off the bluffs while Mimi and I pressed on to the northern Brattstrands to locate a 'dry land' camp site for possible future use. We had been camped on the sea ice for twelve nights now and had successfully weathered a blizzard, but the proce-dure was strange to us and against all established custom. We had as yet too little experience in estimating whether particular areas of fast ice were safe or not and so tended to distrust all of them. Nevertheless, the tents by Gelato were a welcome sight that evening after our eighteen-mile rough-ice trudge and we crawled gratefully into our sleeping bags and slaked our parched throats with mugs of tea. The night was a cold one; we woke up shivering after a few hours and brewed more tea to warm us.

A snowmobile recce to seaward had been arranged for the next day, but had to be postponed on account of whiteout. When the four of us did set out on the 11th the weather was no warmer but the sky was clearer. A wide sweep brought us by late afternoon (when we had to turn back) to a spot eight miles out from the Ranvik and four miles inside the Svenner Islands. The ongoing looked promising ahead, but there was no way of telling if this better section linked up with the smooth ice off Brattstrand Bluffs. 'This is the obvious route to try first in our major attempt,' we noted in the field book.

After several more days fruitlessly searching for an intermediate route, we decided to waste no more fuel at present, and to postpone our big push south for another three weeks, when there would be far better daylight. We would then load up at Cape Drakon and strike directly towards the smooth stretch inside the Svenners, bypassing the Gelato depot altogether.

On the way back to the ship Jannik showed me his big toe. It had been frostbitten on the day of the snowmobile offshore recce and had ulcerated and the skin had sloughed off. The cause: Jannik, anticipating more walking, had worn his Sorrel walking boots on the recce instead of the warmer, insulated 'Mickey Mouse' boots more suitable for vehicle riding in winter.

We reached *Explorer* on 15 August and were mightily relieved to find that all was well. In twenty days away we had covered some 108 vehicle-miles and 70 on foot and had used twenty-one gallons of precious petrol to less purpose than we had hoped. Nevertheless, we had learned a lot about sea ice and how best to cope with it, and we knew that at least there was smooth ice along the Brattstrand coast to aim for on our next attempt, when visibility was better.

Norm and Jamie had enjoyed being on their own with plenty of living space and a relaxed schedule. Greetings were minimal and a voice remarked with satisfaction: 'I knew they wouldn't make it!' Our management strategies were beginning to pay off, but there was still a way to go. There was no emergency blizzard water or even ice on the ship when we arrived, the galley was dirty, the lights were dim for lack of power, the cabin heater had clogged up and the state of the Sørsdal ice was an unknown quantity.

My very restrained criticism of this slovenly neglect of written guidelines was met by Norm with epithets of 'Silly old bugger' for me and 'Bitch' for Mimi. Norm has written in self-justification that 'As Jamie and I were much more sparing in our use of water than he and George, we had only 50 litres on the boat, the nearest suitable sea ice being about 200 metres away. I would certainly have seen to it that there were another 30 litres available a couple of days before their intended date of return, which was still nine days off.'

It is good to be able to report that on our return from the next long field trip everything was in excellent order. The written guidelines had been followed, not only to the letter, but in spirit. Individuals who in April had been alienated from the undertaking had found niches that they could usefully fill. Every one of us was beginning to have cause, we felt, for modest self-congratulation.

9

The Great Breakthrough Southward
– Spring
15 August–28 October

You may recall the sweep of savage splendour,
That land that measures each man at his worth
And feel the memory, half fierce, half tender,
The brotherhood of men who knew the south.

Douglas Mawson, with apologies to Service (inscription in the copy
of *Home of the Blizzard* that Mawson presented to Edgeworth
David, May 1915)

One gale after another became our portion for the next few weeks, putting paid to the last faint hopes of a new ice road off the Sørsdal that would allow of a social visit to Davis by the whole party, delaying the southern venture and restricting activities more than a little. Mimi, assisted by Gill, spent the whole of the day following our return stripping, cleaning and reassembling the heaters. Their next task, a particularly unpopular one, was to impose limits on the use of matches, methylated spirits for priming the stove and some favourite though non-essential items like coffee and cocoa. None of these had previously been restricted, though it had long been pointed out that unrestrained consumption was depleting our stocks. The warnings went unheeded, so that there was no alternative but to issue everyone with personal rations and restrict stove lighting. These restraints, film issues, plus those imposed by the weather and the full occupancy of the boat augmented tensions.

I had to speak out strongly against the use of abusive and obscene epithets. The two offenders curbed their language somewhat in public, though muttered obscenities meant for Mimi's ears continued.

Mimi, who was distraught and profoundly depressed by these snide jabs, insisted that I should not intervene as that would divide the party further. What on earth was the best thing to do? We debated long and bitterly, at times hysterically, and attempted, with indifferent success, to discuss the options with certain of the others.

The sniping at Mimi and me was partly a product of the foul weather. The forthcoming southern venture was the key, we felt, to raising morale by establishing once and for all the success of the expedition. On the positive side, everyone was working better: Gill and Jannik carrying on the biological projects with boundless energy and keenness; Mimi and I on the various sea ice investigations, the hydrophone seal recording and the small-group study; Jamie handling his jobs, and Norm managing the mechanical maintenance and the radio schedules.

Once the long haul south was a patent success it would draw the party back together. Obviously we must get away southward as soon as possible and, in the meantime, pursue off-boat activities whenever we could.

A break in the prevailing bad weather and the consolidation of the new ice outside Filla provided just such an opportunity. This new ice was dotted everywhere with little steaming craters gnawed by Weddell seals where they huffed and puffed as they came up for air. Many were hauled out, taking advantage of the 3–4 hours of spring sunshine. Mimi obtained excellent results from the hydrophone that the Davis technician had adapted to her own tape recorder when the one from Hubbs Sea World had given up the ghost.

Next day Mimi and I witnessed a remarkable battle. Two snow petrels, their beaks wide open and interlocked, fought long and fiercely at the foot of a nesting cliff until both beaks ran with blood. Then the birds, their beaks bright red, would break off to fly round before resuming their contest, which was pursued with the utmost determination for a good five minutes before one gave up and flew away. It was of course in the nature of things that this was the *only* time that we went out without a camera.

The routine of keeping open the trench alongside was continued and we were heartened to find it had succeeded in holding the lateral ice pressure at bay. The angle of heel had been steady for some time now at 8.5° and never grew greater. On the other hand, the ship's bow was forced up two feet into the air by pressure from a new angle, making us fear for the vulnerable propeller and rudder at the stern.

Between storms our preparations for the push towards the Larsemanns and Amanda Bay proceeded. New typed instructions were drawn up for the *Explorer* party, which have too much in common with the previous ones to be worth quoting in full here. We would return by 1 November, I wrote, for in average years the fast ice becomes suspect in November and this would give us a prudent few weeks' grace. This was perhaps over-cautious but there was no field radio and no back-up team. Should we fail to return on time, the likely cause would be a breakout down the coast that cut us off from the ship. Nothing should be done until the helicopters returned in mid-December, when, if we had not fallen victim to some cataclysm, we would probably be found in our tents subsisting well enough on a diet of penguin and seal. This forced reliance on necessarily rigid written instructions and overly conservative schedules in the absence of a field radio was an unwelcome limitation of our flexibility and a reminder of what things had been like in an earlier age of polar exploration. An additional assignment for those on the schooner now that spring was in the air was to make a weekly circuit of southwest Filla to record the return of seabirds and penguins. This was coupled with an admonition not to venture further afield.

The four of us, Mimi and Gill in particular, were kept busy organizing gear and rations, and I typed my Aboriginal manuscript furiously.

Southwestward again

We set out with the labouring snowmobile towing a mountainous load on the Alcan sledge at 12.30 p.m. on 10 September. The temperature was a comfortable − 13°C. The tents were set up at Cape Drakon at 2 p.m., for our already monstrous loads had to be rearranged at the depot, augmented and repacked. By 6.30, when the sorting of the stores, filming and taking pictures were finished for the evening, it was still light. Indeed, the hours of daylight were increasing by something like thirty minutes a day now. The miraculous renewal of the long Antarctic spring was at hand.

All winter long sea mammal and bird life had fled the silent coast, save only for a handful of snow petrels, a few seals lurking in the tide-cracks and the emperor penguins away at Amanda Bay. Soon countless thousands of Weddell seals would be moving in towards the coast, making their way under the ice along the lines of the tide-cracks, where they could most readily break through and breathe. It is on the fast ice inshore that the pups are born, and we hoped to locate major seal rookeries, perhaps off the Larsemanns. Seabirds without number would be coming back to the coast – fulmars, antarctic petrels, cape pigeons, snow petrels, storm petrels and skuas, as well as the little Adélies, who would come trudging in over the sea ice to reoccupy their rookeries. Exuberant life was about to return to the shore of the empty continent.

Next day was spent watching the barometer, for our offshore route southwestward would take us perilously close to a recent breakout line between the Rauers and the Svenners. The glass steadied on the 12th. We were impatient to be gone, so, despite poor visibility, the sledge was packed, in the main by Gill with Jannik's powerful help, and we set off directly towards the smooth ice we had found inside the Svenners. The sledge was overladen worse than ever. Because of the bad light and rough surface Mimi drove all the way, for a solid six hours, covering twenty-two miles. There was more snow cover than in August – a mixed blessing because, while some drifts provided negotiable roads over ice blocks, others led to treacherous drop-offs and walls. Nevertheless, the snow was generally a plus. Visibility deteriorated further during the afternoon. Ever more frequently, encounters with unseen gullies or walls necessitated uncoupling the sledge from the snowmobile and manhandling both onto a new heading, until at last the whiteout became complete and even scouting ahead on foot was not enough. We camped at 5.30, eight miles out from the Ranvik and a mile short of the desirable shelter of the berg complex inside the Svenners, near a prominent seamed iceberg we christened 'cracked berg'.

This was the very first snowmobile trip, I wrote in my diary, when we had been warm. The temperature was − 12.5°C, a far cry from the − 30°C when we had last left Cape Drakon, but our clothing was much the same. Mine this time comprised a sweat shirt, Damart underwear top and pants, two wool jerseys, a Tamar heavy wool shirt and a Fairydown parka with fur-lined hood; track suit trousers, ventile windproof over-trousers and down quilted trousers; wool and Damart socks; Damart and wool gloves, wool wristlets and polar mitts; two balaclava helmets. Gill had on muk-luks, the rest of us 'Mickey Mouse' insulated boots.

A gale blew up in the night, rather frightening in our exposed situation, but, to our relief, the ice held firm. A trumpeting aroused us next morning: eight emperor penguins were solemnly inspecting the camp. We in turn photographed, filmed and made tape recordings of them before they lost interest and plodded off sedately towards the southwest, bound for Amanda Bay, we suspected.

At 3 p.m. the wind dropped as suddenly as it had risen and Mimi and I set off at once on the snowmobile on a recce. The approach to the Svenners was probed first, but rough ice blocked the vehicle. We debated continuing on foot and climbing the nearest island for a view, but the light would be gone well before we could get there. This was a pity because we found long afterwards when we looked out from Stedoy, an island eight miles out from Amanda Bay and midway to the Svenners on the south side, that there *was* a seaward route once a mile or two of rough ice near the Svenners had been rounded. Instead, we followed the smoother lanes southward, crossing two particularly alarming tide-cracks in the process. We had a fright on one. I was driving with Mimi riding pillion. The crack did not look too bad as we approached, being choked with snow, so I took it without a prior recce. As we passed over, the snowmobile's track broke through and Mimi shouted to me to speed up. Fortunately we were going fast enough for our momentum to carry us over because I was slow to open the throttle. Apart from this scare, the way looked promising as far as we went, so the following day we moved camp along the route we had prospected, carefully sticking to the snowmobile's previous tracks as whiteout had closed in again. In fact overcast persisted, so that there was never a day in the next few weeks when visibility was better than marginal.

Our long planks, aided by a little 'bridge building' with snow blocks, took us over the more formidable of the cracks, but not without near disaster. Again it was speed that did the trick, because the crack collapsed under the pressure of the snowmobile track, but Mimi 'gave it the gun' and the sledge planed safely across the break. (When we passed that way again, prolonged reconnaissance discovered a more suitable crossing place.) That evening we camped at the edge of rough ice that disappointingly had reappeared. We were off the northernmost Brattstrand Bluffs and once again about eight miles offshore.

A blizzard raged that night, an anxious eight hours so far out from the coast and with uncomfortable recollections of the wide tide-cracks separating us from the familiar surroundings of Gelato berg. The wind strength, we estimated by analogy to previous storms, was in the region of eighty knots. We learned later that Norm and Jamie had observed from hill 82 that this same blizzard had blown out the new ice that had begun to form off the Sørsdal tip.

Next day was my sixty-sixth birthday. I was now twice Mimi's age, we calculated with a certain bitter-sweet amusement (though it turned out later that the estimate was wrong because Mimi had overestimated her age – she was only thirty-two, not thirty-three as she had supposed). Birthdays at my age are no cause for congratulation, but, more to the point, a day's reconnoitring in towards the coast convinced everyone but Mimi that the field of rough ice we found between us and the smooth going off the Brattstrand Bluffs was too extensive to tackle. We talked over options. The barrier ahead was certainly formidable. What of the alternative – the jumbled mass off the Ranvik tongue that we had only managed to penetrate with much difficulty on foot? There was much more snow cover this far offshore than we had encountered in August and I supposed that the ice blocks off the Ranvik would be snowed-up like those in our present vicinity and thus more passable than they had been. Backed up by Gill and Jannik, I overruled Mimi's objections and made the decision to give up the attempt to break through here far out from the coast, and to return next day to Gelato to tackle the Ranvik fringe.

The road

My assumption was wrong. We found the ice off the Ranvik to be wind-scoured and devoid of snow altogether; the way past these ice cliffs was no smoother than before. But by now it was too late for second thoughts. We had spent the last week motoring some sixty miles to and fro as well as probing twenty miles on foot and using up much precious petrol to no purpose. We could not afford to waste any more time, for we were already late for the emperors, few chicks would be still ensconced on their parents' feet by this time, and before very long the seals would be pupping – and we must not miss that. Equally to the point, we had burnt our boats as far as petrol was concerned, for there was now only enough left for one journey to the Larsemanns and back. It was under the shadow of the Ranvik cliffs or nothing. We set out on foot next day in search of a route.

After having witnessed the calving of the new berg off the Ranvik in August and now coming face to face with the havoc its capsize had wrought, I was extremely leary of venturing anywhere near those tottering cliffs. But hard by them was the only way possible.

Mimi, from the top of a frozen-in berg, mapped out a marginally negotiable way in towards the ice cliffs, and along their foot we came upon a series of glassy smooth pressure ridges and valleys, where the advancing glacier tongue had thrown the plastic sea ice into folds without fracturing it. These pressure-ridge areas were separated from each other by piles of rubble, shattered ice boulders and massive cobbles. All told, the extent of the rough ice we must traverse can have been no more than about five miles. In the course of that long day's recce on 18 September we must have prospected half that distance, covering in the process a dozen or more miles in the ten hours we were out. What with the slipping and sliding and tumbling into masked holes, it was exhausting work, especially for me with my poor balance. When at last failing light constrained us to turn back, the next stretch looked reasonably promising along a line even closer to the ice cliffs towards a triangular berg that fronted an angle in the 150-foot wall. Mimi and I, who had been moving parallel to the other pair but closer in to the cliffs, spotted this likely route, and before turning back we called the others over and pointed it out to them.

Next morning Gill and Jannik set out to reconnoitre the remainder of the route past the triangular berg and on to the smooth Brattstrand corridor. Meanwhile the two 'oldies' found a better route from our Gelato depot camp to the ice cliffs, and Mimi overhauled the snowmobile and cameras for the rough trip ahead. I was frankly exhausted, which was not surprising, seeing that I was as old as anyone else's father and was in need of an easy day. Gill's and Jannik's reconnaissance report was disappointing, since with their energy and eagerness to be away up and doing they paid too little attention to the snowmobile route and carried on unnecessarily far to Brenesholmene Islands, miles away.

I was concerned that the pair had strayed so far from their objective and questioned them closely the next morning (it was 10 p.m. when they got in and they were very tired) about the route near the ice cliffs they had been asked to prospect. They were vague.

'We have only one vehicle,' I pointed out. 'If we drive it across what we prospected the other day, we will be taking the risk of smashing it beyond repair. Now, I will not take that risk unless I know definitely that the rest of the way is no worse. We must avoid the danger of spending the night right under those ice cliffs.' Gill and Jannik rather optimistically gave me that assurance.

After a day spent repacking our loads at Gelato depot, we set out in poor visibility and a temperature of $-22°C$ on 21 September. The sledge was weighted down more heavily than ever with two months' food, fuel and gear. The going was atrocious and we feared for the snowmobile, which took a fearful battering. Mimi drove while the rest of us ran ahead to cut away ice blocks or else pushed and manhandled the heavy sledge. A good part of the time one or other of the snowmobile's skis were off the ground and the independently mounted runners of the Alcan sledge assumed alarming angles. Some hillocks had to be taken with a rush to reach the smooth patches beyond, where the sledge jack-knifed and swung the snowmobile round in its tracks. The little engine howled as the track spun uselessly on the slippery surface and we would have to put our shoulders to the sledge to get it going again. We covered something like two and a half miles that day but the odometer showed ten, an indication of how much the vehicle's track was spinning and slipping. By six o'clock the buckled pressure ridges we had crossed on foot three days earlier were behind us and we had reached the limit of our previous recce.

'Where now?' we asked Gill and Jannik.

They did not know!

There was nothing to be gained in crying over spilt milk. The reconnaissance had been bungled, but, for that matter, I had been wrong earlier in abandoning the offshore route. The real question was what to do now.

'It is no use continuing blindly,' I decided. 'We will have to spend several nights near ice cliffs after all, but we will get as far away from them as we can and then camp. We will stay in that camp until we have prospected every foot of the way properly and have cleared the worst obstacles.' So, bumping and skidding, Mimi manoeuvred the snowmobile and sledge to a safer spot some two hundred yards away from the ice cliffs, where we camped, tired and discouraged.

Prospecting began at ten the following morning, and by the time we all gathered together at 3 p.m. to discuss our findings the rudiments of a plan had emerged. We could weave our way with the vehicle a little further to a better camp site at the start of very rough ice, which extended for nearly a mile to the neighbourhood of the triangular berg. Behind the berg and separating it from the ice cliffs lay an interlocking series of smooth, glassy 'pools', beyond which the going looked possible but had yet to be checked in detail. So far, so good. We broke camp and moved to the new location, a quarter of a mile out from the threatening cliffs this time. 'Our aim,' in the words of the field log, was 'to maintain this camp while constructing a road to the "pools" a mile distant'.

Work began next day. With no pick any more, our tools were limited to an ice-axe and a shovel, with Gill's geological hammer as a rather sorry extra. Only two people could effectively road-build at a time and Gill and Jannik wrought mightily, doing the bulk of the heavier chopping away of obstructions and filling in of gaps with the shovel. Loud rumbles from the nearby cliffs spurred them on. Mimi and I helped, but our first priority was to inspect the rest of the way ahead. Here we made a providential discovery. The exit from the 'pools' was uncomfortably close under unstable-looking crumbling ice cliffs, beneath which a solitary Weddell seal had hauled out and was sunning itself unconcerned. From where it lay a solidly frozen tide-crack led straight out from the cliffs a quarter of a mile to a zone of passable cobbles which, in turn, joined the smooth ice off the Brattstrands. This frozen crack would require very little engineering to make it a first-class pathway. Mimi and I resolved, however, not to move camp again until the whole way was clear, for we had no wish to be forced to spend a night under those tottering cliffs at the start of the crack. It was bad enough where we were!

Between reconnoitring and road building Mimi took hydrophone recordings, pictures and film. The success or failure of our efforts here would largely determine the scientific worth of our expedition, so a good pictorial record was desirable. The still pictures came out well considering the very poor light, but the movie camera, sad to relate, would only run very slowly despite all Mimi did.

By noon the third day the work was finished. It was an exceptionally rough track replete with sharp angled turns and abrupt humps, interspersed with smooth, slippery 'pools'. As a route it was marginal at best, but we all went to bed that night buoyed with high hopes for the morrow.

We woke on 25 September beneath a sky cloaked with thin overcast through which an opalescent light was diffused, so that the atmosphere shimmered all day long. As we began to take down the tents, Mimi gave a cry and pointed. The sun, shining fuzzily through the haze and already high in the southeast, was flanked by a pair of mock suns or sun dogs. Mimi ran for the camera and took a series of pictures, but she need not have hurried; the sun dogs remained for two hours, a good start to the day and a favourable omen, we felt.

The light was very strange and beautiful, unique in our experience, and sometimes little flurries of snow came down, but the absence of shadow did nothing to ease Mimi's task. Each section of the way was marked out as she came to it by markers like gloves or the ice axe, and the sharp turns by one of us directing traffic. Mimi drove for a full five hours without goggles the better to see, and with her eyes aching all the more because her spare contact lenses did not fit properly any more.

The hillocks were so steep that they had to be taken fast; most involved sharp turns into the bargain, and more than a few ran out onto smooth ice 'pools'. Steep descents, especially winding ones, worried me most, for fear the vehicle would topple, pinning Mimi helplessly in the path of the following sledge, which was as heavy as a car.

But her nerve and judgement never failed. Standing high like a steeple-chase jockey, she would come hurtling off the top of a rise, the vehicle's skis airborne; she would accelerate again on the down slope to prevent the sledge over-running her fragile mount. Then out over a glassy 'pool' at speed, where the sledge would jack-knife savagely, slam into the snow-mobile and spin it round and round, while Mimi laughed and cried out in triumph.

Much to our relief, the unstable cliffs by the somnolent seal did not avalanche down at the racket of the engine as we had half feared and the snowmobile was soon speeding away out of danger along the frozen tide-crack.

The camp that night, on a snowdrift, was in Brevika Bay on the smooth ice off the northern Brattstrands. The Ranvikbreen – the Ranvik Glacier – lay behind us. That *five miles* of rough ice had taken us *five days* to cross as well as three days reconnoitring, but we were past the barrier at last that had held us up for so long, complete with our belongings and with the vehicle still intact.

'A triumphant day,' I wrote in the field log, 'and everyone has contributed to the triumph.'

The emperor penguins

The first stop next day was at Brenesholmene Islands, where we cached petrol and food enough to carry us back across the 'road' to the depot at Gelato on our return. These little islands were the site of a great Adélie rookery, which was empty and desolate as yet but would soon be host to a teeming multitude. I took turns with Mimi at driving as we sped along at as much as fifteen and twenty miles an hour. Visibility was poor and decreasing, but the bigger tide-cracks were now generally marked by seals hauled out along them. Then, without warning, a whiteout shut down, making sky and ice one so that, after some abrupt encounters with unseen ice ridges, we called it a day and camped on a convenient snow slope that had formed behind a bergy bit.

Visibility was no better in the morning so the most we could do was to make a recce on foot to the next island, Outer Brattstrandoyane, off the southern Brattstrand Bluffs. We had barely climbed to the summit when the clouds rolled away, so, after a hurried scan of the way ahead, we scurried back to the camp, packed up and got under way. The route now lay through a great bergfield of overwhelming grandeur. Frozen-in giants towered stark and majestic on every hand, most rising sheer a full 200 feet to crenellated summits, some broken with caverns and archways or frozen avalanche cascades. The ice between the bergs was as level as a dance floor and coated thinly with snow, across which the sledge runners hissed. The frozen world was silent apart from the unseemly noise of our passing; we were awed by the majesty of the primeval scene into which we were intruding so brashly.

Out from the shelter of the bergfield and across the mouth of Amanda Bay we sped, all eyes searching for the emperors. A row of distant rocks on the margin of the plateau, which afterwards turned out to be the size of houses, gave rise to a false alarm and a good deal of subsequent merriment.

'There they are!' There was no doubt this time. Long lines of little figures were strung out over the ice, one half stolidly plodding out towards the open water (twenty-three miles away, we later ascertained), the rest returning towards the rookery. The columns, moving in opposite directions and mostly in single file, seemed to be keeping to the left.

'Proper little Australians, aren't they?' I remarked to Mimi with amusement. 'I wonder if the ones at the US base at McMurdo pass on the right?' (Alas, this interesting speculation was not confirmed. The Amanda Bay emperors varied their track according to the time of day and obeyed no consistent 'rule of the road'.)

The rookery had formerly been located off Flatnes ice cape at Amanda's southern boundary, but it was evident from the direction of origin of the columns that the penguins had moved base in towards the head of the bay, so we turned and followed the marching lines until we came on the rookery. It was in two adjacent parts; the older, to judge by the snow stained coal-black with droppings, was on a snow-covered shelf of moraine under low, weathered ice cliffs, the newer was nearby on the fast ice. Fluffy 'spectacled' chicks were swaggering importantly about among the adults, greedily mobbing birds returning from seaward with insistent high-pitched cries. The chicks were just beginning to become independent of the parents and being formed into crèches. Only the smallest chicks still clung to the security of their feathered 'pouches' and the platforms of their parents' feet. We camped that night and for almost a week thereafter on a mound opposite the rookery and went to sleep lulled by the surprisingly musical chorus of what turned out to be 2,450 adults and 2,340 chicks (the other half of the adults were away from the rookery on their way to or from their fishing grounds).

We descended eagerly upon the rookery next morning. The adults were around three feet tall and must have weighed about ninety pounds. They walked with a rolling gait, with flippers pressed in to their sides, so that they looked for all the world like dignified old men promenading. When standing still they rocked back on their heels. There was none of the unseemly scuttling of the Adélies. From time to time the emperors would toboggan on their tummies, pushing themselves up again with their beaks to come erect.

Crèches of a dozen or twenty chicks came together, especially towards evening. Crèches are important for emperors and Adélies alike, because they allow of both parents feeding and bringing back digested fish meal for their rapidly growing and insatiable young at the same time, while a comparatively small number of 'baby sitters' watch over their offspring. Unlike the raucous, ever quarrelling Adélies, that jealously guard their nests of stones, emperors are not territorial at all. They carry their nests with them in the form of their huge feet and they must needs huddle together for warmth in winter darkness and blizzard. The only fights among emperors that we observed were when several adults vied for the possession of a single chick, elbowing each other aside and trying to push the unfortunate chick into their 'pouch' with their beaks.

Our sojourn at Amanda Bay on the fringe of the rookery was sheer delight. The adults' melodious symphony, that reminded Mimi of French horns, punctuated by the high-pitched calls of the chicks, never faded away altogether, although the community's pleasant clamour was muted after midnight. There was rather a bad moment when we found that the ridgepole of our tent (a hollow steel pipe of uncertain vintage) had snapped. Mimi splinted it with a spare pole and bound it with nylon cord and adhesive tape and all was well.

Gill and Jannik did the penguin counting, concentrated and conscientious work, clicking their mechanical counters as they perched atop boulders facing the clamorous throng. Subsequently they shifted their tent to the margin of the penguins' 'high road' and, by dint of sleeping in turns, managed to make a 24-hour count of the wayfarers. Some 500 birds left the rookery in that time and 900 returned, a discrepancy which we speculated might be due to the thirty-knot wind that had sprung up and which must have kept many would-be 'fishermen' at home. The emperors on the march averaged 1.4 m.p.h., Jannik later ascertained, when he trailed a party for three and a half miles. He saw individual birds pass each other in the lines but the columns as a whole remained intact, except when they came to a halt, often to discuss the crossing of a crevice or a tide-crack, pitfalls that these heavy birds obviously dreaded. A fall into a deep, narrow crack could be fatal if there was no way to scramble out, and had been, we found, for a dozen unfortunate chicks (there were two lucky ones that Gill and Jannik rescued). Apart from these periodic conferences, all traffic came to a standstill between midnight and 3 a.m. true local sun time.

Mimi, with me as her assistant, was specially concerned with filming, photographing and sound recording. The emperors' behaviour at cracks and crevices was particularly fascinating. Apart from their usual calls, the marching penguins would occasionally give vent to a series of barely audible murmurs and 'coughing' noises. These sounds were especially in evidence when the birds halted to inspect an obstacle. It was hard to get near enough to record these soft sounds above the noises of the wind and the nearby rookery, but Mimi was able to get on tape an incident that made all her disappointments worth while. This was a confrontation between several older birds and a younger one (distinguished by size and neck colour) that took place at the edge of a crevice. The seniors' murmurs, motions and nudges with beaks and flippers made it abundantly plain that they were trying to persuade the youngster to cross the crack first, an honour it firmly declined for several minutes, until in the end it bowed to the inevitable, flopped down on its tummy and tobogganed across safely. Hubbs Sea World, who analysed the recording of the exchange, described it as 'an excellent aggressive sequence between mature individuals at a tide crack'.

Gill found time away from the penguins for a couple of strenuous outings in search of lichens, on one of which, to the bluffs at the edge of the polar plateau and the nunataks beyond, Mimi and I joined her – not that I was much good as a collector as I lacked the sharp eyes of the other two. It never ceased to amaze me how the tiny yellow, orange, white and black plants grew in greatest profusion on south-facing slopes at the very margin of the continental ice. The sheer beauty of Amanda Bay, with its dark red bluffs and nunataks, blue ice cliffs and the massed grandeur of the bergfield to seaward through which we had passed, took one's breath away. 'We are almost surfeited with splendour,' I wrote in my diary, and was to recall those words as equally appropriate to the bold Larsemann Hills with their huge snow cornices and frozen lakes and fjords.

It was during this first stay at Amanda Bay (for we returned later and camped off the entrance, where we made some exciting observations that we will come to) that Mimi and I had leisure and peace of mind enough to reflect on the great sea-ice journeys of the past, which we had read about and whose lessons we were attempting in some small measure to apply.

Not too much sea-ice travelling is done nowadays, apart from unloading ships at the edge of the fast ice. An exception is the Australian base of Mawson, whence dog teams traverse 150 miles of sea-ice to an emperor penguin rookery. The heroic exploits of the past mostly involved man-hauling.

In 1907 the 53-year-old Edgeworth David, the young giant Mawson and Dr Mackay, all members of Shackleton's expedition, made the longest unsupported man-haul journey in history – 1,260 miles without depots, more than half of it over the sea-ice, to reach the South Magnetic Pole, which was then in the interior of Victoria Land. Their loads were enormous even though they were able to supplement their rations by hunting as long as they were on the coast.

Equally heroic, Scott's northern party in 1911, led by Campbell and Priestly, after surviving a terrible winter of semi-starvation in an ice cave, man-hauled more than 300 miles along the sea-ice of the Victoria Land coast to reach their base at McMurdo – to receive the melancholy tidings that their leader was no more.

In 1913 Douglas Mawson's eastern party sledged for weeks along the coast of George V Land. They crossed the formidable Mertz and Nimitz ice tongues in the process, and the maps they made (which we used aboard *Explorer* in our previous expedition) are still the only ones of that coast – and good ones at that.

Our efforts were very small beer in comparison. We must have covered about 650 miles over the sea ice on our own expedition so far (not counting day trips from the boat), about half of it man-hauling. We had been in the field every month since the sea had frozen, but this seemed all rather feeble in comparison with the giants of the past – especially the heroes of that immortal emperor penguin saga, *The Worst Journey In the World*.

Still, we had learned a few lessons about sea-ice travel, and this seems a good place to pass them on (they are supplemented by satellite data and published reports we saw later). Two practical questions most concerned us: breakouts and the causes of rough ice.

As to massive breakouts, vast areas of apparently fast ice can and do disintegrate right up to the coast at any time of the year. Fatalities have several times resulted. Along the sixty-mile stretch of coast between the Vestfolds (Davis) and the Larsemanns every breakout followed much the same pattern. There appeared to be a great open-water polynia out in Prydz Bay throughout the winter and this broke through to the coast periodically, notably in the region of the Sørsdal Glacier and along a line from the outer Rauers to outside the Svenners.

This observation was afterwards confirmed by ESMR (microwave) data from NASA, which showed a large and persistent polynia in Prydz Bay during the winter of 1983 which met the coast in the Sørsdal region. The reasons for the polynia are obscure. Russian meteorologists list Prydz Bay as an area of stationary anticyclones which must affect the distribution of sea ice, and the Australian researcher Mellor points to the rapid movement of icebergs off the Vestfold Hills (we observed the same off the Rauers) as evidence of strong currents.

We had been told beforehand that bergs calving off the Sørsdal Glacier front tore up the sea ice and prevented its consolidation. This was not so. Systematic observation through the year showed only three tiny bergs breaking off from the side of the glacier, with minimal effect on the sea ice. Moreover, the configuration of the actual snout remained unchanged for at least eight months, strongly discounting any glacial surge.

The deep undersea trench scored out by the Sørsdal in ages past and the complex of waterways nearby would be likely to cause powerful currents and tidal streams, which most probably account for the instability. The precipitating breakout factor is, of course, a blizzard. But there is no evidence that the ones at Sørsdal are any worse than similar storms elsewhere.

The anchoring effect of islands and grounded bergs was everywhere apparent and their presence was a useful guide to relatively safe camping places. What must not be forgotten in all this is that there are wide differences in ice conditions along various stretches of coast and that many factors operate which are not yet understood.

The roughest ice we encountered, and it was through its fringes that we built our 'road', covered a triangular area whose apex was the Svenner Islands thirteen miles offshore and whose base extended from the Ranvik to the Brattstrands (with a smooth strip along much of the Brattstrand coast). Numerous large and small bergs were scattered through the zone, the ice between them being an indescribable jumble of up-ended blocks, ridges and 'tank traps', with here and there a glassy patch where a berg had ploughed its way through. The area was generally within the one-hundred-fathom line of soundings, so the larger bergs would have been grounded. Current eddies off the Ranvik and katabatic storms would probably have churned up the brew of pack ice fragmenting against rock-hard bergs.

The weather was generally fine and sunny at Amanda Bay, the temperatures varying between −15°C and −20°C, and, with the exception of one gale, the katabatics were not too strong for comfort. Apart from the profound satisfaction at having reached one of our major objectives, there was the beauty and interest of our surroundings and our relaxed relationship with Gill and Jannik. Both couples enjoyed the privacy of living in their own tents after the cramped quarters on the ship. Sociable councils of war were held frequently in our tent in the evenings over mugs of tea or cocoa, with the visitors wrapped in sleeping bags. Now that the weather was warmer than in winter, the closed-cell foam Karrymats that were spread over the canvas tent floor as insulation were fully adequate. We chatted happily about the events of the day and our plans for the morrow, firmly linked by our common venture.

On *Explorer* Mimi and I were naturally careful not to upset anyone by public show of affection for each other. Out here it did not matter, we could behave more naturally, a relaxed state of affairs, and very welcome because we are both demonstrative people.

The Larsemanns and seal pups

Much as we would have liked to remain longer in this delectable spot, the Larsemanns beckoned. Apart from anything else, there were the Australian-recommended anchorages to inspect to see how accurate had been our aerial photo assessments, as well as the seal rookeries to find. So on 4 October, Gill and Jannik packed the sledge with their usual efficiency and we set off on the twenty-odd-mile run to the Larsemanns, with Mimi and myself taking turns at driving. We had not gone very far, only four miles in fact, to Inner Hovdeoyane, an island off the southern entrance to the bay, when we came upon a pool broken open by seals in a tide-crack that emperors were sharing with the seals, albeit in no very cooperative spirit. Seemingly ignoring the bemused-looking seals, groups of penguins dived in *en masse* and, after emerging some minutes later, continued as far as one could tell in the direction they had been going before. We tore ourselves away reluctantly, with the promise to camp here on our return, and drove across the bay where *Explorer* had alternately motored and drifted all one night more than seven months before. The going was excellent and we drove fast although, at −21°C, the wind of our passing cut cold and we had to stop once in a while and run around to get warm again.

The heavily crevassed Dalk Glacier at the head of the bay we were crossing had calved off two enormous bergs that dwarfed all other features nearby and, by their seamed and serac-studded contours, unmistakably proclaimed their origin. Their faces were in part blue ice, in other places snowdrifted, and this snow was a distinct and delicate pink colour that so remained throughout our stay. We were concerned that there was a disappointing dearth of seals in the tide-cracks. Perhaps we were wrong and the primary pupping areas were somewhere else altogether.

The immediate problem, however, was to pick a way among the bergs piled up against the windward shore of the Larsemanns, which was made up of Vestodden Peninsula and Vikroy Island a mile offshore. The task was easier than we had feared because the pack ice between the bergs, that had blocked our approach in *Explorer*, was now an integral part of the fast ice, and a route was soon found. We made camp at 6 p.m. on a sheltered snow slope beneath the rocky tip of Vestodden. The latitude was 69°.22′S, the longitude 76°.22′E. It was our southernmost camp site.

Next day Gill and Jannik prospected the seaward margin of the Larsemanns, where they again saw very few seals, while Mimi and I headed inland to Broknes at the root of our peninsula. An unexpected find was an ANARE dump of ATK helicopter fuel. We had known all about this depot except that it was some five miles away from where it had been pointed out to us in Hobart on an aerial photograph. There was a cairn by the depot with a bottle containing a note left by the party who had laid it from the *Nella Dan* two years before, as well as a bar of chocolate. We saw with amusement that the person who had unwittingly misdirected us had been a member of that party. It is embarrassing to admit it, but we could not resist greedily eating the bar of chocolate and leaving only a note of thanks, since we had already eaten our day's ration of muesli bars.

The Larsemanns, we soon found, were very different from the Rauers, much larger in scale and more rugged altogether. The hills, besides being higher, were often separated by steep-walled U-shaped glacial valleys. The abrupt lee or southern drop-offs down to the fjords and valleys had huge cornices and vertical snow slopes that were potentially lethal for the unwary, especially in thick weather.

The second day at the Larsemanns, Mimi and I began an inspection of the winter mooring sites that had been proposed to us in Hobart, and which were nearly all on Vikroy, the island we had visited in the schooner in late February and where Gill and Norm had landed. In general, we considered one and all to be potential death traps, with one single possible exception for a very small vessel, as a last resort only. While we were prospecting anchorages, the other two made an exciting find. A dozen seals had appeared since the day before and had hauled out along a system of tide-cracks in the shelter of the two huge Dalk Glacier bergs. And one of these seals was nuzzling a new-born pup.

From then on Mimi and I spent nearly every day at the rookery with our little fibreglass sledge, loaded with a beach cooler containing heated water bottles to keep from freezing the sound recording and movie equipment, spare clothing and lunch. We photographed, filmed, tape-recorded and observed. Jannik took some pictures too, but, in the main, he and Gill went tagging.

Our first rookery day, 7 October, was bleak. The temperature was $-25°C$ with a bitter northeast wind, so seal-watching and recording was chilly work to say the least. The pup born two days earlier had been joined by another during the night, and the first pair of skuas of the season were already in attendance busily pecking away at an afterbirth. The pups had huge front flippers, big heads and great brown eyes, which filled with tears whenever they gazed at one intently. The touching effect so produced is quite phoney, since seals on land all tend to 'cry' when they want to see more clearly, the watery film apparently aiding their marine-adapted vision.

We very soon found that the pups' individual personalities varied enormously, as did that of their mothers. Some mothers warned us aggressively to keep off. Most didn't seem to care. There was one in particular who seemed to be a nervous case who bellowed like a bullock whenever anyone, Weddell or human, came within fifty yards of her, while her pup cowered close to her side for protection. Other pups flopped right up to us with eager curiosity, which their mothers did nothing to curb. At first we carefully avoided touching the newborns for fear that our alien scent would impair the bond with their mothers, though the temptation to fondle them was hard to resist. (Later we were told that this was an unnecessary precaution as these mother seals do not identify by scent.)

The most adventurous little fellow of all was one Mimi encountered later off Amanda Bay. This pup was no more than ten minutes old but already it was all out to see the world. The mother had bitten through the cord but the afterbirth had not yet been passed, when the pup lolloped towards her with such determination that she had to move the recorder and camera case out of its way no less than three times. She had ultimately to hide behind a snow drift before the persistent little animal desisted and turned its attention towards the seal hole. Mimi was seriously worried as it teetered on the slippery edge of the hole, until the mother finally woke up and called it back.

Within a day or so the number of seals hauled out off the Dalk had risen to around twenty-five, though there was a lot of coming and going among the males as some slid beneath the ice while others emerged. There was a good deal of underwater fighting too, attested by great gashes on flanks and flippers, for Weddell mating takes place as soon as the females re-enter the water after pupping. The foetus, interestingly enough, lies dormant until the time is ripe for it to develop, and this may not necessarily be in time for the following pupping season. If conditions are unfavourable the foetus may not develop for another year. The males off the Larsemanns were plainly excited, some lunging around in circles shovelling snow up with their snouts and bawling at the females. Two-way exchanges also took place between females on the surface and submerged males, and we recorded some of these with a hydrophone three metres down in a seal hole and a hand-held microphone above.

Mimi's efforts to film an actual birth were frustrating. My obstetrical experience was no use at all. The pups seemed to pop out like cherry pips without warning. We would take up station near a restless pregnant female who had shed some blood and watch her intently for hours, during which time nothing whatever happened, only to find that two others we had ruled out had given birth in the meantime. Eventually Mimi got a shot of a pup emerging, but only just. We did, however, see a number of pups still attached to the afterbirth, only seconds after their emergence into the polar world. Their first action once the cord was bitten through was to circumnavigate their mother, nuzzling eagerly all the way round (usually paradoxically the long way) until they found the teat. And since they flopped along so very slowly at first, this might take half an hour or more, but, once the milk store was found, they never forgot its location again. Weddell seal milk is extremely rich and copious, so that the pups appear to swell visibly from day to day and they double their birth weight in a week.

It is during this first week that the newborn pups are most vulnerable to cold. In all the rookeries we visited, we only found three dead pups out of some 350 survivors: one had been stillborn, the other two were victims of first-week blizzards. In one case the poor mother remained with her dead offspring, nuzzling it frequently, for days. The vast majority of the baby Weddells, however, took gales and snow storms in their stride. Within a day or two at most they would begin to play with their mothers, rolling over on their backs and twisting themselves into all manner of lively contortions. The pair would mock-bite and nuzzle each other in play and, when the mother tired, the restless pup, if an adventurous one, would flop off to examine its new world.

While we concentrated on the seal rookery, Jannik, with Gill's help, kept busily tagging seals, and had an impressive fifty Larsemann seals tagged by 11 October. Thirteen pups had been born off the Dalk by then and we had amassed a good collection of visual and sound records, so we tore ourselves away from the seals for the time being to traverse Vestodden and Broknes peninsulas in search of lichens and for the sheer joy of scrambling over these splendid hills. During this period we also completed our investigation of the winter mooring places that I have already described. There was one cramped little bay on an islet that might have done in case of need. Temperatures were beginning to fluctuate widely from the −20°s to around −7°C, much of this variation now being diurnal, with late afternoons much the warmest. The hours of daylight were already long. It was immensely enjoyable, quite apart from lichen collecting, to stride for miles over those miniature mountains, kicking steps on steep snow slopes, skirting the shores of frozen lakes or mountain tarns and clambering up the sides of the U-shaped valleys. The paucity of bird life compared with the Rauers was striking, no doubt because of the much greater distance to the open water polynia out in Prydz Bay, the polynia whose winter-long persistence we subsequently confirmed by reference to satellite imagery in Washington. Indeed, apart from the few skuas, two snow petrels were all that we saw. 15 October, our final day in the Larsemanns, was particularly rewarding. Gill and Jannik prospected Sigdoy Island just south of Broknes, while we made our way to the edge of the polar plateau via fjords and mountain passes and traversed the length of Broknes on the way back.

Seals, emperors and Adélies

The decision to leave the Larsemanns was a hard one, for the continuing cold weather and the unimpaired condition of the sea ice made it certain that there would be no very early breakout and that, on the contrary, the ice might be expected to remain intact longer than usual. Moreover, we had ample food and cooking fuel even if there was no petrol to spare. We were morally bound, however, by my written schedule in the schooner's log, that obliged us to be back by the end of October after seven weeks. No matter what the temptation, it would be a gross dereliction of responsibility deliberately to overstay the deadline we ourselves had set. The only question to be decided was how best to spend the two weeks remaining to us. Jannik was all for a man-haul push to the southwestward. The chance of seeing new country beyond the horizon was very appealing. But desert lay in that direction, progressively further away from the Prydz Bay open-water polynia. There would be no birds and not even many seals, for, even as far as we had walked towards the southern Larsemanns, their numbers diminished rapidly. So there was absolutely nothing to be gained and we were, after all, a research expedition. On the other hand, the increasing numbers of pregnant seals, and their interactions with emperor penguins at their common watering place off Amanda Bay, that we had glimpsed in passing, cried aloud for study. We would head back then, on 16 October, to Amanda Bay and camp by the seal hole.

By the time we left that morning the indefatigable Jannik and Gill had raised their tagging total to an impressive 103 seals. They took time off to tag five more during pauses *en route*, one of which was occasioned by me, when driving, having to be persuaded that I was heading towards the wrong island.

Despite this embarrassing involuntary detour, it was still early when we camped thirty yards from the seal/penguin hole off Inner Hovdeoyane, the island that lay a mile outside Flatnes, the ice cape bounding Amanda Bay on the south. The afternoon was sunny and windless and Mimi was eager to see and record on film and tape all that was going on. Jannik and Gill's blood was up now, and the sight of a hundred or more seals in the tide-cracks to seaward had them hurrying away clutching tagging pliers. To my companion's surprise I showed no enthusiasm to be up and doing. Instead, I crawled into my sleeping bag as soon as the tent was pitched, and found, when I removed my frozen headgear, that the left side of my jawline was distorted by a hot, throbbing swelling. It was another flare-up of the dental abscess and the worst yet. I felt very sorry for myself indeed. Dosing myself with Mysteclin V antibiotic and Dymadon for the pain, I was apathetic to all the exciting sights that awaited the others. The one thing I did enjoy during the next few days while lying in my sleeping bag was the seal chorus that was transmitted upwards through the ice. Long descending melodious whistles, chirps, pulses and clicks (male Weddells use five calls exclusively and six are used by both sexes) all came through loud and clear to my naked ear.

The tale for the next few days is Mimi's, since I had nothing but self-pity to contribute:

Leaving the invalid to try to doze off, for it came out that he had had a sleepless night with toothache, I took the cameras and recorder to the seal hole. The emperors appeared to be breaking their journey to or from the sea at this and another hole that I found later. Sometimes they would swim around on the surface for 5–10 minutes, but many times all the swimming penguins would dive together and not return for up to 10 minutes. Often a bevy of them would shoot out of the water together. At other times the pool would be literally seething with penguins, so that there seemed to be not a millimetre between them, yet a dozen or more, who had been contemplating the churned-up pool from the ice margin, would without warning dive *en masse* into the midst of the maelstrom. Astonishingly, none was ever hit or hurt.

A little drama was enacted that first afternoon almost as if it was for my benefit. A male Weddell, that had been hauled out five yards from the hole, began to hump his way purposefully towards the water. Emperors were swimming in the pool and more were standing around the edge when the seal began to move. When he was less than two yards away, several birds in succession shot out of the hole, landing within two feet of his face and tobogganing off, startling him and stopping him in his tracks. He made some guttural clucking sounds and moved forward again, eventually getting far enough to stick his head into the water. He withdrew it abruptly and backed up hastily as the emperors swimming underwater 'buzzed' him and threatened to peck his nose. The sequence was several times repeated until at long last, after thirty-five minutes, he finally did get in with a desperate lunge. The penguins got out then and stayed out for two hours.

The seal came off worst on this occasion but, more often, it was the penguins that stood aside while the seals were in the water. Unlike the Weddells, who echo-locate with sonar clicks, emperors are generally believed to be silent under water, a fact confirmed in our hydrophone recordings. No underwater sounds were recorded, as American, French and Russian researchers have also elicited. Again unlike the Weddell seals with their dialectal variations, the emperors' sounds on the ice at Amanda Bay differed no whit from those in other parts of Antarctica.

I noticed that evening that a male seal who was lying near the hole bore one of our Rauers tags in its tail flippers. We had spotted others in the Larsemanns. In fact, a total of forty-seven Rauer-tagged seals were re-sighted during our field trips along the forty miles of coast south of those islands, good evidence of the mobility of the Weddell population – evidence which, incidentally, was not available to the more static Davis zoologists who had been tagging seals for over nine years.

The only disappointment to mar this happy day (David's toothache apart) was the final demise of the movie camera. I had managed to get it going again after a fashion and had high hopes for interesting footage of the swimming emperors and seals, for the camera was a Eumig underwater, which had done yeoman service on David's 1981–2 expedition and had, goodness knows, stood up to unprecedented abuse on this one. The chance of filming the emperors under water was too good to pass up, though, with hindsight, I should have been more wary. I removed my gloves and jacket, lashed the camera to my wrist and lowered it into the water. Sadly, the O-ring was worn out and it was waterproof no longer, so that was the end of my filming until a new movie camera arrived by helicopter in the summer.

This seems a good place to report that the 110 seal recordings we made each month between March 1983 and February 1984, as well as those of zoologist Rhys Puddicombe at Davis, revealed that the underwater sounds of the Prydz Bay seals were different from those of both McMurdo and the Antarctic Peninsula. This could well be an indication of there being three separate breeding populations.

One unlooked-for finding on the seal taped from Amanda Bay was only revealed on analysis at Hubbs Sea World. The sounds of killer whales and great whales were both recorded on our tape. The nearest open-sea ice edge was, we later found out, a good twenty miles away.

Two days later I came rushing back to the tent, where David was slowly recovering. I was so excited at what I had seen I just had to share it at once.

'Guess what I saw?' I cried out as I pushed through the tent entrance. 'A mother seal teaching her baby to swim and,' I added proudly, 'I got pictures!' The news was enough to shake David out of his misery.

'How did she teach it?' he asked eagerly.

'The pup was about two weeks old, maybe a little less. She nosed it into the water and slid underneath it to hold it up. It didn't look happy at all, but after a while it seemed to gain confidence. They both came out after about ten minutes. It wasn't easy getting the pictures because the ice all round the hole was rotten so I had to crawl like a seal myself to spread my weight.'

'That's why your front is all wet!' exclaimed David, concerned. 'Come on, mate! You'd better get changed right away. You're no baby seal.'

The seal rookery here was a good deal larger than the one off the Larsemanns and there was another the same size about a mile further seaward. There being so many pups around, it was a little disappointing that I only saw one other first swim. I had been keeping an eye on this mother and baby, just as I had on the first one. The second mother did not exactly 'push the baby in off the deep end' but floated beside its offspring giving it more moral than buoyant support. The third pup I watched swimming had probably been in before. Nevertheless, the mother swam beside it and kept on it a watchful eye while emperors swimming in the same 'pool' kept a respectful five metres distance.

The Adélies had now begun to return to Antarctica, for we saw several little figures looking lost and bewildered among the emperors. It seemed that there must be an Adélie rookery near by, though none had been recorded in the vicinity, and that these confused little folk had strayed. Indeed, they kept rushing back and forth without clear purpose. Penguins navigate by the sun and become disoriented in overcast, but, even with the mostly clear weather we had been having, some not surprisingly must have deviated from the correct line on the long trek in from the ice edge. The dignified emperors tolerated their little cousins and even seemed to feel protective towards them. In fact one emperor warned us aggressively from a pair of Adélies it was walking with and which I wanted to photograph.

Time was now running out. So, for that matter, were seals for Jannik and Gill to tag. In the six days we spent outside Amanda Bay they tagged an amazing total of 205 seals, 94 of them pups. By 20 October they were turning their attention back to the emperor rookery and embarking on a recount which disclosed rather fewer birds, a not unexpected result of increased crèche formation. Meanwhile we used the last surplus of petrol on a trip to Stedoy Island.

Stedoy is six miles out from Inner Hovdeoyane, where we were camped, and halfway to the Svenners, that we had previously approached from the opposite, northeast direction. From sixty-metre-high Stedoy as a vantage point, we were able to trace the limits of rough and smooth ice as never before, though we were not much nearer elucidating why some parts were so rough and others smooth and undisturbed. Obviously the jumbled regions had been subjected to much turmoil – breakup in storms, re-freezing, piling up through pressure and, we suspected, rogue bergs charging about and committing general mayhem. But the mystery of the very sharp boundaries of the rough areas remained.

Not only were bergs, islands and ice fields laid out before us, but open water was visible on the horizon away to the northwest, an estimated fourteen miles from Stedoy and twenty-three from the Amanda Bay emperor penguin rookery. We calculated the distance to the polynia from the formula: distance in miles to the sea horizon is the square root of the observer's height in feet multiplied by 1.15. Now, walking down from the sixty-metre-high summit of Stedoy, we lost sight of the sea at an estimated altitude of 145 feet. The square root of 144 is 12. Twelve multiplied by 1.15 is approximately 14. The distance from Stedoy to the emperor rookery was of course read off from the odometer. In order to learn more about the emperors' route towards the sea we resolved to make a detour on our return to camp (we had just enough petrol for this) and to cut the emperors' track four miles or so outside the geographical constraints of the deeply indented Amanda Bay. Meanwhile, there was much else doing on Stedoy.

Unlike on most offshore islands, lichens were profuse among the summit rocks and there were many varieties too. On the lower slopes we found two separate Adélie penguin rookeries, the southernmost especially being only part occupied as yet, for many stone nest circles were still unclaimed and others often guarded by a single bird. An equal area of former rookery territory (droppings and stone nest rings) was not so far colonized at all. But it obviously would be very soon. Little groups of Adélies were hurrying towards the island from seaward, something like fifty being scattered over the approaches at any one time. All were coming from the northeast (315° True by the compass), the direction in which we had sighted the open water fourteen miles away. None was observed going the opposite way. As they neared the land the penguins speeded up their pace, scuttling up over the tide-crack pressure ridges at a run and on up the rocks as fast as their little legs could carry them. You would have expected them to be out of breath when they got to the nest sites, but without pause they launched into clamorous territorial squabbles.

The two Adélie rookeries, which seem not to have been previously reported even by a 1980 helicopter survey, had the following populations according to our field notes. Southwestern rookery: 399 birds, mostly single at nests. Birds spread very widely, only a few in pairs, many collecting stones. About half the area that had been previously used as a rookery was occupied. Northeastern rookery: 340 birds, many more pairs – about half were paired. More closely aggregated than on the southwestern rookery but still thinly spaced. About three-quarters of the space that had previously been used as a rookery was occupied. At a rough estimate, full occupancy would triple the number of birds from the 730 we counted to something over 2,000.

After visiting a couple of rather sterile neighbouring islets and being warned off by an aggressive mother seal, we moved on to the bird cliffs on the south side of Stedoy. A hundred feet above our heads fulmars were burrowing nest holes in a steep snow slope while others flew in circles off the cliff face. They kept changing places with a group rafted on the sea ice below, who numbered twenty-four on average. However, it was quite impossible to estimate how many there were on and around the cliff up above, so constant was their movement.

Back on the snowmobile again, we went roaring away southwestward through an echoing gap between two bergs towards the line of march of the emperors. We had already established the precise direction being taken by the rather straggling Adélies. The main question that intrigued us about the emperors was whether they fanned out once they had left the restricting confines of Amanda Bay or maintained their strict formation over the open sea ice.

We came up with the columns well out from Inner Hovdeoyane and eight or nine miles out from the rookery. The lines were as close-packed laterally as they had been in Amanda Bay. We counted groups coming and going that numbered anything between thirty-five and three as well as a few individuals. Three Adélies had attached themselves to the largest party, who, to keep up with the longer tread of the emperors, had to scamper along at a run in unconscious caricature of their 'betters'. The emperors were marching in a straight line but, true to their nature, bunched up at easily crossed tide-cracks and conferred a while before moving on. There was one small berg flanking their line of march before completely unrestricted sea ice stretched to the edge of the polynia fourteen or fifteen miles further on. There was no other visible obstacle, but the birds trudged away over the horizon out of sight still keeping their tight formation, their tracks in the snow spanning a width of no more than 250 yards. Their road, like that of the Adélies, was an undeviating northwest, or 315°.

Thus both Amanda Bay emperors and Stedoy Adélies marched parallel to each other with the Adélies about two miles north of the emperors. The emperors walked twenty-three miles from their rookery to the sea, the Adélies fourteen.

One more day at this magic camp was all we could afford, though we were more than reluctant to move on. We had been privileged to observe at close quarters scenes from the lives of the emperors and Weddells who were both true year-round denizens of Antarctica. They neither feared us nor were overly friendly, for this was *their* land. We were mere irrelevant intruders, a well-deserved put-down for us humans, the most predatory and destructive of all animal species.

So, on 22 October we sadly packed up and headed back towards the Rauers, scouting *en route* Inner Brattstrandoyane, an island a few miles north of Amanda Bay that Mimi and I had singled out from air photographs in Canberra as the only really promising winter mooring south of the Rauers. When we had passed that way in *Explorer* in February the island had been invisible, hemmed in by the icebergs of the Amanda Bay bergfield, which we had assumed to be impenetrable. Now we were not so sure. Bergs surrounded the island, true enough, but with space between them, and the sheltered bay on the southeast lee side of the island was free from screw ice or pressure and had attracted no intruding bergs. We appeared to have missed the one and only opportunity of spending the winter in close proximity to Amanda Bay and not very far from the Larsemanns.

'You can't win every bet,' was Mimi's comment. That night we camped at Brenesholmene Islands in the Ranvik approaches, thankful to pick up the cached petrol left there on the way south, for we were down to our last few pints.

The formerly silent and deserted islets had been transformed out of all recognition by the raucous, seething throng of Adélies that had fully populated all the rookeries on the islets, 4,100 of them, as we counted next day. The birds were mostly paired and there was a good deal of displaying and mating. The latter proceeding, as might be expected from such natural clowns as the Adélies, is ungainly in the extreme. The female lies down on her tummy. The male, facing forward, climbs precariously on her back, stumbling to and fro to maintain his balance but steadily backing towards her rear end. The moment when he gets past her upraised tail he begins to fall off and, during that crucial fraction of a second, the two cloacas are opposed to each other and impregnation takes place. Such a ludicrous and seemingly inefficient procedure should not work in a thousand years, but quite clearly from the results it does work very well indeed.

Other birds were coming back now besides the Adélies and their attendant skuas: tiny black-bodied storm petrels swooped about the more northerly bluffs and Antarctic petrels, snow petrels and fulmars arrived every day in increasing numbers. There was even one rare solitary dominican gull. It was sad to be leaving this spectacular ice-bound coast when the sun was long hours in the sky and the shores of Antarctica were throbbing with renewed life, but there was no help for it. We moved on and made camp alongside a bergy bit in Brevika Bay at the threshold of the 'road'. A single long day sufficed to take us through, now that several small snow falls had improved the going, and we camped, tired but relieved, at our depot at Gelato berg, where a blizzard held us for three days. Then we were off again, having heaped on the sledge all that remained at Gelato. Most of the stores at Cape Drakon were also picked up *en route* and we arrived back at the ship on 28 October on the last of our petrol.

We had covered 206 vehicle miles and, at a conservative estimate, another 150 on foot in the fifty days we had been in the field. Jannik and Gill had tagged 344 seals, 137 of them pups. No praise can be too great for their tireless energy and dedication and we all had much to be proud of besides. The success of the expedition had been fully assured in those seven weeks, which had been among the most rewarding of our lives.

10

Breakout and Storm
28 October 1983–11 March 1984

Hung with hard ice flakes, where hail-scur flew,
There I heard naught save the harsh sea
And the ice-cold wave . . .
    Ezra Pound, 'The Seafarer' (from the Anglo-Saxon)

The recent blizzard had, as might have been expected, blown out any ice that had formed off the Sørsdal. One last chance remained of collecting the drum of petrol cached at Kazak Island that would enable us to return southward again, if only as far as the Svenners, to take advantage for continued field work of the exceptionally good condition of the sea ice. This was to make the ten-mile passage in front of the glacier in the Beaufort inflatable. The project was frought with risk. The fabric had taken a fearful punishment in the course of two consecutive Antarctic seasons. So it behoved us to set out before even a partial refreeze and the return of fragmented floes blown out to sea by the blizzard should render the seaway unnavigable. It had to be soon or not at all. All our efforts, therefore, were immediately bent to this end; the two outboards were put back into commission and tested; cuts and tears in the rubber duck's skin were repaired; float suits and emergency gear were collected. All to no purpose. A mild sea breeze next day was enough to bring the pack back in and close the way.

If this setback was disappointing, the improved morale we found aboard the schooner was heartening. This time our return was met with positive remarks and a festive air. Norm and Jamie had done well. The trench had been kept open and, as the schooner was nearly back on an even keel, it could be discontinued; the mooring warps had been kept free from the ice; there was fresh water aboard. Jamie had done weekly bird walks and kept notes, especially as to the dates of arrival of each species; he had caught fifteen fish for the stomach sampling programme. Norm was full of the jobs he had been doing round the boat: the seventh repair he had made to his ice-axe, his mending of a broken wooden spoon, his skiing.

The two men had come full circle from initial enthusiasm in Australia to alienation and now enthusiasm again. This had nothing to do with the success of the southern party, about which they had no way of knowing. Both men had done their best and a very good job it had been: we were a complete expedition again. That night at dinner I could sincerely congratulate everyone and was hard put to it to hold back tears of relief.

There were problems, of course. The diesel generator's water pump belt was wearing badly, no big deal in itself for the steps to take were plain, but explosive in human terms. In six weeks at most a new belt would be delivered by the first helicopter. Meanwhile the wind generator, which Norm had set up on the rail in the autumn, gave a trickle charge, the small Honda generator was capable of supplying our power and we had ample petrol for its miniscule needs. The Honda would be on standby, I decided, and the diesel generator used for the time being, but with great care; Mimi or Gill would inspect the belt with their sharp eyes before and after it was run and someone would remain in the engine room while the machine was in operation.

Norm's resistance to this plan was puzzling until he showed me a rope belt he had made, which was palpably very much weaker and more vulnerable to friction than the damaged rubber belt with its remaining three integral wire strands. Norm was so keen to 'go down in history' as the man who had saved the ship's electrics with his impractical makeshift that he took every opportunity for weeks to come to evade my instructions.

'As mentioned previously,' he wrote, 'after many hours of experimentation I produced a replacement pump vee belt made of spliced polyethylene rope coated with silicone rubber which worked well.'

This had its amusing side, but the real stakes were the possible wrecking of the diesel generator.

Our long radio report to the ORF on the seven weeks field trip, transmitted like all the others by the patient Norm to the long-suffering Davis operators, elicited a warm comment from the base leader: 'David Lewis and company. Have read your message with admiration and envy. Congratulations indeed. Briggs.'

Even more welcome was a message from Professor Grahame Budd, one of Australia's greatest living explorers: 'Greatly appreciated copies reports especially the interesting scientific results Amanda Bay and elsewhere. Impressed and envious extensive field work, especially the splendid Larsemanns trip. You may count me as one of those "Gentlemen in England now abed" who Henry V predicted on the eve of Agincourt would "think themselves accursed they were not here". A very nice expedition.'

The ice, at this stage, still held firm, so there was no dearth of practical things to do. Jannik took over the fishing for specimens again. We ultimately caught a total of 197, a record, we were told, for any Australian expedition. A first priority was to arrange field trips in the Rauers for the two who had perforce been confined to the vicinity of the ship. Neither had yet seen a seal pup, for instance, though three had been born within half a mile of the schooner. Jamie was delighted at the first one he saw. He and Jannik set off to a rookery we had observed at Cape Drakon on what proved to me a particularly fruitful seal-tagging exercise. On 17 November Gill, Jannik, Jamie and Norm went to spend five days at the Adélie rookeries on Hop Island, and in their absence I was able to complete my Aboriginal manuscript – a potential lifesaver, we hoped, for our lamentable finances.

Afterwards the two of us went away for eight days man-hauling to Cape Drakon and the moraine. We were anxious to finish prospecting snowmobile routes down from the plateau, since Davis had again suggested that they might in future want to bring snowmobiles to the Rauers across the plateau, bypassing the head of the Sørsdal. There was also lichen collecting to be done and inspection of anchorages now that summer was fast approaching. Without exception the winter's pressure ridges had disappeared without trace. We clambered up the salient red nunataks behind Cape Drakon and happily trudged on crampons up the steep flanks of the continental ice sheet to where it began to level off at 1,500 feet, roping up when skirting crevasses. The verdict was the same as on our earlier visits: snowmobiles could only be manhandled down these slopes with care and difficulty. This man-hauling and climbing trip was enjoyable in the extreme, for the sun hardly set now and the weather was warmer. At the edge of the ice cap we came upon a sight we had all but forgotten – the snow had melted to form a clear pool of fresh water in a rocky basin. Eagerly we bent down and drank.

Later lichen-collecting forays to the line of bluffs fringing the plateau by the agile Gill and Mimi, with me puffing up the steep slopes far behind them, were timed, not so much for daylight, because it was light all the time, but rather to avoid the morning katabatics. Thus we would leave the boat at noon and only return eighteen or twenty hours later when the keen winds had begun to blow again.

Particular interest focused on the teeming Adélie rookeries on Filla and Hop at this time. By late November most of the nesting pairs had one, or more often two, dark brown, fluffy, pear-shaped chicks that varied enormously in size, though some birds were still incubating their eggs. Gill and Jannik staked out sample areas, which they monitored weekly to record the breeding success of the pairs. They also continued with the stomach sampling. Mimi and I camped for a whole week at the edge of one of the Filla rookeries, so near that preoccupied birds would occasionally trip over the guy-ropes, turning round swearing and smartly belabouring the offending ropes with their flippers.

Adélies space their nests just out of pecking range of each other, so that any bird having to cross a rookery presses its flippers in tightly to its body and runs the gauntlet rapidly. If it is lucky it provokes no more than baleful sideways stares and token pecks (we were treated in exactly the same way, being pecked whenever we trespassed within the forbidden range). The problem arises when birds returning from the sea are searching for their mates. Often there are several false starts and scuffles before the reunion is effected with rapturous mutual neck-stretching displays.

Two pairs of skuas, each with their own fluffy chick that they fiercely guarded by 'dive bombing' intruders, were preying on this segment of the rookery. Eggs and chicks were their targets. We did manage to rescue one Adélie chick that had been dropped by a skua and that had a neck wound but seemed otherwise intact. The real difficult was to have it accepted back into the rookery, for there was no telling from which nest it had strayed. In fact, it was pecked mercilessly by the nesting adults for a time until the poor bedraggled little thing found refuge in the anonymity of a crèche. The Adélies mostly cowered away when a skua swooped down to steal a chick or an egg. Not always, though. Once when a skua alighted to finish a half-eaten penguin's egg, an enraged Adélie rushed out at it, beak agape and striking out with its flippers; the robber hurriedly took off.

The penguins were continually engaged in pilfering stones from each other's nests. An ecstatically displaying bird was a particularly open invitation to theft because it was unconscious of what was going on around it. Not uncommonly, too, while a penguin was straining forward to craftily appropriate a stone from a nest, its neighbour in the rear would be sneaking some of *its* stones away. Mimi and I tried the experiment of collecting a pile of stones and leaving them in front of our tent. Snatching stones by stealth from each other's nests must have become such an ingrained habit that, if the tent door was open and a passing bird thought we were watching, it would shuffle by with no more than a sideways glance at the treasure. But when we pulled the tent flap to, every penguin that passed would first look round furtively, then make a quick dash for a stone and scuttle off guiltily with it clutched in its beak.

Skuas were not the only enemies of the penguins. As the fast ice below the rookeries shrank, a pair of ten-foot leopard seals took station in the water beyond. Hard lines on any unwary penguin that swam too close to where one was lurking. There would be a swirl in the water, a squawk as the leopard seal's monstrous jaws crushed the bird, then, thrashing its head from side to side with unbelievable violence, the seal would tear it to pieces, literally shaking it out of its skin. Hunting must have been good for that pair of seals since they would often eat no more than the breast meat of the birds they caught.

Jannik never tired of watching and photographing the gory business. He very nearly paid for this fascination with his life on one occasion when, as he stood at the ice edge scanning the sea, a leopard seal hurtled up at him from below, jaws wide. Only Jannik's quick reaction saved him as he instinctively leapt backwards and then ran across the ice with the seal in pursuit. Out on the ice the great creature was no match for him in speed and it abandoned the chase after about thirty feet.

By the end of November the ice outside Filla to the west had broken out, so that waves now lapped just past the bird cliffs, and the blue sea beyond was littered with drifting floes that were dazzling white in the sunlight. The sounds and fjords inside the Rauers remained hard-frozen, however, not least the firth outside Winterover Bay. The days were almost uniformly fine and storms were notable for their absence. This good weather, while pleasant enough in all conscience, augured badly for an early unlocking of the ice that enclosed the ship. Open water was tantalizingly close, only one and a half miles away. Yet, in default of a major storm to break up the fast ice, the barrier between the schooner and the freedom of the open sea was likely to persist for a long time before it finally melted away. It was particularly galling that our range of movement was becoming progressively so restricted that it was soon limited to the nearer Rauer islands themselves. Frustration began to affect the whole party.

The bird cliffs were still mostly accessible, as were the Filla Adélie rookeries and the mainland lichen bluffs. Nesting seabirds, some with eggs or even chicks, fully occupied the steep faces – Antarctic petrels, fulmars, snow petrels, storm petrels, cape pigeons and skuas. A number of skua pairs 'worked' the bird cliffs, just as they did the Adélie rookeries. Their main prey here seemed to be adult birds, especially the lovely snow petrels that they struck down in flight, so that the ice beneath the cliffs came to be littered with remains: wings mostly, since the rest of the carcasses were consumed or scattered.

It was now time to say a last farewell to the disgusting salami, as well as the burnt and flattened cans and the ashes of the rest of our rubbish, by dint of sledging the lot out to the ice edge. With the aid of liberal applications of kerosene we managed to set the salami on fire, after which it smouldered for days. Ultimately, the ice with its burden of trash duly drifted out to sea, to deposit the unsightly detritus of our visit in deep water.

Together with Mimi, I worked out plans for a summer programme in *Explorer*, which was entirely dependent, of course, on just when we would be able to break out. The main item on the agenda would be a visit to the Soviet base of Mirny, if time allowed and the ice permitted. Gill and Jannik were enthusiastic at the prospect, Norm neutral and Jamie 'couldn't see the point'.

Jamie, to our disappointment, had again begun to dissociate himself from the rest of us. On 30 November he made his first open breach with the expedition by repudiating his agreement to send all exposed film to the *National Geographic Magazine* for processing. Mimi was collecting and packaging the exposed film to send off once the summer sea routes were open.

'I won't give you my film and I won't send it to the *Geographic* either. I'm sending it back to Australia.' When I reminded Jamie of his undertaking, he snapped back.

'I won't keep any agreements. I don't trust you,' and much more that was inventively obscene.

'Give us one single instance when Mimi or I have broken our word,' I challenged him. He could not.

'Not the letter, but the spirit,' he muttered.

Jamie's new level of antagonism to Mimi and me and the expedition itself showed up as well in his refusing to record his views on the expedition for the small-group study. Everyone else, Norm in particular, enjoyed being interviewed.

An attitude of non-cooperation was potentially disruptive on a small-scale venture such as ours in which everyone had to pull their weight, and we hoped that the imminent arrival of ships and helicopters that would renew our contact with the outside world might restore a sense of proportion. (We were to be disappointed.) I appealed to the group to maintain its unity.

'What for?' asked Jamie.

'Because we have been through a lot together and have succeeded in all our projects, to which everyone has contributed in one way or another. We should keep working together on the last lap.'

The supply ship *Nella Dan* moored up to the fast ice off Davis on 16 December and the same day we had our first visitors in two helicopters (they always flew in pairs for safety). This was an exciting occasion but it was subtly distracting too. The privacy of our already shrunken little world had been breached. It was no longer our own any more. In the ensuing weeks zoologists from Davis became regular visitors and the place that had been our special preserve was now open to all. Not that we were not grateful for the new opportunities. We sent off the first loads of fish stomachs, penguin 'chucks' and lichen specimens for delivery to ANARE scientists in Australia.

The effect on Jamie was distressing. Since our visitors knew him to be a zoologist, they naturally deluged him with questions about the wildlife and the work we had done. There was little he could say and he became even more withdrawn and sullen.

The Davis base leader generously air-ferried petrol to us. Welcome though it was, we had less use for it now that the snowmobile's role was increasingly limited and the rubber duck was still cut off from its native element. A radio technician, Dick Sibthorpe, kindly spent a whole day with us working on our ship's radios, which badly needed re-tuning. He installed in the VHF radio the output module that the ORF had sent us, so that rather belatedly we had field communications once more.

Every single thing we had requested from the ORF – a generator vee belt, heavy duty batteries and sundry spares – they had laboriously collected and consigned to us through the good offices of the Antarctic Division and *Nella Dan*. With such loyal back-up we must needs give of our best and not let down the 'home-based part of the expedition'.

The seaward ice edge seemed to our impatient eyes to be inexorably fixed near the bird cliffs, but inside the islands things were happening, even if with maddening slowness. The sun warmed rocks and the ship's warm hull melted the ice in their vicinity. *Explorer* became semi-afloat, in part supported by ice spurs. We saw with some relief that the propeller and rudder were intact.

The ice melted in layers. On top would be a fragile crust overlying a foot of water, beneath which again was a foot of firm ice. This lower layer may not have been altogether residual but in part new deep ice, which is formed whenever there is a layer of fresh water below the sea's surface caused by the melting of ice floes. This fresh melt water is still liable to freeze (for summer sea temperatures remain below the freezing point of fresh water), forming ice-under-ice and adding to the floes from below at the same time as they are melting from above. This explanation from Nelson's book on Arctic sea-ice hunters applies equally to Antarctica.[1] An analogous process seemed to have been at work round *Explorer* herself. When the ice began to melt around the ship we found that the propeller, rudder and keel were encased in their own ice sheath four inches thick, which came away as a series of casts complete with rust and paint. Apparently the relatively warm hull had caused melting of abutting ice and the melt water had trickled down and re-frozen as a cocoon around the ship.

As the great winter pressure ridges against the shore melted away, bottom ice was revealed. This, as its name suggests, is an ice layer formed under water with much of it below the silt and gravel of the beach. It is quite different from the deep ice mentioned above. The Soviet glaciologist N. N. Zubov (quoted by Nelson) has described how 'ships found themselves surrounded by ice which had suddenly risen from the bottom of the sea; this was proved by sand and bottom objects that had floated up with the ice'.

Walking on the sea ice, especially crossing the disintegrating tide-cracks, demanded increasing and unremitting care. A system of plank and empty fuel drum bridges became necessary for crossing between the schooner and the shore.

This is a good place to take stock of our studies of winter mooring

[1] R. K. Nelson, *Hunters of the Northern Ice*, University of Chicago Press, 1969.

places. There were seventeen of them, eleven of which were in the Rauers. The only really possible one outside the archipelago was the one on Inner Brattstrandoyane a few miles north of Amanda Bay. At least half a dozen of the Rauer anchorages would have been excellent. Let us try to summarize the good and bad points to look for in wintering a small vessel.

We have described the local pressure effects as the ice thickened to something like two metres, which were so unexpected and alarming. The phenomenon is most pronounced in shallow bays with gradually shelving shores, where the ice throws into folds and sometimes fractures into walls, like the nine-feet-high one on Shelyf Island. *Explorer*, moored fifty metres from the shore, was tilted about 9° away from the land. She was also squeezed up a good metre into the air. A sheath of ice formed as a cast round the hull and its appendages. All this had gone without trace by the beginning of summer.

Wintering a ship is such a versatile technique that there is little doubt it will become increasingly popular with small expeditions in large yachts and fishing boats. What should they watch out for?

Naturally the chosen bay must be sheltered, aligned away from the prevailing wind and current that drives the ice before it and piles it up against any obstruction (I have seen an ice 'sandwich' fifty feet high at Cape Adare). The cove should not be too deep, since a twenty-foot-high bergy bit would have a draught of 60–80 feet, so could not drift into a bay fifty feet deep. A depth of water of 20–30 feet would be ideal, and 50 yards from the land would be more than adequate even if the shores were shelving.

The next question to consider is how enclosed by rocks, islets and so on the bay should be. If it is too landlocked it may not unfreeze at all, and a preliminary study of aerial photos might help. On the other hand, we saw six-inch-thick ice break out of exposed bays during the autumn blizzards in the Rauers. What the effect of this would be on a little ship I do not know. Our examination of these bays after they had refrozen suggested that the ice had fragmented before washing out to sea, so that unless an anchor chain fouled, the vessel would probably have remained secured to the shore.

Without doubt, the essential precaution would be to have no anchor on the bottom with its chain running down through the ice, but to moor ashore to boulders, anchors set above high water or to ice bollards. The warps must be kept from freezing in.

We had at least avoided the most serious mistakes and hopefully had learned some useful lessons.

On 20 December the Davis base leader dropped in on his way down the coast. He took the two of us aside. 'Would you all like to join us for Christmas dinner?' he asked. 'I'll send the choppers for you that morning, we have to pick up our bird man [who was camped near the Filla Island bird cliffs] anyway.' We accepted gratefully. A break like this was just the thing to raise everyone's spirits, we thought. But did he really mean it? Eventually we decided to tell the others of the invitation. However, Christmas approached and we heard no more, so Mimi and I prepared to cook Christmas dinner just in case. This was as well, for no helicopters arrived. It turned out that the o/ic had asked Hobart to approve his invitation and they had turned him down. Despite everyone's disappointment on the schooner and, we subsequently heard, on the base as well, Christmas Day was friendly and happy and gave hope for the future.

As our world constricted further there was less and less we could usefully do in the ANARE-related programmes. Mimi and I were lucky in that we had plenty to occupy us in monitoring the incipient breakout at such winter moorings as were still accessible, and Mimi's involvement with the human dynamics study was as time-consuming as ever. Gill and Jannik were busy with the Adélies and even so were frustrated, but the other two rarely left the boat now except to gather drinking ice and to go for short walks.

The restriction of our activities, plus continued tantalizing contacts with a world outside that we could 'see but not touch', further upset Jamie. All would be well if only we could break out soon, but this was impossible. In the meantime, we must needs plan projects for everyone. Together with Gill and Jannik we racked our brains and eventually came up with a scheme to monitor the proportion of skuas to Adélies, an idea not without merit, and a good one for Norm and Jamie.

At the same time we discussed with the other couple Jamie's possible dismissal. By now they were heartily sick of him. It would be best, they both felt, if he were sent away. Mimi and I did not quite agree; only as a last resort, we insisted.

Matters came to a head on 4 January 1984. Gill, Jannik, Norm and Jamie were due to leave for the Adélie rookeries, Gill and Jannik to study the breeding pairs, Norm and Jamie the skuas. The ice edge by this time was in bad shape and very dangerous. In fact it was an open question whether it would be possible to cross on to the land from the bay ice at all, in default of which the party must take a circuitous route overland. Gill would be in charge of the group and would make the decision whether or not to attempt the crossing of the shore lead, I said. Jamie thrust his face into mine.

'I know just as much about ice as Gill. I will make up my own mind.' He launched into a familiar litany of abuse, that was utterly irrelevant. I explained as temperately as I could that his field experience with ice was far less than Gill's. She would decide, I repeated. He ranted some more. Gill was reliable, I countered, and reminded him of his recent statement that he would not be bound by any agreement. He made no reply to this, only abused me for lying, he did not say what or when, and insisted that he would make his own decisions about doing whatever, when and where he pleased.

I could take no more. Disregarding safety instructions could mean the loss of our lives. We could not afford to risk crossing the Southern Ocean with this man.

'I am dismissing you from the expedition,' I said and turned away from him. I reiterated that Gill would be in charge of the field party and presently they went off. Jamie followed them, having apparently forgotten the original cause of his outburst. The o/ic Davis, when contacted by radio, was immediately helpful.

'I made arrangements when you saw me in Davis in July,' he said. 'Hobart agreed then to return any misfits to Australia. Have him pack his gear and I will pick him up by helicopter this evening. I am going direct to Melbourne on the *Nella Dan* in two days and I will take him with me.'

That evening I duly signed a document taking personal responsibility for any costs incurred in the repatriation and a sad and sorry Jamie with his belongings was flown out to Davis. No one except Norm even waved goodbye. We were all a little subdued and sorry for Jamie that he had brought things to this pass, but we were relieved too – a cloud had been lifted.

Norm's opinion of the incident was once more different. 'Lewis dismissed Jamie. For some time Jamie had been our regular and willing supplier of ice for melting into fresh water. The sea ice was now broken into floes, and agility and sure-footedness were needed when man-hauling ice blocks across the tricky surface. Jamie had proved to be safe and reliable on this chore, and, naturally, he objected when Lewis tried to insist that he follow the lead of Gill across rotting ice to the bird cliffs.' Norm goes on to say how conscious I was of the 'little empire' that I headed.

Such misconceptions show how necessary was firm leadership. Drinking ice was collected just outside Winterover Bay. Jamie had not been anywhere near the bird cliffs for weeks and not since the ice had deteriorated. Gill was there nearly every day. Her 116 man-days in the field and her general responsibility contrasted with Jamie's thirty-one and his unimpressive performance record.

Norm's comments apart, the dismissal of one of the party was a serious step which had only been taken after consultation with the four most responsible people. Once again, as when I had decided to call *Polar Star* to our aid, I was forced to face a decision that would inevitably reflect on independent expeditions and my own reputation. It was the lives of the party against my good name, so there was no real choice.

Was the decision right? Yes, it was. A better leader with a stronger party could perhaps have 'carried' Jamie. But I myself could not; the safety of the enterprise demanded that he go.

We were no longer surprised at how avidly the ANARE press spokes-man made hay with this poor man's dismissal. Every year misfits are evacu-ated from Australian and other national bases, always discreetly so as not to cause them added pain. Not so this time. *News* of Darwin of 25 January 1984, for instance, reported:

> Martin Betts, information officer with Australian National Antarctic Expeditions (ANARE), said the bill for returning Mr Miller would be sent to him or the Sydney-based Ocean Research Foundation which sponsored the trip . . . He said 'personality clashes' aboard the *Explorer* had caused Mr Miller's early return. He said the bill would be round $1000.
> 'They should all be thankful we're not billing them for the other services we provided,' he said. 'U.S., Australian and Russian icebreakers had been called to help the expedition last year.'

Who would have guessed that we had, unpaid, made major contribu-tions to the ANARE research programme, which would have cost the Australian taxpayer several hundred thousand dollars? It is only fair to add that, as was eventually admitted, the threat to bill ORF was un-authorized. We have a host of similar press cuttings with which we will not bore the reader.

There was still a frustrating wait before we could extricate *Explorer*, but the shipboard atmosphere had improved out of all recognition. The well-tried snowmobile was hoisted on deck, dismantled and lowered into the hold. The propeller was reconnected to the shaft. The dump ashore was dismantled and its contents loaded aboard. The sails were overhauled and all rents were carefully repaired; the navigation instruments were checked.

Norm's natural good humour and willingness to be helpful increasingly asserted itself and he became a much more cooperative member of the team. He was not required to stand watches at sea, which were difficult for him, but he was generally pleasant and did his best.

Mimi insists on inserting a personal note here on her own performance as deputy leader: She writes:

> David has already mentioned a number of his mistakes, and I, of course, was far from being error free. I want to make plain what I see as my own worst shortcoming.
> The expedition would not have stood so good a chance of success if I had been in charge because I tended to be far too sharp in handling sloppiness, especially early on in the venture. All my life, whether at sea, at work or in academia, I had interacted with fairly responsible people who were striving to do things well, or else I washed my hands

of them. The experience of having to constantly manage irrational and negative attitudes had never before come my way.

David, with more experience and understanding, grasped from the first that we must not ask too much. He was more prepared to accept the limitations of people who were ultimately victims of circumstances for which they were unprepared, and for which we were responsible. David would have given more 'perks' (like film) to promote harmony, whereas I responded to poor performance too rigidly. I did not see why Gill and Jannik, who kept to the simple rules, should yield precious film to those who flouted them. David, on the other hand, saw sooner and more clearly than I did that personal limitations must needs be accepted and that management consisted largely of nurturing whatever was positive and letting slide everything that was not absolutely necessary.

David's sense of proportion in these human matters, as well as his mastery of general strategic planning, were the real keys to our success as an expedition.

Both of us were at fault in failing to establish better 'one to one' relationships with the others. They felt, I am sure, that there was a lack of access to us as individuals. We did make an effort to overcome this, by going on day trips with the others in turn, for example, but we did not do it consistently enough.

Despite our mistakes, all research goals had been achieved and everyone was happier. More specimens were boxed up and piled ashore to be picked up by Davis helicopters for shipping to Australia. We ourselves were amazed at the sheer bulk of what we had collected. The corpse of a 60lb emperor penguin, that had died of mysterious natural causes at Amanda Bay and which we had brought back with us, was disinterred from the snowdrift where it was buried and forwarded to Davis for a post-mortem.

Gavin Johnstone, chief biologist at the Antarctic Division, expressed his appreciation of our work in a long telegram. Our biological information was 'of real value to our [ANARE's] programmes in particular and to the biology of the region in general'. He congratulated us especially on our first-hand observations at Amanda Bay.

But as January wore on we watched the slow melting of the ice with increasing impatience. It occurred mostly around the edges of the bay and round *Explorer* herself, so that she floated free, linked with the shore by her warps and the rubber duck. A most welcome visitor was Captain Gisli Gunnarson, master of *Nanook S*, who very kindly flew down to acquaint us with pack ice conditions. There was an unusual amount of fast ice along the coast, he told us, but the pack to seaward was relatively open. Even Mirny would probably be accessible if we broke out in time to make the passage. This was good news indeed; though frustrating because we could not immediately make use of it.

If the ice did not break out at all, which was unlikely but not impossible, Mimi and I decided we would let the others go home and stay with the ship.

'We would only need more gas and some birth control pills,' said Mimi. 'Some more coffee and chocolate for sledging rations would help too. With what we have learned, we could make some terrific over-ice journeys next winter, at least as far as the Amery Ice shelf, and further – who knows? It would be great to find out if the rough ice was still in the same place. We could see if the anchorage at Inner Brattstrandoyane looked as good two years in a row.'

We were not to get the opportunity. Leads began to open up in the ice sheet that blocked the entrance to Winterover Bay and we went sounding in the rubber duck. The depth of water at the ice margin was seven feet, just our draught. Perhaps we could make it at high water? On 26 January we made our move.

We break out

The day was warm and windless. We made one final check with the Beaufort, then *Explorer* was swung round on her lines until she faced seaward, the warps were cast off and we steamed dead slow out of Winterover Bay, our home for eleven eventful months. It was half an hour before high water. The margin was desperately thin as we edged along a narrow shore lead. Twice we grounded, but by dint of pushing with the rubber duck and going full astern we got off again and were able to get past by crunching through the edge of the bay ice. The next stage was easier, down a lead that had opened across the middle of the sound to where we found to our dismay that the ice had moved in since the day before and now abutted against a rocky point of land in our path.

The ice between the schooner and the next stretch of shore lead appeared weak, however, so we backed up for room to get up speed, and charged it. *Explorer*'s bow slid up over the ice edge and four feet beyond until the ice broke under her weight. Cracks opened up ahead. Again and yet again the manoeuvre was repeated until the ship was able to squeeze through.

'Didn't know we had an icebreaker, did you?' Jannik laughed.

There was not far to go now, but the same ice movement that had necessitated the 'icebreaking' had brought a huge floating ice sheet hard up against the rocky shore ahead. There was no way past for the moment, so we positioned the ship in a lead, put out anchors on to the ice and settled down to wait for a change. The change came abruptly early next morning. A strong northeast wind came up without warning, blowing the ice clear of the land but simultaneously rapidly narrowing the lead in which we were moored. There was only enough time to get in the anchors, start the motor and squeeze out between the closing margins before the lead was obliterated.

At last *Explorer* was in the clear. Mimi and Gill motored ashore in the inflatable, bouncing over the miniature whitecaps to climb the bird cliffs to take photographs of the schooner emerging from the sound into the open, then rejoined us where we drifted, waiting for them. It was with nostalgic memories that we skirted the bird cliffs and penguin rookeries, passed Lookout Islands and motored along the long front of the Sørsdal, all places replete with mixed memories. I for one had the greatest difficulty in equating these same places at sea when we had so recently traversed them on six feet of ice. The two Sørsdal ice caves and the tottering bluff beyond, that we had thought about to collapse at any moment, and that we had squeezed past with such trepidation last winter, were still intact, we noticed with amusement; our alarm on that memorable occasion had been uncalled for!

But if one stage of the expedition was completed, our involvement with Antarctica was far from over. Motoring up the Vestfold Hills shoreline with its indentations and off-lying islands in the teeth of a brisk north-easter, I stupidly steered in too close. There was a violent thump and a screech of tortured metal and we were aground on a rocky shelf. Fortunately the steep waves and the strong wind helped us bump our way astern and back off. The bilges remained dry; the hull was not holed. No credit to me. Carelessness is never excusable in the Antarctic and I had been guilty of relaxing my vigilance. The ship could easily have been lost on that rock and I would have been entirely to blame.

Two LARC's (amphibious vehicles) escorted us into Davis and to a warm welcome from Phil Elliott, the cordial and extremely competent new o/ic, and from all the station personnel. The base's hospitality on this occasion surpassed, if that were possible, anything we had previously known.

Towards Mirny

The Canadian supply ship *Lady Franklin*, under Australian charter, dropped anchor off the base, bringing with her the film and cameras that *National Geographic* had arranged to be shipped to us by the first ship of the year, but which had been unaccountably delayed in Hobart. Captain Gordon Williams of *Lady Franklin* was able to give us the latest ice information, including the news that there was relatively open water clear to Mirny, the Soviet base 700 miles to the eastward. N. K. Dimitriev, leader of Mirny base, radioed me: 'We will be glad to see you at Mirny. Sorry but this year ice conditions here are very bad. Today our cargo vessel the *Mikhail Somov* with its ice protection cannot yet pick the way to Haswell Island [three miles to seaward of the base]. Your visit may be fulfilled with the help of our helicopter . . .'

After four enjoyable days we bade farewell to our friends at Davis on 31 January and skirted the main pack until we could lay course more or less direct for Mirny. With a great deal of ice about and predominantly head winds, conditions were tricky. I took Jannik on my watch, Mimi took Gill. The passage was trying and hazardous and arduous in the extreme with only four people to work the ship, but the morning of 8 February found us working our way between bergs and fields of old heavy pack to within a stone's throw of Haswell Island, no more than three miles from Mirny. The buildings of the base were clearly visible on the mainland beyond. Further progress was blocked by a hell's brew of jostling floes that could be threaded neither by *Explorer* nor by the rubber duck. Nor could they be traversed on foot. After ascertaining that the lee side of the island was totally inaccessible, we moored to a stranded berg, setting two anchors firmly into the crystalline surface of a ledge. A watch was set while we waited on events. Gill, whose turn it was, suddenly cried out. The berg was moving and had evidently floated off at high tide. There was not a moment to be lost, for the iceberg, with us in the van, was rapidly bearing down on a massive wall of consolidated pack, against which we would be crushed. With desperate haste, Gill and I wrenched out the anchors, flung them aboard anyhow and scrambled over the rail as Mimi, who was at the helm, gunned the motor and we slid clear just in time. We were all a bit shaken at our narrow escape. We had reason to be grateful to Gill for her vigilance. It began to snow heavily and a rising gale set in.

The Mirny radio operator, speaking in excellent English, gave us the worst news of all. The helicopter, that could have picked us up from Haswell Island, which we could have reached with the rubber duck, was no longer at Mirny. It had gone out aboard *Mikhail Somov* a few days before so there was absolutely no means of access to the base. Well, there was no point in risking the ship any longer in its exposed and dangerous position, especially with the weather deteriorating. It had to be a case of 'hello-goodbye', so, with expressions of '*Dos Vedanya*', we took our departure and shaped course direct for Sydney, 3,250 miles to the northeast.

There came an unpleasant surprise. The fuel pump to the header tank in the engine room sucked dry. According to the engine log there were supposed to be 800 litres still in the tanks, but when the inspection covers were removed we found them to be bone dry. Galley kerosene had to be used to run the motor. The only comfort was that once clear of the pack there would soon be wind and to spare to speed us on our way.

Storm-driven

Antarctica, of course, did not release us all that easily. Every iceberg in the world seemed to be drifting outside Mirny, interspersed with great rafts of pack that stretched across our path, necessitating frequent changes of course. Sea fogs and blinding snowstorms compounded our difficulties for days. Without the radar things would have been very difficult. Icebergs showed up with perfect clarity, so that there were only the growlers, bergy bits and pack ice to worry about. Some forty miles beyond Mirny is Drygalski Island. We passed within two miles of it and saw nothing through the fog, though the radar revealed an iceberg that was at least twelve miles long fronting the island's position.

That first week from Mirny, which lies astride the Antarctic Circle in 66°.30'S, and where the variation of the compass is upwards of 90°W, took us 600 miles northward through the zone of the polar easterlies. Shortly thereafter, the westerlies began and steadily increased in intensity. On 16 February the last iceberg was seen in 58°.30'S and we entered the kingdom of storms.

Every one or two days, intense low-pressure frontal systems drove by. The wind would peak at the very edge of hurricane intensity, with the schooner, snugged down to jib alone, surging and surfing at eight and nine knots when, unlike a modern maxi ocean racer, she was almost unmanageable. The days that followed were a veritable ride of the Valkyries.

It was full dark in the night watches now and we were mightily relieved to be clear of the menace of growlers – hard ice cores of melted bergs rolling awash and invisible on radar, that could split the ship open at the speed she was often going. To balance things, a module, for which there was no replacement aboard, went out on the autopilot. It was hand steering all the way from now on and exhausting it was for the four of us.

On 19 February *Explorer* was racing along eastward under big jib alone beam-on to a force ten northerly gale. As the barometer bottomed at 981 mb, the wind backed suddenly to northwest in a furious line squall of force twelve, hurricane strength. The tops were blown off the waves and came at us horizontally so that the sea was white with driving spray and foam. Visibility was minimal. By an old nautical definition hurricane force (65 knots) winds are those in which 'no sail can stand'. Despite the strength of modern materials, ours were to be no exception. A sheet parted and within seconds, abetted by my dithering, the sturdy jib had flogged itself to pieces. This was a blow. The tiny storm jib that remained to us was adequate for these latitudes but no more than a pocket handkerchief for the temperate breezes we should encounter further north. Despite this mishap and the lack of an autopilot, *Explorer* logged a creditable 829 miles that second week out from Mirny.

Plankton sampling was scheduled at the Antarctic Convergence, which we found centred on the 53rd parallel and crossed on 21–22 February with sea temperatures climbing from +4.8°C to +7°C. Sampling was complicated by a rising gale. Gill gallantly performed at the plankton pump on deck, pumping sea water through filters until it grew too rough for her to continue safely and the project had to be terminated. The continuing heavy weather was taking a toll of the courageous young woman, who was a prey to seasickness whenever the weather was bad. Since this was almost all the time now, she became progressively paler and more wan. She would force herself to come on watch like a walking zombie. But she never once failed to turn up on time ready and willing to play her full part. It hurt to watch her suffering so bravely, but there was no one else to take her place. It was not until the last quiet night before land that we were able to send her to bed for a whole night while the rest of us split her watch between us.

The wind kept increasing beyond the Convergence, and in the early hours of 24 February, in 50°S latitude, a northwest gale was once again reaching force twelve. The seas were confused and broke unpredictably across the deck, occasionally crashing right over the wheelhouse. As daylight strengthened we saw that a small rip had opened in the foresail; we hastily downed it and continued under our 'pocket handkerchief' alone. So strong was the wind that, despite this minimal rig, the noon to noon day's run was 120 miles. As soon as the weather moderated a little we stowed the torn foresail below and replaced it with the mizzen, the least useful sail on the ship. Before long the schooner was making nine knots again in the squall, even with this small sail double reefed.

A few days later, however, we were approaching Tasmania and the winds eased, leaving us under-canvassed without big jib or mizzen. An unfamiliar problem confronted us. Hitherto only wind, ice and weather had dictated our timetables; now things were different. The ORF, which was arranging a welcome in Sydney, important to the thousands who had contributed to make the expedition possible, was naturally anxious to set a deadline for our arrival, preferably at a weekend. But since we had only the little fuel which remained in the galley kerosene, and because the winds would become lighter and more variable the further north we went, it was going to be no easy matter to time our landfall. The ORF was able to arrange, by special dispensation of customs and immigration, that we should be met at Wollongong, sixty miles short of our destination, by a Channel 7 crew bearing with them extra fuel necessary for the detour. This would allow us to arrive at Pier One in Sydney, whence we had departed so long ago, at noon the day after.

So far, so good. But could we make the Wollongong rendezvous on time? We pressed on in light winds as February drew towards a close. If only there were one more day, we were sure we could make it! To our delight, there was one. Instead of 1 March, 29 February came up on the clever sat. nav.'s computer. It was Leap Year!

Four days on into March and three and a half weeks from Mirny, the dim outline of Maria Island off Tasmania's east coast broke the horizon. The breezes became erratic but never failed altogether, and we hove-to off Wollongong in bright sunshine on the morning of 10 March. This was a different world from that to which we had grown accustomed, one full of half-forgotten delights. The scents of the land; the city backed by bush-clad ranges; the golden beaches thronged with bathers. Two friendly coastguards in a motor boat came alongside and, when they learned who we were, departed for a favourite fishing ground, returning with a load of fish they had caught for us. Welcome Australia!

The camera crew brought us red wine, and the last night at sea was spent in holiday spirit motor-sailing up the coast. The welcome in Sydney on 11 March from the crowd that awaited us was unforgettable. Dick Smith and other notables spoke and afterwards we were whisked away as guests of the Ramada Inn.

But for me the most touching greeting was from my granddaughter Jaquie and my daughter-in-law Roslyn. My son Barry was at sea. Vicky was on tour in Western Australia and Susie, now living in Paris, was also studying dance. My eldest daughter, Anna, was also far away, in Oxford, where she is a lecturer at Trinity College.

'Grandpa!' cried Jaquie, as she threw herself at me, and 'Grandma!' as she hugged Mimi.

It was hard to realize that the expedition was over. We had traversed 4,000 miles of ocean since the Rauers. During the past sixteen months of endeavour and experience each person's individual dream had not perhaps turned out as imagined. Nevertheless, all could hold up their heads; the trials had been severe and few would have had the guts to tackle them. Our experience had, in a real sense, been the stuff of sagas, the raw material of poetry. Despite setbacks and disappointments, nothing could take that away from us.

Taking stock

This was the moment to look back on what we had done. Four of us had been on field trips sledging over sea ice and living in tents in all weathers and in all seasons for 124 days, or four months in all. Two others had done increasingly useful work over a more restricted range. Over-ice field trips had been mounted in each of the eleven months (March to January inclusive) that the sea had been frozen. Our activities had been conducted along a sixty-mile stretch of coastline. The total distance travelled over the sea ice while living in tents during those eleven months had been 830 miles, half on foot and half with the snowmobile, and of this 830 miles 650 had been outside the shelter of any islands. We had a systematic record of our experiences as a small group under stressful conditions. The party had to its credit the tagging of 720 seals, a total in excess of that of Davis, the collection of lichen specimens from twenty-five remote bluffs and islands, and much more.

In terms of sea-ice travel and year-round field work in rigorous condi-

tions with simple equipment, no women in the history of Antarctic exploration could match the accomplishments of Mimi and Gill.

The research results were positive beyond expectation. All major
objectives were accomplished. The next party to winter a small ship need
not make the mistakes we did. The fast ice of Prydz Bay proved eminently
suitable for safe winter and spring travel between the Rauers and the
Larsemanns. The view southwest from the Larsemanns, together with
satellite imagery, suggests that the ice would be more stable and very
possibly smoother all the way to the Amery Ice Shelf. Thus a party put
down by helicopter, with a prefabricated hut and snowmobiles, to winter
at Amanda Bay, say, would have over-ice access to more than 100 miles
of coastline that would otherwise be inaccessible for at least nine months
of the year.

Apart from the intriguing connotations of people's interactions with
distant frontiers that Mimi discusses in Appendix One, and our over-ice
and ice wintering studies, research carried on in cooperation with outside
bodies like ANARE played a big part in our story, as the narrative makes
clear. What should be pointed out again here is that our volunteer party
did work which would normally have occupied several highly paid scientists with expensive logistic support and that we functioned in places which
for most of the year were beyond their reach.

Norm has written, 'We have proved the viability of wintering in a small
vessel and leaving the land mass unaltered at our departure, suggesting
that in the interests of conservation and economy, a large ice-strengthened
ship could also be used as a base, to be moved to new locations as
required.' He goes on to criticize my 'denigrating' two of the crew. This is
the question I would like now to address.

In any account of an expedition, the decision on how fully to reveal
shortcomings is a thorny one. I have tended towards frankness for the
very good reason that our experiences will be worthless to others if I gloss
over them. What was deemed commendable restraint in the days of
Shackleton and Scott has been shown by modern scholarship to be
downright misleading, and people are no longer content to wait three-
quarters of a century to learn the truth. I have certainly made no secret of
my own mistakes: the groundings at Flinders, in Wintercover Bay and off
the Vestfolds; my poor judgement in entering the pack in the wrong place
in February 1983 and, earlier still, using slipshod selection procedures.

There is an Antarctic myth which has arisen because of too-restrained
reporting (for this continent, only 165 years old in terms of human aware-
ness, has spawned its myths and sagas aplenty) about the 1946–8 Finn
Ronne Expedition. The myth is that Edith (Jackie) Ronne and Jean
Darlington, who we mentioned were the first women ever to winter in
Antarctica, split the expedition, and this myth was used to keep out women
for the next twenty years. Conflict did develop, it is true, but the cause of

it was not between the women at all. It was over the issue of command, not over some supposed 'women's empires' as has been pretended for so long.

Jackie Ronne effectually managed the base during her husband's absences in the field, because a deputy who had challenged Ronne's leadership had in consequence been relieved. In other words, polarization occurred round loyalty to the expedition itself and the causes were not personal relationships or gender at all. But the myth that things had been otherwise, and the male exclusivism it helped to reinforce, has persisted now for upwards of thirty-seven years, all *because the real facts were not clearly stated at the time.*[2] We have tried to avoid such a failure of communication, for Antarctica deserves to be engaged only with honesty and humility. It is up to the reader to judge how well or ill I have succeeded.

We are repeatedly asked about the cost of the expedition. This is a difficult question to answer because so much was donated, but I will do my best.

In round figures the total costs of the two expeditions, 1981–2 and 1982–4, were:

Capital costs		
Purchase of schooner		$90,000
Fitting out, alterations,		
Instruments, etc.		$110,000
	Total	$200,000
Running costs of the two		
expeditions		$140,000
	Total	$340,000
Estimated cash value of		
donations of food and equipment		$100,000

By way of comparison, the cost of maintaining an official base for a year runs into millions.

[2] Finn Ronne's later book, *Antarctic Command*, more than made up for this deficiency. It is one of the frankest stories ever written.

II

Whither Antarctica?

One last task awaited us after our return. The very success of the previous 1981–2 expedition, together with flowery press coverage beyond our control, had impelled a few individuals to play fast and loose with the media. Channel 7 TV, making use of the film Mimi had taken, and the ORF Board, publicizing our radio reports, had done their best to disseminate the truth and had had not a little success.

There were red faces among our detractors, but to make doubly sure and to build firmer bridges of cooperation, the two of us hired a car and repaired to Canberra and then Hobart prepared to do battle if necessary. It was not. The responsible Federal Minister and the newly appointed Acting Director of the Antarctic Division were in tune with our ideas and the one-time information officer had been transferred to other duties. The scientists were grateful for our specimens and data. The role of independent expeditions was now better appreciated, as, indeed, it always had been by the majority of ANARE. While prejudice and double standards will never completely go away, there is every reason to anticipate that the more harmonious relationships that are already in evidence will continue in the future. More on this subject later.

Antarctic Treaty perspectives

This is a larger question, of course, than the role of independents; what is being currently debated concerns the very future of man's engagement with Antarctica. A World Park idea was put forward by New Zealand in 1975, but was turned down flat by the other countries. *Euphausia Superba* or rill, the little shrimp upon which the great whales, fish, penguins and winged seabirds all feed, was then being lauded as mankind's future sea food bonanza. Since then, krill's high fluoride content, its swarming behaviour, winter retreat beneath the sea ice and reverse growth pattern in bad years has led to second thoughts. Claims as to krill's ultimate potential have become much more muted but it is still being harvested relentlessly, prompting fears that heavy capital investment in specialized trawlers may lead to disastrous over-fishing. Much depends on the renegotiation of the treaty, which is on the agenda for 1991. Third World countries have often been critical of the monopoly exercised by the treaty powers and some are lobbying for the continent to be declared 'the Common Heritage of Mankind'. However, as we mentioned in Chapter 1, several developing countries have now become consultative members, India, China, Uruguay and Brazil having established bases, and small nations like Papua New Guinea and Cuba having acceded to the treaty. Environmentalists, for their part, have entered a plea that Antarctica be declared an International Wilderness Park, where activities such as mining would be strictly controlled.

Fortunately for the cause of conservation (which the treaty powers have generally supported), Antarctic oil and minerals are unlikely to be commercial propositions for some time to come. The continent is 95 per cent overlaid by ice and the ores so far found in the exposed areas have been uniformly low-grade. Icebergs, depth of water and pack ice render offshore oil drilling hazardous and costly, though perhaps most imminent off the Antarctic Peninsula for political reasons, namely the intense national rivalry between Argentina and Chile, who are both doing everything they can to bolster their territorial claims – to the same area. Krill and fish apart, the danger to Antarctica's fragile ecosystem by commercial development, while real, seems to have been exaggerated.

Let no one forget, however, that the ecosystem *is* fragile, nor must we underestimate mankind's potential for suicidal environmental mischief. In Chapter 1 we mentioned some dangers: there are more. The West Antarctic ice sheet, for instance, presses the underlying land down below sea level (East Antarctica is considerably higher), so that the ice rests, somewhat precariously, it is believed, on the sea bed. This potential instability is borne out by a geological history of wide fluctuations. Total disappearance of the west ice sheet would raise the level of the oceans by twenty feet. Though any such cataclysm is unlikely to occur suddenly, the scenario for a slow melt is a very real one and a resulting rise in sea level of only six feet or so could have distinctly awkward effects.

Perilous frontier

While the dangers of Antarctic living and of travel by land, sea and air have been used as an excuse for keeping outsiders at bay, they are nevertheless very real and must never be underestimated. The point is, of course, that they strike at governmental and private projects equally.

By way of illustration, here is a random selection of mishaps due to pack ice during the 1985–6 season.

Nella Dan, that was mentioned in our story, and whose complement included Jenni Bassett and Paul Ensor from our Mawson Anniversary Expedition, was trapped for fifty-two days. The powerful German *Icebird*, under Australian charter, failed to free her and was herself beset for a time. Eventually the Japanese icebreaker *Shirase* released her.

Then *Kapitan Bondarenko* was stranded in the ice for 133 days off Marie Byrd Land and broke her rudder. Helicopters from her sister ship *Mikhail Somov* flew off 100 three-ton loads to lighten her, and the rudder was repaired by the ship's own divers and engineers.

Meanwhile the British *John Biscoe*, on which I 'hitched a ride' south in 1973, was trapped and abandoned, her crew being taken off by the US *Polar Duke*. The more powerful German *Polarstern* later was able to put the crew back aboard and break the ship out.

A private British expedition ship was crushed in the ice of the Ross Sea and sunk; this we will come to later. The point is made, I think, that no single ship, no matter how strong, is ever completely safe in pack. It is only the magnificent cooperation of vessels of all nations, such as we ourselves experienced, that keeps the supply lines open. It will also be apparent that independent vessels have no monopoly of the sea ice troubles.

Colonization and independents – democratization of Antarctica

Presumed danger is by no means the only reason why independents have so often been hampered by officialdom. Here is the reason, told by Paul Dalrymple, editor of the Antarctican Society Journal of Washington DC, why Sir Hubert Wilkins never got to fly over the South Pole. This Australian explorer and North Pole overflight pioneer was the first man to fly in Antarctica, the first man to go under the ice in a submarine, and was Stefansson's loyal lieutenant when in command of the schooner *North Star* (which he winched up onto the floes whenever she was beset). But 'he had made the mistake,' writes Paul, 'of giving an honest interview to a reporter, which soon found its way back to McMurdo, resulting in his being ostracized by the admiral whose ego matched his drinking, and who was not receptive to anything derogatory'. We were in good company!

Why, it may well be asked, out of all the private expeditions in the field during the two-year span of our expeditions, was ours the one singled out for attack? Both Heard Island ventures took place while we were in the south. So too did Rick Ridgway's and Chris Bonnington's daringly conceived ascent by a new route of Antarctica's highest mountain, the 4,897-metre Vinson Massif, when they used for their approach a three-engined turbo-prop DC3, refuelled by the Chileans. This Seven Summits Expedition was an international one, including Americans, Japanese and

English. The plane's pilot was Captain Giles Kershaw, who had made a name for himself with the British Trans-Globe expedition. The Trans-Globe party had already crossed Antarctica and was approaching the North Pole when we were at Commonwealth Bay and were in radio contact with them. But these were more adventures than scientific undertakings; could this be the reason we were singled out? Were we seen as trespassers in a closed preserve? We do not know.

Roland Huntford, whom we quoted in Chapter 1, has written: 'The National Science Foundation in Washington virtually dictates American Antarctic policy. It has worried countries like Britain, New Zealand and Australia, which maintain a modest presence in Antarctica, by banning private expeditions in favour of an official monopoly.... Chile and Argentina, however, have ignored American remonstrances, and blithely allow private expeditions to use their bases on the Antarctic Peninsula. It is the first visible crack in the treaty structure.' It is significant that it was Chile that supplied fuel to Ridgeway's and Bonnington's DC3.

Nevertheless, there are signs of a more liberal attitude even where America's writ runs most strongly. In the summer of 1984–5 *Explorer* was back in Commonwealth Bay in an operation called Project Blizzard, whose aim was to survey Mawson's historic hut to find out how best to save it. The schooner's skipper was Don Richards and the veteran Arctic and Antarctic explorer Colin Putt (who is now president of ORF) was engineer. The undertaking had the full backing of the Australian Government, a far cry from 1978, when an identical proposal by the ORF led to us being sternly warned off. In the following 1985–6 season the Government went further by allocating Project Blizzard a grant of $20,000 and providing logistic support.

Independent expeditions apart, representatives of non-governmental, primarily conservation organizations have been included as observers on several of the official delegations that are currently discussing the future of Antarctica.

But while Australian policy has been becoming more liberal, the same cannot be said of the American naval bureaucracy at McMurdo. The 1985–6 season was the worst for ice in the Ross Sea for twenty years. The British Footsteps of Scott expedition ship *Southern Quest*, an ice-strengthened Icelandic trawler, which had landed the sledging party and their prefabricated hut on Ross Island the previous year, was returning in January 1986 with a ski-equipped Cessna 185 to bring back the successful sledgers from the South Pole. The redoubtable Giles Kershaw, who flew the plane, is widely considered Antarctica's premier pilot, but the McMurdo authorities asked him not to fly and US aircraft brought back the trekkers from South Pole Station.

Meanwhile *Southern Quest* was beset and sunk. The twenty-one men and women aboard set up tents on a floe, from which they were picked up by helicopters from our old friend *Polar Star*. The castaways were subsequently flown to New Zealand. This praiseworthy rescue was somewhat marred by the McMurdo command. Paul Dalrymple writes: 'However, there were some ruffled feathers, supposedly including some of the personnel at both McMurdo and Scott, about the treatment of the private expedition. A letter with 56 signatories told their tale. The Royal Geographic Society sent a long letter to the London *Times* on 24 March . . . about "Obstacles in the steps of Scott." They got a bunch of knights (Fuchs, Hunt, Scott, Shackleton, Hemming and Bishop) . . . to sign the letter. The only residual seems to be that authorities have banned the three expedition members wintering over from visiting Scott and McMurdo, except for the use of the post office at Scott! Who would want to visit a post office when no mail is incoming or outgoing?'

Letter to *The Times*:

Obstacles in the steps of Scott

From Lord Shackleton and others Sir, There have been a number of statements and criticisms of the 'In the footsteps of Scott' expedition, both as to the competence of its members and their right to be in the Antarctic. We believe these criticisms are unfair and unjustified.

'In the footsteps of Scott' was a unique expedition. Robert Swan, Roger Mear and Gareth Wood set out to walk to the South Pole manhauling their sledges, recalling Captain Scott's epic journey. While it never pretended to be anything but a commemorative adventure retracing Scott's and Shackleton's route, it did have a limited scientific programme.

In view of its exceptional nature, extra care was taken to examine the membership and logistics of the expedition before the Royal Geographical Society decided to support this highly professional venture. On January 11, 1986, the three men reached the South Pole.

Simultaneously with the arrival at the Pole, the support ship Southern Quest was crushed by the ice and sank off McMurdo Sound. Whatever its limitations may have been, the ship had been ice-strengthened and passed to Lloyds Ice Class III. Stronger ships than Southern Quest have encountered serious trouble in Antarctic waters this season.

The Institute of London Underwriters paid the full £100,000 for total loss within four days of her sinking. Arrangements have also been made through the same route to pay the bill rendered by the United States authorities for £21,000, for subsequently flying the expedition from McMurdo to New Zealand.

The captain, Graham Phippen, with eight years' experience with the British Antarctic Survey, was duty-bound, after the loss of his ship, to take up the offer of American helicopter assistance. Had that help not been available, the crew could have made landfall themselves; but the prudent choice was to accept the generous help offered.

Meanwhile the aircraft which had been dismantled in Australia and shipped down on Southern Quest had already been offloaded and flown. Thus Captain Giles Kershaw (one of the most experienced of polar pilots) was fully prepared to take off for the Pole to retrieve Swan, Mear and Wood. But the United States officials, who had already accepted that his flight plan was feasible, asked him not to fly. He agreed to this as a matter of courtesy after the assistance given by the United States to the crew of Southern Quest. Consequently, the US authorities undertook to return the polar party to McMurdo.

Regretfully, we feel bound to comment on the quite extraordinary reaction to the expedition from certain Antarctic authorities arising out of their declared policy that they would not support 'private expeditions'. A letter signed by 56 members of McMurdo and Scott Base stations we think tells the tale.

After warmly congratulating the expedition the signatories went on to say: 'What we cannot accept is the shamefully hostile treatment of your group, the failure to extend to you access to communication facilities and restrictions placed upon personal interaction among us.'

Those who have heard the recording or read the transcripts of the official exchanges can only regard them as an aberration in stark contrast to the warm and generous reception of the expedition by those manning the South Pole, McMurdo and Scott Base Antarctic stations.

The expedition has left three men in the Antarctic to care for their hut and aircraft and to make sure that everything is removed next year, so as to leave Antarctica as they found it. These three men have been banned by the authorities from visiting Scott and McMurdo bases, except for the use of the post office at Scott Base. This means that normal Antarctic hospitality cannot be accorded to them without special permission.

The view has also been expressed by certain authorities that only governmental expeditions should participate in Antarctic work. We strongly support the scientific effort of the Government-based expeditions within the Antarctic Treaty, but to exclude properly planned and supported expeditions approved by societies such as ours is something that we cannot accept.

We write with two objectives in mind. One is to set the record straight. The expedition has been called 'a group of enthusiastic amateurs'; enthusiastic they are, but amateur certainly not. Secondly, in the light of the unfortunate happenings described above, we wish to see an understanding established that will preclude bureaucratic difficulties in the future.

Then we can expect the time-honoured amity that has always existed among polar explorers and scientists to continue within the Antarctic Treaty.
Yours sincerely,
SHACKLETON,
GEORGE BISHOP,
VIVIAN FUCHS,
JOHN HEMMING,
JOHN HUNT,
PETER SCOTT,
Royal Geographical Society,
Kensington Gore, SW7.
March 24.

The Ross Sea ice frustrated another venture, that of Greenpeace to set up a base on Ross Island. The nearest the ship could get was twenty miles away and, even with the use of her helicopter, the attempt had to be abandoned for that year.

In fact the only really successful Ross Sea venture seems to have been that of my son Barry and his four-man crew in the 47-foot steel yawl *Requita*. Advised by the experienced Jim Caffin of Christchurch, he did not leave Sydney until 10 January, and in consequence had an almost ice-free passage to Cape Hallett in 72°19'S. There 'the self-propelled tourists' (Barry's phrase) landed, but, being unable to obtain ice reports from McMurdo, prudently decided to retreat, having already been further south than any other yacht. They called at Cape Adare and Macquarie Island on the way home. 'A model expedition,' Jim Caffin told me.

On the Antarctic Peninsula at the other side of the continent, independent expeditions were making their mark this same 1985–6 season. No less than three parties, American, Canadian and South Korean, successfully climbed the remote Vinson Massif, all with Chilean Air Force logistic support. Two were flown in by Giles Kershaw.

For many years tourist ships and tourist overflights have been features of the polar scene. We may deplore or welcome these developments, but Antarctic tourist resorts can be anticipated in the near future. During the 1985–6 summer the tourist ship *World Discoverer* visited the British bases of Faraday twice and Signy once and the Society explorer visited Faraday four times. At least two hundred tourists went ashore at Faraday. Meanwhile Kershaw's Twin Otter aircraft became a familiar visitor to the British Rothera base.

But by far the most intriguing development to my mind has been the setting up of Adventure Network International (ANI) by a distinguished group of two Canadian climbers and one American in conjunction with the ubiquitous pilot Kershaw. They plan to open up Antarctica to teams of private explorers and mountaineers, and already operate research vessels, base camps and expedition services. Their 1985–6 season's operations, two Theron ascents and the air support for the Footsteps of Scott Expedition, have not been a bad beginning.

In January 1978 a new era opened for the ancient Antarctic continent, that had first felt the step of man only 156 years before. Emilio Marcos Palma was born on the Argentine base of Esperanza. He was the first native-born Antarctican.

Since then other children have been born at Esperanza. In 1984 Chile set up its own 'Village of the Stars' with six families at Teniente Marsh base (which peacefully shares a common water supply with the Soviet base of Bellingshausen in the same bay). Whatever the political-military motives for the setting up of these rather artificial settlements and no matter how marginally they skate past Antarctic Treaty provisions, men, women and children have clearly come to Antarctica to stay.

Family settlements, permanent tourist enclaves and the independent ventures scientific or sporting of men and women who feel the challenge of this land must necessarily become a part of the continent's future. Antarctica cannot, therefore, without grave detriment be allowed to become the ward of an international bureaucracy. There has to be a niche for adventure too.

Scott and his heroic men lugged 37 lb of geological samples all the way to their deaths. Amundsen, who was a professional explorer first and foremost, cared little for science and did no geological collecting. It seems to us that Scott's and Amundsen's approaches are equally valid; there is room for both attitudes.

The scale of man's wilderness activities is increasing all over the world. The Soviet school teachers who skied to the North Pole and their female colleagues who are planning a like private venture to the South Pole, the small expeditions we have been discussing, the growth of back packing and the like, show that the spirit of Amundsen and Scott is more alive than ever – and increasingly turning towards Antarctica. It is becoming a major target for adventurers, perhaps *the* target, until overtaken by outer space.

It is up to the treaty powers, therefore, to cooperate with responsible sport, tourist, environmental, private research and adventure organizations, to ensure that this wider human involvement with Antarctica develops with maximum harmony and safety. For it can no more be stopped than Canute could hold back the sea.

In conclusion I would like to quote a 1986 resolution passed by the highly respected New Zealand Antarctic Society and communicated by them to the Government.

> The New Zealand Antarctic Society fully supports the concept of private expeditions to Antarctica where these expeditions have an emphasis on planning and safety. History has shown such expeditions have played a valuable role in expanding our knowledge of the region. Further in recognition of the terms and principles of the Antarctic Treaty all parties involved in or with such expeditions should engage in frank and constructive consultation with a view to achieving mutual cooperation where possible.

We have already suggested that a clearing house for information and coordination of private/official projects should be set up by SCAR with representation from independent bodies like the ORF and polar tourist and aviation agencies. This would go far towards fulfilling our responsibilities to the last continent.

An appeal for participants

The ORF is carrying on. After the government-supported Mawson's hut survey in Commonwealth Bay, *Explorer* sought warmer climes, the Bismarck Sea off Papua New Guinea from May to September 1985, under charter to the Australian National University Prehistory Department. Mimi and I were members of the ANU party, a most rewarding research experience, though it seemed strange to be aboard the schooner again as passengers.

The ORF, which is tax-deductible in Australia, has continuing projects in hand and would welcome supporters and participants. The address is: PO Box 247, Windsor 2756, Australia.

The Inter-Polar Research Society

Light-hearted suggestions for a name like 'polar bear–penguin friendship society' had to be reluctantly turned down. This new group, non-profit and tax-deductible in the USA, has been set up by the McCune family, the Boelcskevys, Mimi and myself with other close friends, all of whom are potential expedition participants. Its membership is international, currently including Americans, Russians and Australians, and particular efforts are being made to recruit indigenous polar people. The accent of research is on the humanities and education, rather than the ORF's 'harder' science. A stout vessel has been acquired and expeditions are planned to Arctic Alaska, the Antarctic Peninsula, the Siberian Arctic and the tropical Pacific. Participants are welcome.

The society's address is: 3451-B, Vincent Drive, Pleasant Hill, California 94523. Telephone 415-9325809.

Appendix 1

The High Frontier – Antarctica and Space
by Mimi George

The two women and four men of our party, whose ages ranged from 24 to 65 and who had five national backgrounds, spent three months at sea and thirteen months in the Antarctic, of which eleven months were in physical isolation. The general relevance of our experience has been brought home to me by the spate of letters I am still receiving from the most diverse sources: space scientists, sailors, housewives, underwater researchers, an Everest mountaineer-psychologist, Antarcticans, climbers, wilderness adventurers, explorers in general, and one courageous Black man who for ten years has been an inmate of Georgia's death row. Many of these letters have contained requests for detailed data and clarifications about the small-group research project and its methodolgy. But many simply offered comments and criticism, or simply sought to exchange views on 'what it's like' under an astounding range of 'similar' conditions.

In presenting our preliminary findings here[1] I will draw on accounts from comparable situations. In 1983–5 Boeing published three space-station habitability studies, which reviewed the experiences of Soviet cosmonauts, US astronauts, US nuclear submarines and US Antarctic personnel as well as our own.[2]

When I read these reviews I better realized how relevant to space prob-

---

[1] These findings are based on preliminary analysis of *non-confidential* data only – i.e. ship's and field log entries, public events and discussions and systematic observations. Furthermore, much nominally non-confidential data supporting the preliminary conclusions is not presented here in order to avoid possible personal embarrassment. The untimely death of Professor Victor Turner, co-investigator of the project, has materially delayed more conclusive analysis to date. Some of the materials are still being evaluated by psychologists, sociologists and other specialist experts. Eventually I will complete the analysis, taking into account the specialist findings, from a broad anthropological point of view.

[2] *Space Station Habitability Design Recommendations*, Vol. 2, prepared by H. V. Jones, Boeing, Seattle, WA, 1984.

lems our experience was. Specifically, the dangers, isolation and time scale of our expedition made it a much better analogy to the human challenges of space station life than that of the modern Antarctic bases. Almost all of today's nationally sponsored Antarctic bases are virtually detached segments of America or Australia sealed off from the harsh surrounding environment. There can be little doubt that if our party had been living in such comfortable circumstances, significant polarization would not have occurred among ourselves and there would have been fewer lessons.

An observation from the Frozen Sea Expedition which reflects credit on every member of the group was that there was *never overt panic in the face of very real dangers*. The stresses were much greater than on large national bases. Our circumstances demanded a high standard of reliability. By the same token, there was ample scope for initiative and an imperative for meticulous performance. In short, it was a higher risk, higher gain enterprise.

Our worst difficulties were not with the environment, but with human problems, both within and without our expedition group. A major catalyst for low morale was when people were unable, because of the weather, or were unwilling, to leave the ship and engage the environment.

In our demanding situation, the party tended to polarize, and most noticeably so when the members felt themselves to be under stress of circumstances or the need to perform. This polarization occurred primarily around positions of *adherence to or dissociation from* the aims of the expedition, rather than around personality, sex, or nationality differences.

Disaffection manifested itself in antagonism to the objective purposes of the expedition and to the efforts of the leadership to have them fulfilled as well as unwillingness to engage the environment. Thus the number of man-days spent sledging in tents away from the ship for the four active people was 124, 124, 116, 116; for the other two, it was 31 and 19. Other symptoms of poor morale were staying in bunks much of the day in winter, not washing for months at a time, and further deterioration of performance.

General health correlated positively [3] with the degree of outdoor activity, two expeditioners tending to deteriorate in fitness, while four improved. There was a strong psychosomatic element here; for instance, a 58-year-old felt himself far more handicapped by moderately troublesome arthritis than did a 64-year-old with an artificial hip, damaged retina and sundry other physical disabilities.

On the other hand, the only physical damage was suffered by the more active expeditioners, in the form of an incident of hypothermia, a frostbitten big toe, and a tooth which succumbed to a frozen fruit bar and became the source of recurrent dental abscesses.

Ability to orient spatially and general competence in the field, as might

[3] The term *correlated* is used in its general sense as this is not a statistical study.

have been expected, correlated positively with the degree of engagement. It is noteworthy that the two least active people had in most respects the greatest previous snow experience. This appears to contradict Colin Irwin's conclusion that some people were good route-finders and others bad in any situation,[4] but in this case psychologically negative attitudes and unfamiliar stresses of field conditions clearly outweighed previous experience and skills.

Tensions which derived from normal personality differences and differing spheres of interesst as well as sexual frustrations and jealousies were only secondary factors in alienation, though their importance was certainly increased by stress and isolation. I offer the narrative, particularly the discussions of the role of sex, in support of this conclusion. Of even less importance were age, nationality and previous expedition experience.

Issues relating to mixed-sex parties that are currently being debated by a variety of researchers are performance, pairing, and sexual tensions. The performance of the women in our party compared favourably with that of the men. They did as much or more hard physical labour and field work, including every job that needed doing, and they carried out executive and coordinating responsibilities for every major programme of the expedition. The mixed-sex pairs were highly stable and effective working teams in which the women played crucial and often leading roles. This was true whether the paired persons were sexual partners or not. We have pointed out in Chapter 1 that the 1981–2 Mawson Anniversary party, which consisted of three couples, two unattached women and four unattached men, was exceptionally harmonious and free from sexual tensions. In the longer 1982–4 expedition, one couple (George and Lewis) long antedated the project of which they were organizers. The other couple formed en route, but polarization among the party was evident well before they paired, and the formation of this couple was observed to have had the effect of helping to stabilize the party as a whole.

The Boeing report reveals divergent opinions on the inclusion of women. At one extreme there is an Antarctic case of 'threats of aggression that bordered on murder'. On the other hand, the presence of women was thought by several US Antarcticans to 'exert a civilizing influence' and by Soviet cosmonauts to 'elevate relationships in a small team'.

The Soviets too have been hesitant to fully integrate women into their programmes, though it was they who put the first woman into space. Thus, the woman cosmonaut Savitskaya, who visited the 211–day Salyut space station in a Soyuz-T spacecraft, commented on women's participation: 'A hundred years from now no one will remember it, and if they do, it will sound strange that it was once questioned whether a woman should go into space.'

Neither American nor Soviet space organizations, nor the American

[4] Colin Irwin, 'Inuit Navigation', *The Journal of Navigation*, Vol. 38, No. 2, May 1985.

Navy, have as yet included married couples on their missions or on nuclear submarines. The opinion was expressed by some American Antarctic personnel that women in a party improved its tone but only if they avoided pairing. It should be recognized, however, that they were referring to a highly artificial situation, one or two women among thirty or so men, and thus tailor-made to cause tensions. An obvious solution is not to view women askance as potential sources of all evil, but to ensure something like equal numbers of each sex. The harmony of the Mawson Anniversary Expedition, when there were five women and seven men, and successful relations on innumerable mixed-sex long-distance yacht voyages, attest this common-sense view.

In the Frozen Sea Expedition, the more alienated expeditioners needed greater encouragement, imaginative management and support. They required organized recreative and escape activity and a higher frequency of communication with the outside world than their more positively involved team mates. There were varying attitudes towards radio contacts in our own party, two needing frequent messages from home and the others finding them to be more of a distraction.

Differences of opinion on this subject are equally apparent in the accounts quoted by Boeing and others. Some American researchers, including anthropologist Ben Finney,[5] think it likely that future space colonies will tend toward increasing cultural autonomy. Some Soviet experts say that it is 'still unclear whether it is better to facilitate or inhibit normal ground-based ties'. One pair of cosmonauts certainly had strong feelings on the matter, for they switched off all radio communications with mission control for *two whole days*!

During the first single-handed transatlantic yacht race David Lewis had no radio and, after a few days' adjustment, felt relaxed and at ease. Felicity Ann Davidson, the first woman to sail the Atlantic alone, felt the same. In the second race daily radio schedules quite upset Lewis's peace of mind. This was more or less our own experience on the Frozen Sea Expedition.

We have discussed leadership strategies at some length in the narrative. The degree of formal leadership required seems to correlate inversely with the level of homogeneity in the party. Thus only low-key management was needed in the 1981–2 venture, and even less was required on recent American Himalyan mixed-sex expeditions on which every member was an elite climber. The reverse was the case in 1982–4, when people's skills and motivation varied so widely. Command structure was felt by US astronauts to be a likely area of conflict, but they considered that in general the kind of management should be determined by the tasks involved. One American Antarctic base manager sensibly advocated 'few rules and a lot of common sense'. All agreed on the need for more authoritarian leadership in the face of crises.

[5] Ben R. Finney and Eric M. Jones, *Interstellar Migration and the Human Experience*, University of California Press, Berkeley, 1985.

In selecting expedition personnel we feel strongly that more emphasis should be placed on dedication to the undertaking than on technical credentials, no matter how impressive. Necessary qualities in an expeditioner are a high degree of motivation, integrity, reliability and initiative. He or she should also exhibit resourcefulness in the face of unforeseen circumstances.

Personality and compatibility are generally seen as particularly important in the selection of both American and Soviet space personnel. When training cosmonauts the Soviets insist on the importance of learning to function coolly in conditions of real-life stress. For instance, every cosmonaut has to carry out a minimum of 100 parachute jumps while performing tasks that become progressively more difficult. This is reminiscent of the US astronaut's emphasis on 'the right stuff'.

In conclusion I would like to express thanks to all those whose comments and suggestions have been so helpful at the talks and seminars I have given. In particular I would like to mention the personnel at NASA's Ames Space Station Research Center, the Antarctican Society, the Alaska Anthropology Conference, and various departments and organizations at the University of Virginia and the Institute of Ecotechnics in Aix-en-Provence.

Appendix 2

Rates and Mechanisms of Iceberg Ablation in the D'Urville Sea, Southern Ocean

By J. R. Keys and K. L. Williams

Introduction

Icebergs are a conspicuous and significant element of many polar seas. They drift and melt in euphotic surface waters influencing the upper part of the water column and hence may be biologically important, at least locally (Jacobs and others, 1981). Some Antarctic icebergs are potentially a valuable source of fresh water, if they can be successfully selected, transported north, and converted into economic quantities of water (Weeks and Campbell, 1973; Job, 1978). Icebergs transport and drop sediments contributing to marine sedimentary records which are valuable indicators of past climates. Iceberg formation and decay have applications to theoretical discussions of iceshelf disintegration caused by climatic warming.

The rates and mechanisms of ablation are important aspects of an iceberg's life history, but in general are poorly known. Although laboratory and theoretical studies are useful, extrapolation by several orders of magnitude to real icebergs may not be appropriate (Neshyba and Josberger, 1980). Few close field studies have been made because of practical difficulties.

We studied iceberg ablation in the D'Urville Sea (Fig. 1) during January and February 1982. We measured sea temperature and salinity close to drifting icebergs, and monitored ablation rates mainly around the waterline of a small iceberg over an eight-day period. Seven icebergs were studied in most detail during periods totalling four weeks. Their positions, and number designations used herein, are shown on Figure 1. Icebergs 1, 5, and 6 were 100–200 m long and numbers 2, 3, 4, and 7 were 40–100 m long. Operations were based from the 21 m schooner *Dick Smith Explorer* but activities up to the edges of icebergs were carried out from a 2.5 m inflatable dinghy. At all times a second inflatable stood off about 150 m in case of emergencies but was never needed.

Subaerial and Waterline Ablation Mechanisms

Iceberg ablation takes place in three overlapping zones; subaerial, waterline, and submarine. Calving of ice from iceberg sides and splitting of icebergs into two or more smaller icebergs are the most significant subaerial processes (Orheim, 1980). Minor subaerial processes include slab

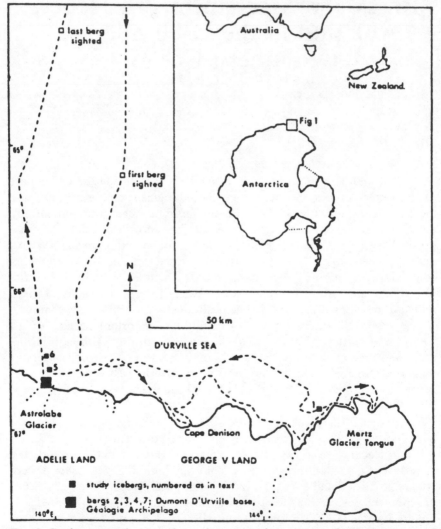

Fig. 1. *Study area and route of expedition in iceberg waters, showing positions of icebergs referred to in text.*

avalanches from tabular bergs that become tilted, plus sublimation, melting and deflation. Waterline mechanisms include wave action, current action, and melting. These cause horizonal grooves (notches) to form in the iceberg at the waterline, promoting calving from the undermined sides. Wave-cut platforms (terraces) or spurs, and caves growing upwards by roof and wall collapse are common results of these waterline and subaerial mechanisms, especially on tabular bergs where soft snow or firn are present at the waterline.

Submarine Ablation and Effect on the Water Column

Submarine ablation acts over the largest part of an iceberg and is believed to occur mainly by melting adjacent to a generally turbulent, convecting boundary layer (Huppert and Turner, 1980; Josberger and Martin, 1981). Water currents, iceberg wallowing, and roll-over enhance this melting by causing turbulent forced-convection (Job, 1978). Melting causes the rounded surfaces that are normally visible from a distance on icebergs that have recently tilted or rolled over, and which often predominate over angular cleavage faces on the smallest icebergs.

We saw some evidence for underwater calving including blocks of ice 1–2 m wide about to calve from submerged water-worn surfaces, and shallow, rounded depressions up to 1 m in diameter on recently emerged surfaces. However, it seems that relatively little ice is lost from icebergs in this way.

Submarine melting is significant apart from causing mass loss, because the water which results from it potentially has important oceanographic effects. The convecting melt-influenced water may move upwards, downwards, or spread sideways as layers, depending on ambient temperature, salinity, and vertical density gradients (Huppert and Josberger, 1980; Josberger and Neshyba, 1980). Thus, the iceberg can affect the stability of the surrounding water column, potentially influencing nutrient levels and primary productivity (Jacobs and others, 1981).

Differential motion between a drifting iceberg and surrounding sea-water may also affect the movement of melt water and the upper part of the water column. This was investigated by measuring surface (0.3 m) water temperature around two icebergs drifting in water 400–500 m deep (icebergs 1 and 6) using a Leeds–Northrup 8078 precision temperature bridge. Figure 2 illustrates the temperature distribution around iceberg 6 during a period with no wind, a calm sea (like a mirror), and 0.3 m high, long-period swells from the north-west and east. The sharp temperature gradient centred to the south-east and south of the iceberg (Fig. 2A) is suggestive of colder sub-surface water mixing with warmer surface water as the iceberg moved south-east relative to the sea-water.

The broad temperature minimum to the north-west appears to represent a wake of mixed water, similar to the result of Foldvik and others, (1980). This iceberg was slightly domed with a mean freeboard of 15 m, had been overturned, and apparently was entirely composed of ice. From buoyancy considerations it would have had a draft of about 100 m, and therefore would have locally affected this much of the upper part of the water column.

This apparent relative motion of iceberg 6 was confirmed using dye. Powdered Rhodamine-B dye in a weighted flask held on a line at 3 m depth, 3 m from the iceberg sides, was released by pulling out the stopper, so letting sea-water *in situ* mix and remove the dye from the flask at that depth. The dye moved diagonally upwards with a horizontal component of 0.2 m s^{-1} (Fig. 2A) consistent with the inferred movement of the iceberg, although the density of the dye could not be measured.

Slightly diluted surface salinities were detected around iceberg 6. Figure 2B illustrates the diluting effect, measurable on all four sides, of the iceberg, obtained using a Yeokal Hamon S-T bridge. Fresh water is not found beside icebergs because the melt water produced at the ice face is mixed with surrounding sea-water in a generally turbulent convecting boundary layer (Huppert and Turner, 1980; Josberger and Martin, 1981). S-T depth profiles were made but usable results were not obtained at the positions shown on Figure 2A. Time did not permit further measurements. Nevertheless, it appears that drifting icebergs do trail a plume of turbulently mixed, melt-influenced sea-water in their wake.

Ablation Rates

Grooves marking former waterlines on icebergs that have tilted or rolled over show that ablation takes place most rapidly in a narrow belt around the waterline. The development of these grooves was examined over a 13 d period to obtain quantitative field data for wave energy transfer, waterline and submarine ablation rates, and by inference, subaerial calving rates.

Groove height differs depending on wave conditions. In sheltered waters of the Géologie Archipelago (Fig. 1), groove heights of 1–3 m were measured on icebergs 2, 4, and 7. These icebergs were subject to waves whose mean maximum amplitude was 0.1 to 0.2 m with wavelengths of about 2 to 14 m respectively (periods of 1 to 3 s). Mean ambient sea temperature was −1°C and salinity about 34.1% during the monitoring period. A groove height of 10 m was estimated by sounding on an iceberg (5) grounded with others just north of the Archipelago. In the open sea further north, the mean maximum wave amplitude was about 1 m with a wavelength of 60 m (6 s period) during the 14 d preceding the visit to that iceberg, but mostly these parameters were less than this. In the wave-induced heat transfer model of Martin and others ([ᶜ1978]), the groove height, z, is given by

$$Z = 4a + \lambda/6 \tag{1}$$

where a is wave amplitude and λ is the wavelength. Equation (1) predicts the groove heights quite well, within the limits of the field data.

The rate of horizontal deepening of the waterline groove was monitored on a small (40 m × 40 m) irregular iceberg (no. 4, Fig. 3) trapped, in 15–25 m of water in a 220 m wide channel, by sea-floor topography and grounded icebergs. Sea waves raised by the predominantly south-east wind, and a west-setting current of approximately 0.1 m^{-1} ran through the channel, situated between two islands of the Géologie Archipelago. After the iceberg tilted about 40° exposing fresh non-grooved sides, it became evident that the iceberg was now trapped (floating), not grounded, because the developing groove generally maintained the same horizontal attitude and height irrespective of tides. Grounded icebergs in the vicinity would often rock back and forth (up to three degrees) with tides, and varying amounts of groove would be exposed at different times of the day. The fastest rate of deepening measured at iceberg 4 was $0.30 \pm 0.02 \text{ m d}^{-1}$ taking place at site 5 (Fig. 3) during a storm from 19–21 February. A rate of $0.28 \pm 0.04 \text{ m d}^{-1}$ was measured at site 4A during a period with smaller waves and similar sea temperature ($-1°C$). Measuring at this site had to be discontinued because of danger from calving ice. Ablation was slowest at sites 6 and 1 on the lee sides where rates of 0.063 and 0.068 (± 0.006)m d^{-1} respectively were obtained. Thus, waterline ablation was most rapid on the windward sides of the iceberg where waves transferred most heat to the ice.

These groove measurements can be used to estimate the efficiency of heat transfer from the incident wave train to the ice melting as done by Martin and others ([^{c}1978). Here, the groove is assumed to be a half-ellipse in cross-section perpendicular to the wave crests, with major radius (1.5 m) constant at half the groove height, and minor radius growing up to 0.3 m d^{-1}. This represents a maximum ice loss of $1.5 \times 10^{-5} \text{ m}^2 \text{ s}^{-1}$ per metre length of groove after the first day, or $4.4 \times 10^3 \text{ j m}^{-1} \text{ s}^{-1}$ of energy F_1, assuming the ice is all at the melting point. Martin and others ([^{c}1978]) model gives the wave-induced heat flux per unit length of wave crest, P_w, as

$$F_w = \tfrac{1}{2}p \ cp(T_w - T_i)\sigma a^2 \tag{2}$$

where $_p$, c_p, and T_w are the density, specific heat and temperature of sea-water respectively, T_i is the melting point and temperature of the iceberg, and σ is the wave frequency. T_w and T_i are assumed to be uniform and constant. Conditions at iceberg 4 give a heat flux of $2 \times 10^5 \text{ J m}^{-1} \text{ s}^{-1}$. Comparison of F_w and F_i suggests a heat-transfer efficiency from waves to the ice face of up to two per cent, compared to one per cent for the particular laboratory experiment of Martin and Others ([^{c}1978]).

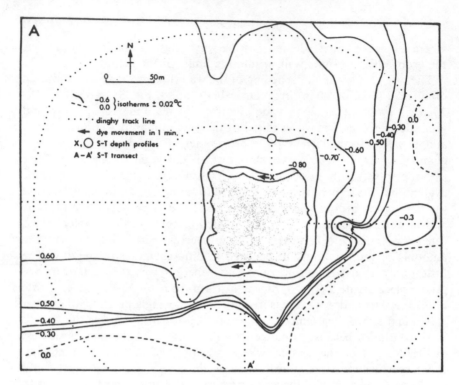

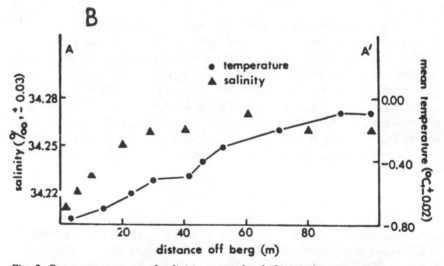

Fig. 2. Sea temperatures and salinities around a drifting iceberg (no. 6).
A. Time-averaged isotherms at 0.3 m depth, and horizontal vectors of dye movement.
B. Surface (0.3 m) salinity and temperature along a 100 m transect up to the south side of the iceberg.

The average rate of subaerial calving averaged over a long time is probably similar to the rate of ablation of the waterline, in terms of the rate of backward retreat of the side of an iceberg. On actively calving iceberg sides, groove depths vary from at least 5 m to zero. There, in the short term, waterline ablation is faster than calving but in the long term the two are probably similar. During the monitoring period at iceberg 4, one calving event per day was recorded on average (Fig. 3). Calving rates were estimated to be less than 0.1 m d^{-1} averaged over the vertical sides.

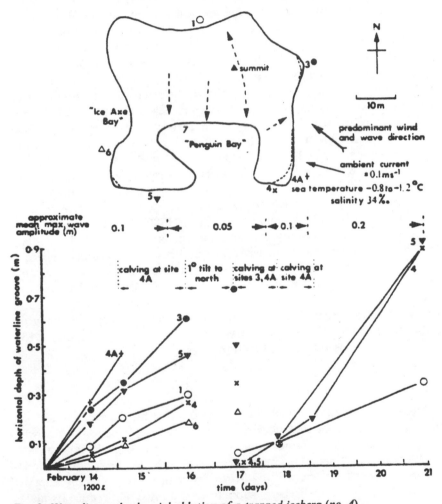

Fig. 3. Waterline and subaerial ablation of a trapped iceberg (no. 4).
Top. Plan diagram of iceberg showing ablation measuring sites (1–7), calving zones (dashed lines), and paths of calved debris (dashed arrows). This orientation with respect to north changed by no more than 20° during the measuring period.
Bottom. Measurement of melting at six sites on the waterline.

However, a long-term rate of up to 0.3 m d^{-1} may be more appropriate for the water conditions pertaining to this iceberg.

Subaerial calving rates will be much higher for icebergs in rougher, warmer waters. Waves about 2 m high with 5 s periods in water of $+3°C$ were recorded in the open D'Urville Sea in January and February. These data, with Equations (1) and (2), and heat-transfer efficiencies of one to two per cent, give waterline ablation, and hence calving, rates up to 5–9 m d^{-1}. Robe and others (1977) produced data which show that a drifting Arctic tabular berg decayed at about 2 m d^{-1} in sea-water of 2–4°C, mainly by wave action causing undercutting and subsequent calving. Rates of 2–5 m d^{-1} at 1–4°C were obtained by Job (1978) assuming temperatures typical of Southern Ocean waters. Equations (1) and (2) do not seem reliable for real conditions, with high waves, and iceberg temperatures not at the melting point throughout.

The rate of submarine ablation varies with sea temperature and relative velocity of water past the iceberg, although iceberg wallowing is also likely to be significant. At iceberg 4, submarine melt rates were estimated to be about 0.04 m d^{-1} on the down-current end, and about twice as fast on the sides and up-current end. The slowest measured rate of waterline ablation, about 0.06 ± 0.01 m d^{-1} (Fig. 3) is probably a reasonable estimate of the average rate of submarine ablation under these conditions. This is consistent with the range of iceberg melt rates at $-1°C$ (0.02–0.08 m d^{-1}) determined statistically by Budd and others (1980), and reasonably consistent with rates derived for ice melting in currents 0.04 m d^{-1} for a 40 m long iceberg melting under the environmental conditions around iceberg 4 (Weeks and Campbell, 1973). Side-wall melt rates in the absence of any current, calculated for iceberg 4 using equation (7) of Neshyba and Josberger (1980), are several times less than those measured here. In open waters offshore, ocean swells of long periods will promote wallowing of icebergs up to several hundred metres long (Kristensen and Squire, 1983) which will increase submarine ablation rates.

Conclusion

Submarine melting is considered to be responsible for the greatest loss of mass from an iceberg that does not split. Although it acts more slowly than wave action and calving, submarine melting acts over the largest part of an iceberg. For a medium-sized level tabular berg, dimensions 800 m × 500 m × 250 m, drifting in sea-water of $-1°C$, 34%, moving at 0.1 m s^{-1} relative to the iceberg, submarine melting could reduce its mass by up to 0.06% per day assuming side wall and basal melt rates are similar. This is one and a half times the daily loss caused by wave action and subaerial calving combined. However, as an iceberg becomes smaller, waterline ablation and calving become relatively more important, especially in rough seas. Nevertheless, splitting is likely to be responsible for gross reduction in mass of many Antarctic icebergs.

This study has provided field data to test theoretical models. Martin and others ([^{c}1978]) wave-induced heat-transfer model adequately describes the action of waves at the waterline of small icebergs in cold, sheltered waters where ablation rates are low. However the model does not seem reliable for higher, mixed-wave conditions in the open sea. Melt rates derived theoretically by Weeks and Campbell (1973), and statistically by Budd and others (1980), are in reasonable agreement with submarine ablation rates obtained here.

Drifting icebergs trail a plume or sea-water, that has probably been mixed, slightly cooled and very slightly diluted, in their wake. Precise measurements are needed to determine the structure and stability of this plume water. The many thousands of Antarctic icebergs could have a small but measurable effect on the upper 100–200 m of the water column in coastal seas.

If icebergs are ever towed to arid lands, it may be preferable to moor them before they ground. Our observations show that grounded icebergs are not necessarily stable platforms even in calm water, where irreversible tilts of more than 40° may occur. However, knowledge of the iceberg's underwater shape could indicate how stable a grounded iceberg would be. Controlled wave energy could be used to undermine the iceberg sides and promote calving of portable-sized iceblocks for conversion to water ashore.

Acknowledgements

We sincerely thank Dr David Lewis, Margaret Huenerbein, Dick Heffernan, and other fellow expedition members and Joel Bonnett, the Oceanic Research Foundation and its many supporters for making this project feasible. The expedition's generous sponsors are too numerous to mention but we thank: Leeds–Northrup, AWA, Yeokal Electronics (Sydney), Beaufort, Metzler and Outboard Marine companies of Australia; Met-Co Ltd of Wellington, New Zealand; Antarctic Division and Bureau of Meteorology of the Department of Science and Technology, Australia; and Commonwealth Scientific and Industrial Research Organization, Marine Laboratories, Cronulla, N.S.W., Australia; for donating or loaning equipment. An unidentified referee did much to improve this manuscript.

References

Budd, W. F., *and others*. 1980. Antarctic iceberg melt rates derived from size distributions and movement rates, by W. F. Budd, T. H. Jacka, and V. I. Morgan. *Annals of Glaciology*, Vol. 1, p. 103–12.

Foldvik A., *and others*. 1980. Measurements of the radiation temperature of Antarctic icebergs and the surrounding surface water, by A. Foldvik, T. Gammelsrød, and Y. Gjessing. *Annals of Glaciology*, Vol. 1, p. 19–22.

Huppert, H. E., *and* Josberger, E.G. 1980. The melting of ice in cold stratified water. *Journal of Physical Oceanography*, Vol. 10, No. 6, p. 953–60.

Huppert, H. E., *and* Turner, J. S. 1980. Ice blocks melting into a salinity gradient. *Journal of Fluid Mechanics*, Vol. 100, Pt. 2, p. 367–84.

Jacobs, S. S., *and others*. 1981. Thermohaline steps induced by melting of the Erebus Glacier tongue, by S. S. Jacobs, H. E. Huppert, G. Holdsworth, and D. J. Drewry. *Journal of Geophysical Research*, Vol. 86, No. C7, p. 6547–55.

Job, J. G. 1978. Numerical modelling of iceberg towing for water supplies – a case study. *Journal of Glaciology*, Vol. 20, No. 84, p. 533–42.

Josberger, E. G., *and* Martin, S. 1981. A laboratory and theoretical study of the boundary layer adjacent to a vertical melting ice wall in salt water. *Journal of Fluid Mechanics*, Vol. 111, p. 439–73.

Josberger, E. G., *and* Neshyba, S. 1980. Iceberg melt-driven convection inferred from field measurements of temperature. *Annals of Glaciology*, Vol. 1, p. 113–17.

Kristensen, M., *and* Squire, V. A. 1983. Modelling of Antarctic tubular icebergs in ocean waves. *Annals of Glaciology*, Vol. 4, p. 152–57.

Martin, S., *and others*. [ᶜ1978.] Wave-induced heat transfer to an iceberg, by S. Martin, E. Josberger, and P. Kauffman. (*In* Husseiny, A.A., ed, *Iceberg utilization. Proceedings of the first International Conference and Workshops on Iceberg Utilization for Fresh Water Production, Weather Modification, and Other Applications, held at Iowa State University, Ames, Iowa, U.S.A., October 2–6, 1977.* New York, etc., Pergamon Press, p. 260–64.)

Neshyba, S., *and* Josberger, E. G. 1980. On the estimation of Antarctic iceberg melt rate. *Journal of Physical Oceanography*, Vol. 10, No. 10, p. 1681–85.

Orheim, O. 1980. Physical characteristics and life expectancy of tabular Antarctic icebergs. *Annals of Glaciology*, Vol. 1, p. 11–18.

Robe, R. Q., *and others*. 1977. Iceberg deterioration, by R. Q. Robe, D. C. Maier, and R. C. Kollmeyer. *Nature*, Vol. 267, No. 5611, p. 505–06.

Weeks, W. F., *and* Campbell, W. J. 1973. Icebergs as a fresh-water source: an appraisal. *Journal of Glaciology*, Vol. 12, No. 65, p. 207–33.

Appendix 3

Variations in Underwater Vocalizations of Weddell Seals (*Leptonychotes weddelli*) at the Vestfold Hills as a Measure of Breeding Population Discreteness

Jeanette Thomas, Rhys Puddicombe,[1]
Mimi George and David Lewis

Introduction

The vocal nature of Weddell seals (*Leptonychotes weddelli*) has intrigued researchers throughout the history of Antarctic exploration. Early accounts of explorers mention seals making 'musical noise' (Wilson, 1905). Lindsey made phonograph recordings of Weddell seals at the Bay of Whales in 1937. Schevill and Watkins (1971) and Ray and Schevill (1967) made numerous recordings of underwater sounds in McMurdo Sound. Thomas and Kuechle (1982) quantitatively examined the acoustic characteristics of Weddell seal sounds in McMurdo Sound and classified them into discrete categories. These underwater sounds consisted of numerous frequency-modulated sweeps, chirps, pulses, and clicks. Functions of Weddell seal sounds were determined using playback studies (Thomas *et al.*, 1982) at McMurdo Sound. Ian Stirling during the same period made recordings of vocalizations of Weddell seals near the Palmer Peninsula. Upon examination, distinct geographic variations in vocalizations between Palmer Peninsula and McMurdo Sound were documented (Thomas and Stirling,

[1] Present Address: Whales and Marine Section
Australian National Parks and Wildlife Service
GPO Box 636
Canberra ACT 2601, Australia

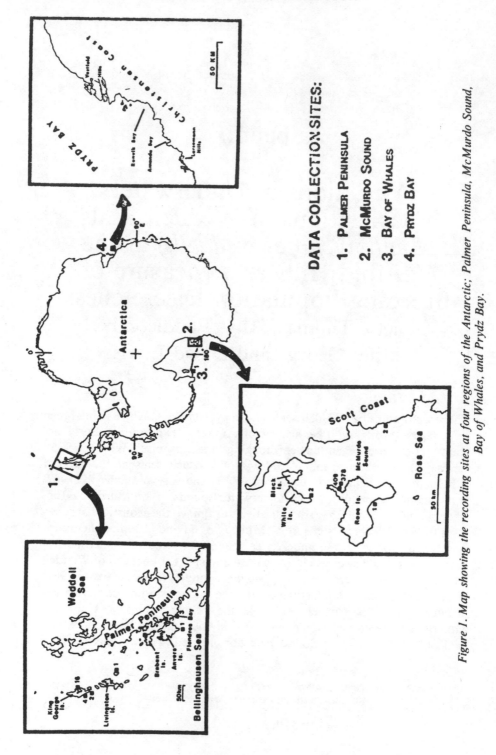

Figure 1. Map showing the recording sites at four regions of the Antarctic; Palmer Peninsula, McMurdo Sound, Bay of Whales, and Prydz Bay.

1983). In addition, the unique usage of mirror-image vocalization patterns and calls in trios at Palmer Peninsula were documented.

We predicted that the degree of vocal differences reflects the extent of geographic isolation between breeding populations of Weddell seals. We hypothesized that the amount of variability in vocalizations around the continent reflects the degree of mixing between breeding colonies and would allow us to identify discrete populations. The Australian station at Davis in East Prydz Bay is approximately between McMurdo Sound and Palmer Peninsula and makes an ideal site for sampling vocalization of Weddell seals and testing our hypothesis (figure 1).

Materials and Methods

Breeding colonies of Weddell seals occur near Davis Station; about 3,000 Weddell seals inhabit the near vicinity of Davis Station (Lugg, 1966). Two research teams were conducting studies in East Prydz Bay during 1983 and recorded underwater vocalizations of Weddell seals using similar sampling schemes and equipment to those used by Thomas and Stirling (1983). Rhys Puddicombe made monthly recordings near Davis station from May to September and fortnightly recordings from October to December (144 samples). The recording equipment was a Marantz C207-LP cassette recorder, coupled with an ITC 6050C hydrophone (system frequency response linear to 20 kHz). The recording method was to erect a tent near a natural breathing hole in the ice, lower the hydrophone into the hole, and record. During each recording session, a 24-hour cycle was sampled using ten-minute recordings every two hours. He made recordings at five sites: Brookes Hut, mouth of Long Fjord, opposite Brookes, Gardener Island, and Trynne Fjord in and off Vestfold Hills.

At approximately the same time, Mimi George and David Lewis made underwater recordings of Weddell seals along the coast extending from 30 to 100 km southwest of Davis Station. Recordings were made using a Sony cassette recorder and a Yak-Yak hydrophone (system frequency response linear to 15 kHz) with a 40 dB preamplifier. One hundred and ten fifteen-minute recordings were made in an opportunistic manner during the months of March 1983 to February 1984. On three occasions, sampling was done every two hours for a 24-hour period at the same location. Sites included colonies at: Cape Drakon, Rauer Islands, Brattstrandoyane Islands, Hovdeoyane Islands off Amanda Bay, and Larsemann Hills.

In the laboratory, sonograms of sounds were made using a Unigon SC104A real time analyser and a Tektronix hard copy unit. Frequency, time, and amplitude characteristics of vocalizations were compared. Calls were classified into corresponding categories reported from McMurdo Sound and the Palmer Peninsula or were assigned to a new category if no

similar sounds had been reported. Comparison allowed us to determine
the degree of similarities between vocalizations of Weddell seals at Vestfold
Hills and McMurdo Sound or Palmer Peninsula.

Results and Discussion

As initiated by Thomas and Kuechle (1982), vocalizations of Weddell
seals were classified using a three-place code: the first letter represents
the site, the second letter represents the major call category, and the
ending number represents the type within that call category. Major call
categories at both McMurdo Sound (sounds designated with an M) and
at Palmer Peninsula (sounds designated with a P) include:
T,C,P,G,K,R,W,B,J,O,H,A,E,Z. Types within a category vary from a
single type up to eleven variations (e.g. MT11). To classify vocalizations
of Weddell seals near Davis Station in a similar form, the location was
designated with a D. Only one vocalization (DD1) did not fit into an
existing major call category and was assigned a new letter.

Table 1 compares similarities of calls at Davis Station to those at
McMurdo Sound versus Palmer Peninsula. As at McMurdo Sound and
Palmer Peninsula, the most common vocalization of Weddell seals was the
T vocalizations (or trills as they are commonly called). Thomas *et al.*
(1982) reported that T sounds serve a territorial defence function and
therefore are prevalent during the breeding season. DT3 and DT7 are
both ascending in frequency, which makes them more similar to trills at
Palmer Peninsula. McMurdo trills are always descending. Use of prefixes
in some trills at Davis Station is similar to trills at McMurdo Station,
whereas use of prefixes is absent at Palmer Peninsula. Use of an initial
sweep frequency in some trills at Davis Station is similar to some trills at
McMurdo Station.

W or whistle vocalizations are absent from the McMurdo repertoire,
thus making all DW vocalizations more similar to Palmer Peninsula vocalizations. Like the Palmer Peninsula whistles, whistles at Davis Station
can be either ascending or descending in frequency and can be single or in
series. The function of this sound is unknown.

G or guttural glug vocalizations are absent from the Palmer Peninsula
repertoire. DG1 is very similar to MG2 both in acoustic structure and in
the use of a two-part suffix. Thomas *et al.* (1983) reported this sound as a
low-intensity aggressive sound.

The DO1 or 'ooo' vocalization is very similar to PO1 in frequency and
harmonic structure. Similarly, both DO1 and PO1 are used as single
sounds or in evenly repeated series. 'Ooo' vocalizations are absent at
McMurdo Sound. The function of this sound is unknown.

The DC1 or chug vocalization is similar to both MC3 and PC3 in having
a retarding repetition rate; however, in terms of frequency structure DC1

Table 1. Comparison of similarities between vocalizations from Weddell seals near Davis Station to those in McMurdo Sound and in Palmer Peninsula, Antarctica.

	Similarities of Vocalizations	
Davis Station	*McMurdo Sound*	*Palmer Peninsula*
DTI	initial frequency sweep similar to MT1 and MT5	harmonic structure similar to PT1
DT2	—	—
DT3	—	ascending frequency similar to PT2
DT4	harmonic structure and frequency similar to MT9	—
DT5	use of prefix and frequency sweep similar to MT6	—
DT6	similar frequency sweep to MT2	—
DT7	—	ascending frequency similar to PT2
DW1	—	single, & ascending frequency similar to PW1
DW2	—	series, & descending similar to PW3
DW3	—	—
DG1	acoustic structure & suffix use similar to MG2	—
DO1	—	harmonic structure & use singly or in series similar to PO1
DC1	similar retarding series to MC3 and similar frequency structure to MC4	similar retarding series to PC3
DR1	similar to MR1 in frequency and accelerating repetition rate	—
DD1	—	—

is most similar to MC4. According to Thomas *et al.* (1983), chugs are a very common vocalization and are used in aggressive encounters. At both Palmer Peninsula and McMurdo Sound several types of chugs were present, but at Davis Station only a single type was examined.

The DR1 or 'cricket call' vocalization is very similar to MR1 in both frequency structure and the accelerating repetition rate. This sound is absent in the Palmer Peninsula repertoire. Thomas *et al.* (1983) assigned a non-communicative function to this sound because they could not elicit a response to playbacks of this vocalization.

DD1 is a unique Weddell seal vocalization, occurring only at Davis Station. It has a descending frequency structure, but two separate components. The initial component is an almost pure tone sweep and the ending component has harmonic structure. The function of this sound is unknown.

As with vocalizations at McMurdo Sound, the use of mirror-image sounds (similar to PT1 & PT2, PW1 & PW2, PW3 & PW4, and PB1 & PB2) and trio vocalization patterns (similar to PT4, PT5, and PT6) was absent in Weddell seal vocalizations at Davis Station. These vocalization patterns appear to be unique to sounds at Palmer Peninsula.

Based on the number of similarities in vocalization characteristics, it appears that sounds at Davis Station have an affinity for both McMurdo Sound and Palmer Peninsula vocalizations. However, no vocalization at Davis Station is identical to Weddell seal sounds at either McMurdo Station or Palmer Peninsula. This degree of difference indicates another geographic variant in their repertoire which probably reflects the existence of a distinct breeding population.

Conclusions

1. Vocalizations from Davis Station have some similarities to sounds from both McMurdo Sound and the Palmer Peninsula.
2. All major categories seem to be variable in acoustic structure at different sites.
3. Ascending vocalizations occur at both Davis Station and the Palmer Peninsula, but not at McMurdo Sound.
4. Dependent auxiliary sounds (affixes and suffixes) occur at Davis Station and McMurdo Station, but not at Palmer Peninsula.
5. The predominant vocalization category at all sites is T (trills).
6. All sites have at least one unique major call category. DD1 category is unique to Davis Station.
7. The use of 'mirror-image' vocalizations is unique to Palmer Peninsula.
8. The use of sounds in 'trios' is unique to Palmer Peninsula.
9. Vocalizations used in series can have an even, accelerating, or retarding repetition rate.
10. Underwater vocalizations are probably a good indication of the degree of mixing between breeding populations of Weddell seals around the Antarctic continent.
11. Further sampling is needed to determine the minimum distance over which vocal variations could be detected.

Acknowledgements

Analysis of data was conducted at the bioacoustic laboratory at Hubbs Marine Research Institute. Data collection by Mr Puddicombe was supported by the Australian Antarctic Research Programme and Davis Station. Funding for the expedition by Ms George and Dr Lewis was from public donation and sponsorship of the Oceanic Research Foundation.

Literature cited

Lindsey, A., 1937. The Weddell seal in the Bay of Whales, Antarctica. *Journal of Mammalogy*. 18: 127–144.

Lugg, D. J., 1966. Annual Cycle of the Weddell seal in the Vestfold Hills, Antarctic. *Journal of Mammalogy*. 47(2):317–322.

Ray, C. & W. Schevill, 1967. Noisy underwater world of the Weddell seal. *Animals*. 10: 109–113.

Thomas, J. & V. Kuechle, 1982. Quantitative analysis of the underwater repertoire of the Weddell seal (*Leptonychotes weddelli*). *Journal of the Acoustic Society of America*. 72: 1730–1738.

Thomas, J. & I. Stirling, 1983. Geographic variation in Weddell seal (*Leptonychotes weddelli*) vocalizations between Palmer Peninsula and McMurdo Sound, Antarctica. *Canadian Journal of Zoology*. 61: 2203–2210.

Thomas, J., Zinnel, K., & L. Ferm, 1983. Investigation of Weddell seal (*Leptonychotes weddelli*) underwater calls using playback techniques. *Canadian Journal of Zoology*. 61: 1448–1456.

Watkins, W. and W. Schevill, 1971. Directionality of the sound beam in *Leptonychotes weddelli*. *In* W. Burt (ed.), *Antarctic Pinnipedia*.

Wilson, E., 1905. 'On the whales, seals, and birds of the Ross Sea and South Victoria Land'. *In* R. F. Scott (ed.), *The Voyage of the Discovery*, Vol. 22, Smith, Elder, and Co.: 269–294.

Index